JESUS BEFORE THE GOSPELS

Also by Bart D. Ehrman

How Jesus Became God: The Exaltation of a Jewish Preacher from Galilee

Did Jesus Exist? The Historical Argument for Jesus of Nazareth

Forged: Writing in the Name of God—
Why the Bible's Authors Are Not Who We Think They Are

Jesus, Interrupted: Revealing the Hidden Contradictions in the Bible
(And Why We Don't Know About Them)

God's Problem: How the Bible Fails to Answer Our Most Important
Question—Why We Suffer

Misquoting Jesus: The Story Behind Who Changed the Bible and Why

The Orthodox Corruption of Scripture: The Effect of Early
Christological Controversies on the Text of the New Testament

The New Testament: A Historical Introduction to the Early Christian Writings

Lost Christianities: The Battles for Scripture and the Faiths We Never Knew

Lost Scriptures: Books That Did Not Make It into the New Testament

Jesus: Apocalyptic Prophet of the New Millennium

JESUS BEFORE THE GOSPELS

*How the Earliest Christians
Remembered, Changed, and Invented
Their Stories of the Savior*

BART D. EHRMAN

HarperOne
An Imprint of HarperCollins*Publishers*

HarperOne

HarperCollins books may be purchased for educational, business, or sales promotional use. For information please e-mail the Special Markets Department at SPsales@harpercollins.com.

HarperCollins website: http://www.harpercollins.com

FIRST EDITION

Designed by Janet M. Evans

Library of Congress Cataloging-in-Publication Data is available upon request.

ISBN 978–0–06–228520–1

16 17 18 19 20   OV/RRD   10 9 8 7 6 5 4 3 2 1

I have dedicated this book to the memory of my very good friend Darryl Gless, who died nearly a year ago after a valiant and courageous fight with an illness that racked his body but left his mind intact and incisive to the end. He left behind a wife, my also-very-good-friend Frieda Seeger, and their then-yet-to-be-born daughter Leni. Darryl was a much-beloved, committed, and influential professor of English at UNC, a onetime dean in the college, an insightful and creative scholar, and an extraordinarily beloved and generous human being. We constantly remember and miss him.

CONTENTS

INTRODUCTION

JESUS DIED IN ABOUT the year 30 CE, but our earliest surviving accounts of his life did not start to appear until some forty years later (beginning with the Gospel of Mark). During the intervening years— and even in the years after our Gospels were written—stories about Jesus were in oral circulation, starting with tales told by those who were eye- and earwitnesses to the things he did and said. I am deeply interested in how Jesus was being "remembered" and "misremembered" by those who were telling such stories, both those who actually knew him and those who heard stories from others, some years, or even decades, later, before our written Gospels appeared.

This book, in short, is about the historical Jesus, memory, and distorted memory. I have been interested in the historical Jesus since, well, since I first started studying the New Testament from an academic perspective in the late 1970s. At that time, I heard views from some of my teachers that many people continue to hear today: the Gospels are based on eyewitness reports; they can therefore be accepted as historically reliable; people in oral cultures (such as in the ancient Roman world) had better memories than we do today; and such people always preserved their traditions about the past accurately, since they were not literate and so could not learn about the past from writing.

Are these views correct?

It was just a few years ago that I came to realize that the study of memory, as pursued by scholars who did not work on the New Testament, could provide some valuable and keen insights into such matters. These other scholars work in a number of disciplines well represented in the academy, such as psychology, sociology, and anthropology. Their insights may be especially relevant to understanding how the earliest Christians told and retold the stories about Jesus after his death but before the Gospels were written. This was a mysterious period of oral transmission, when stories were circulating, both among eyewitnesses and, even more, among those who knew someone whose cousin had a neighbor who had once talked with a business associate whose mother had, just fifteen years earlier, spoken with an eyewitness who told her some things about Jesus.

How were such people—those people at the tail end of the period of transmission—telling their stories about Jesus? Did they remember very well what they had heard from others (who had heard from others who had heard from others)? Were the stories they told accurate reflections of what they heard? Or, more remotely, of what Jesus said and did? Or had their stories been molded, and shaped, or even invented in the processes of telling, remembering, and retelling the stories? During the forty to sixty-five years between Jesus's death and the first accounts of his life, how much had the stories been changed? How much was being accurately remembered? Modern studies of memory may possibly provide us with some much-needed insights into the question.

For about two years now I have spent virtually all my free time doing nothing but reading about memory—what cognitive psychologists have to say about individual memories, what sociologists can tell us about collective memory, and what anthropologists have written about oral cultures and the ways they preserve their unwritten traditions.

The more I read, the more surprised I became that so many scholars of the New Testament—the vast bulk of them, so far as I can tell—have never explored this research, even though it is so fascinating and most immediately relevant. Even those New Testament specialists who have delved into such fields have in many instances limited themselves to just one, or possibly two, of them. But they are all important. In this book I try to bring them each to bear on questions about memory and the historical Jesus.

Memory and Jesus

When it comes to Jesus, all we have are memories. There are no lifelike portraits from his day, no stenographic notes recorded on the spot, no accounts of his activities written at the time. Only memories of his life, of what he said and did. Memories written after the fact. Long after the fact. Memories written by people who were not actually there to observe him.

Critical scholars have long argued that the surviving records of Jesus—the Gospels—are not memories recorded by those who were eyewitnesses.[1] They are memories of later authors who had heard about Jesus from others, who were telling what they had heard from others, who were telling what they had heard from yet others. They are memories of memories of memories. To understand what the Gospels are, and to know anything about the man Jesus himself, we have to know about memory.

Our own memories are, on the whole, reasonably good. If they weren't, we would not be able to function, or even survive, as human beings in a very complex world. We count on our memories for the thousands of things we do every day, from the moment we wake up in the morning to the time we shut down at night. But we forget a lot of things as well—not just our keys, and the names of people we

JESUS BEFORE THE GOSPELS

are sure we ought to remember, but also factual information that we used to know and events, even highly important events, that have happened in our lives. Even more disturbing, we misremember things. The older we get the more we realize: we sometimes remember clearly what took place and how it took place. Then it turns out we are wrong.

It happens to all of us. And it has happened to everyone who has ever lived. Including the followers of Jesus. Including the ones who told the stories about him. Including the ones who heard those stories and then passed them along to others. Including the ones who heard these thirdhand stories and told them then to others, who told them to others, who told them to others, who then wrote the Gospels. Each person in that link of memory from Jesus to the writers of the Gospels was remembering what he or she had heard. Or trying to do so.

When it comes to knowing about the Gospels and about the historical Jesus himself, it is all about memory. And about frail memory. And faulty memory. And false memory.

Memory is not simply about us as individuals, as we remember things in our world and information that we have learned, or when we recall events that have happened to us and persons we have encountered. Memory—"calling something back to mind"—also involves groups of people as they remember what has happened in their collective past. Society itself cannot function without a memory of the people and events that have bound and continue to bind it together. As a society we have to remember our origins, our history, our wars, our economic crises, our mistakes, and our successes. Without a recollection of our past we cannot live in the present or look forward to a future.

It is astounding how we, individually or as a society, have such different memories of events and people from the past, and how often our recollections of important moments and figures are so far removed from historical reality.

Let me give an example of "social memory" to demonstrate my point. This will help set the stage for what I want to say about memories of Jesus.

Remembering Lincoln

In 2014 a poll was taken of 162 members of the American Political Science Association, asking them to rank all the past presidents of the United States, from best to worst.[2] Probably to no one's great surprise, the top-ranked president was Abraham Lincoln. Most of us—though certainly not all of us—remember Lincoln as a truly great and noble man who did remarkable things for his country. But he was not always thought of in that way. In his own day, Lincoln in fact was not seen as a great president. And not only in the southern states, whose inhabitants, as a rule, truly despised him and what he stood for. Even among his supporters he was not wildly popular. As social historian Barry Schwartz indicates in his pivotal study *Abraham Lincoln and the Forge of National Memory,* "When Abraham Lincoln awoke on the last day of his life, almost everyone could find something about him to dislike."[3]

Schwartz's book tries to show that Lincoln did not come to be considered "great" until after his death, and even then his fortunes in memory rose and fell depending on what was happening more broadly in the country as a whole. Every turning point in American history led to a revised image of Lincoln, both who he was as a human being and what he tried to accomplish (and did accomplish).

I think it is fair to say that most of us today remember Lincoln as one of the first great heroes of civil rights, as one who aggressively promoted the idea that "all people are created equal," that whites and blacks deserve to be treated the same before the law, that black slaves should be set free and allowed to have the same rights and freedoms as their white owners.

We generally do not remember another side of Lincoln. Prior to the Civil War, Lincoln is clearly on record for not favoring civil rights. His views changed over time, of course. Our views often do. But why do we remember only one part of his life—not the part that is discomforting to our modern views? We don't remember that Lincoln publicly stated that blacks should be set free and then deported to a colony. That he declared that blacks should not be allowed to vote or to serve on juries or to enjoy the privileges and responsibilities of the whites in society. That he explicitly opposed the idea of racial equality, in no small measure because he believed (in his words) that there was a "physical difference" between blacks and whites that would make it impossible.

This is a memory of Lincoln that most of us have never had, and as incredible as it seems to us today, it is easy to document from Lincoln's own speeches and writings. As he said quite plainly, and somewhat shockingly, in his fourth debate with Stephen A. Douglas in 1858:

> I am not, nor ever have been, in favor of bringing about in any way the social and political equality of the white and black races . . . and I will say in addition to this that there is a physical difference between the white and black races which I believe will forever forbid the two races living together on terms of social and political equality.[4]

If Lincoln publicly stated such views—which would be seen as hideously racist by us today—why is he so widely thought of today as a champion of civil rights? Is it, as some historians claim, because Lincoln eventually reversed himself and became an advocate not only of abolition but also of complete equality? This is a controversial issue. Schwartz himself argues that we remember Lincoln the way we do today because the leaders of the civil rights movement in the early 1960s latched onto Lincoln as a voice from the past who could provide a rationale and moral justification for their push to provide full equality under the law for African Americans, a push that almost all of us realize came many, many years too late.

Whether we think Lincoln completely reversed himself or not, this example of our own selective memory can be instructive. When we remember the past, whether we are thinking simply our individual thoughts or are reconstructing our previous history as a collective whole, as a society, we do so, always and necessarily, in light of our present situation. The past is not a fixed entity back there in time. It is always being transformed in our minds, depending on what our minds are occupied with in the here and now. As Schwartz claims, the somewhat ironic portrayal of Abraham Lincoln as a civil rights prophet "demonstrates the malleability of the past and justifies Maurice Halbwachs's claim that 'collective memory, is essentially a reconstruction of the past that adapts the image of historical facts to the beliefs and spiritual needs of the present.'"[5]

The Maurice Halbwachs that Schwartz invokes here is one of the truly great pioneers in the study of memory—specifically, memory as held by social groups, "collective memory."[6] We will meet him again in chapter 6. Halbwachs had a rather extreme view of how we remember. He thought that literally all of our memories are social memories, that we can't actually have any personal, private memories, but that every memory we have is necessarily influenced by, shaped by, and provided through our various social contexts. Not everyone agrees with that view, but on one point there is much wider consensus. We—whether as individuals or as members of a collective— "remember" the past because of its value in the present. Otherwise we have no reason even to think about the past—whether it is our own past lives and experiences or the lives and experiences of our society. And—this is the key point I am trying to make—sometimes, often, or always our memories of the past are distorted precisely because of the demands of the present.[7]

Schwartz in particular wants to emphasize that this reality of memory does not mean that what we remember about our past—as individuals or as social groups—is simply fabricated and unreliable. On the contrary, most of what we remember is accurate and historical. But the way we remember it is highly selective and sometimes distorted by the reasons we choose to remember in the first place. In Schwartz's words, our modern way of remembering Lincoln "valuates history by lifting the morally significant elements of Lincoln's life above the mundane."[8] In other words, we remember the past not only as it actually happened, but also in light of what is most important to us in our own lives.

Remembering Columbus

Much the same can be said about most of the historical figures that we revere, from Caesar Augustus to Joan of Arc to Christopher Columbus. Columbus is an interesting example. He is not always remembered today in the same glowing terms that we remembered him when I was a child growing up in the '50s and '60s. In those days, we remembered Columbus as one of the great heroes of our past, the one who "discovered America," who made it possible for civilized people to expand into the New World and to bring their Christian ideals into a backward and pagan wilderness that stretched from shore to shore. It was Columbus who made possible all the good things that have come down to us in our democratic, wealthy, and noble society. Among other things, he was a good and kind man who treated the native populations with dignity and respect.

Columbus is not always remembered that way anymore. For one thing, today when people talk about his "discovery" of America, they tend to put it in quotation marks. America, in the more widespread view today, was not "discovered." It was already here, and was populated by civilized peoples, even if their form of civilization was markedly different from the civilization of Europe. And Columbus was not even the first European here. He was preceded by many others.

More than that, Columbus today is often remembered not as a good and beneficent man but as a rather ruthless and violent one, a man responsible for the massive destruction of enormous numbers of human beings and the ill treatment of many others. In the words of one historian who has carefully rethought Columbus's contributions, James Loewen:

> Christopher Columbus introduced two phenomena that revolutionized race relations and transformed the modern world: the taking of land, wealth, and labor from indigenous people in the Western Hemisphere, leading to their near extermination, and the transatlantic slave trade, which created a racial underclass.[9]

In his attempt to portray Columbus in a different light, Loewen shows not only how the diseases of Europe devastated the tribes of Native Americans, but also how Columbus implemented and followed a completely ruthless treatment of the people he found on American shores, sanctioning rape, pillage, and bodily mutilation.

Why then were those of us in my generation taught to remember him with such reverence? In Loewen's opinion:

> The worshipful biographical vignettes of Columbus provided by most of our textbooks serve to indoctrinate students into a

9

mindless endorsement of colonialism that is strikingly inappropriate in today's postcolonial era.[10]

For my purposes here, I am not saying that Loewen is either right or wrong in his revisionist understanding of Columbus. What I am saying is that we were raised to remember Columbus in a way that is disputed by historians today who are wearing glasses of a different tint. Columbus is often remembered today very differently from when I was a child.

My ultimate point is not directly related either to Abraham Lincoln or Christopher Columbus. My point is that what is true of them is true of every historical figure. Our memories of them are shaped by our present interests and concerns, and partly—though not exclusively—because of that, these memories are sometimes frail, faulty, or even false. For historians, of course, it is important to know which memories are accurate and which are not. But it is also important to understand why people have the memories they do—especially the distorted memories—as such memories can tell us a good deal about what people value and cherish in their lives. By studying the memory of the past we can learn about the importance of the present.

Remembering Jesus

As we will see extensively throughout this book, these reflections also apply to memories of Jesus. People today—both believers and nonbelievers—remember him in very different ways. And people always have. Even the first people to remember him. Even his disciples. Even the authors of our Gospels. Some of these memories are no doubt accurate. Some may be distorted. All of them will be helpful both for reconstructing the past and for understanding the personal and social forces that drive people to remember the past the way they do.

One of the historical difficulties posed by our Gospels is that they were not written during Jesus's lifetime or within a few weeks, months, or even years after his death. Critical scholars for centuries have realized that the Gospels were written decades later. Since at least the early twentieth century, scholars have recognized that these earliest written accounts of Jesus's words and deeds were based on stories about him that were being circulated by word of mouth in the forty to sixty-five years after his death.

This raises a number of very big questions that many people have never thought about: Who was telling the stories? Was it only the twelve disciples and other eyewitnesses? Or would it have been other people as well? That is, did people who heard stories from eyewitnesses also tell the stories? Is it possible that stories were told by people who knew people who knew people who knew people who claimed that they heard stories from people who knew people who knew eyewitnesses? What happens when stories are circulated orally, from one person to the next, not just day after day, but year after year, and decade after decade, among such people, before being written down?

Many people have never thought of this as an issue of concern, but it obviously is an enormous problem. We all know from personal experience how much news stories get changed in the retelling (not to mention stories about us personally) just in a matter of hours, let alone days, weeks, months, years, and decades. Were the stories about Jesus exempt from these processes of alteration and invention that we ourselves experience all the time?

Some people, including some scholars, have thought that the answer is yes. They have maintained that it must have been different with Jesus, a man from first-century Palestine. Some have argued that it is different because the Gospels were not written by authors who had gotten their information from others who had gotten their information from others who had gotten their information from others—

over the course of decades. In their view, the Gospels were written by eyewitnesses to Jesus's life. Is that true? It is certainly a question worth exploring.

Some have argued that even though stories might change in our current age, it was different back then, especially in oral cultures. For one thing, the apostles of Jesus themselves would have made *certain* that no one ever changed any of the stories significantly. Right?

Others have argued that in oral cultures, people were more skilled in memory and worked hard to preserve traditions accurately without changing them. Since such people could not rely on writing, and only had oral communications to rely upon, they had to make sure that nothing of any importance came to be changed in the process of telling and retelling. Is there any way to know if that is in fact the case?

Some people have gone so far as to claim that the disciples of Jesus in particular memorized his teachings during his lifetime. As a first-century rabbi, Jesus would have been intent that his words were learned with scrupulous care so that when they were told to others, they were told with great precision and accuracy. So too, the stories of his deeds became accounts that were firmly committed to memory and passed along to others who memorized them, prior to the writing of the Gospels. Is there a way to know if this is correct?

Obviously, this book will not be the first to address such issues. They first came to scholarly prominence, and in fact became something of a scholarly obsession, almost exactly a century ago among German New Testament specialists who today are known as the "form critics" (they are called this for reasons I will explain later in this book). One of these form critics was arguably the most influential New Testament scholar of the twentieth century, a professor at the University of Marburg known as Rudolf Bultmann. Bultmann and his colleagues were intrigued by questions of how the traditions about

Jesus came to be circulated, and they argued (against what many people think) that the sayings of Jesus and the stories about his life had been seriously changed, transformed, "improved," and even invented by storytellers in the years before any of them was written down in our surviving Gospels.

Thousands of books and articles have been written on this topic since Bultmann and his colleagues were pioneering their work. That makes it all the more striking that there is not a single book available on the topic for a general-reading audience, a book that explains the form-critics' views or delves into the issues they raised in a non-technical (and interesting!) way.

That is, however, what this book is about. It is about how Jesus was being remembered by the Christians who told stories about him, year after year after year, before being presented in the Gospels, and about whether the stories had been invented, or at least altered, in the process.

Moreover, the book will ask whether it is necessarily a bad thing if stories were changed as they were told and retold. Don't we often change a story based on the context in which we are telling it? And based on the people we are telling the story to? And based on what we find to be most important, fascinating, and gripping about it? We're not necessarily doing something deceitful when we change stories. We are often doing something very useful: telling a story in light of the situation at hand and the needs of the people we are speaking with. Would it have been any different with the early story-tellers who were passing along memories of Jesus?

The study of memory is thus not only about seeing what gets changed over time; it is also about the people who remember things the way they do. It may be possible to look at how later memories of Jesus were presented to their audiences to help us understand what the storytellers considered to be the most important points for their own contexts. And by doing so, we may be able to appreciate better what these storytellers and their hearers were dealing with and experiencing in their worlds.

These issues are, to my mind, among the most pressing and important ones that can be asked both about Jesus and about those who followed him in the early years after his death. As I will be pointing out repeatedly, we do not have direct access to what Jesus said, did, and experienced but only to later stories told about him. Originally the stories would have been told by eyewitnesses to his life. And so we will ask if the Gospel writers themselves were actually eyewitnesses. Even if they were, would that mean that their accounts are necessarily reliable? Is, in fact, eyewitness testimony always reliable? Legal scholars and psychologists have long explored that question and have a lot to say about it. Their answers are both very interesting and immediately germane to any investigation into the life and death of Jesus. We will want to see what such scholars have to say.

Once the ancient Christian eyewitnesses told stories about Jesus, their hearers then repeated the stories—obviously in their own words. Those who heard these new stories told them again, in their own words. And others then told these stories to others—and so on, year after year. The stories of Jesus, in other words, were circulated in the "oral tradition" before our Gospel writers produced their accounts. What do we know about oral traditions as circulated in nonliterate or semiliterate cultures? Do oral cultures tend to preserve their traditions accurately, since they cannot write them down to ensure that they remain the same every time? As it turns out, anthropologists have dealt with that question by studying such cultures. As we will see, their answers are highly illuminating for anyone interested in the oral traditions of Jesus.

All of the people who told stories about Jesus—eyewitnesses, people who heard from eyewitnesses, and people who heard from people who heard from people who heard from people who heard from eyewitnesses—remembered what they saw and heard. And their own stories were based on those memories. What do we know about memory? Psychologists have intensely studied this question since the end of the nineteenth century and their findings are intriguing and often unexpected—not to mention directly relevant to the question of early Christian recollections of Jesus. If we are interested in the stories behind the Gospels, we will do well to pay heed to what experts have told us about memory.

Even more, as I have already indicated in my discussions of Abraham Lincoln and Christopher Columbus, memory is not simply a matter of a person's individual recollection of what happened in their personal past. There is a social component as well. Social groups—families, organizations, nations—"remember" things based on their social environments and the social influences in their lives. Sociologists have studied this phenomenon since the 1920s. Anyone who wants to see how groups of people (the various early churches) remembered Jesus would do well to pay heed to this kind of sociological research.

In short, this book is different from other books about Jesus that are available to the general reader. In it I deal with some of the most significant and fundamental questions that we can have about the figure who stands at the head of the entire Christian tradition. These questions are deeply rooted in what I, and most critical scholars, take to be a historical reality: there are forty to sixty-five years separating Jesus's death and our earliest accounts of his life, and we need to know what was happening to the memories of Jesus precisely during that time gap. I approach these questions from fields of study that I have never written about before and that many New Testament scholars have simply never explored, including cognitive psychology, cultural anthropology, and sociology. The intriguing research done in these other fields can help us unpack some of the greatest mysteries confronting both scholars of the New Testament and general readers: what can we know about the man Jesus and about how—and why—the memories of Jesus were altered in the years before the Gospels were produced?

The issues I cover in the book are obviously of enormous importance for all those who claim a personal attachment and allegiance to Jesus. But not only for those. Whatever you personally think and believe about Jesus, whether you consider yourself to be one of his followers or are simply an interested "outsider," you can't deny that Jesus has been and continues to be massively important to our world and our way of life. He is worshipped as God by more than two billion people today, and the church founded on his name has for many, many centuries been the single most powerful religious, cultural, social, political, and economic institution in the Western world. Both faith in Jesus and the church institution established in his name are rooted in stories told about him in the New Testament Gospels. How can we use the later memories of Jesus to the establish facts of his life, the things that he actually said and did? Were details changed here and there when they were being circulated by word of mouth? Were stories changed drastically? Were some invented? In short, were some early Christian memories of Jesus frail? Or faulty? Or even false? If so, can we determine why the memories of Jesus's life and death came to be changed over the course of time? By doing so, can we gain any insight into the lives, values, commitments, conflicts, and concerns of the followers of Jesus who remembered him in these ways? Those are the questions we will be addressing in the chapters that follow.

CHAPTER I

Oral Traditions
and Oral Inventions

As I have talked about memory with people over the past couple of years, I have come to realize that not everyone means the same thing by it. Some people are confused by the very idea that we, today, have a "memory" of Jesus or Abraham Lincoln or Christopher Columbus. None of us ever met these men. How can we have a memory of them? This will be a crucial question to address when considering how Jesus was "remembered" in the years and decades between his death and the first accounts of his life.

To deal with the issue we first have to explore a bit what scholars mean when they are discussing memory—both personal, individual memories that all of us have (and that all thinking people have had, including the earliest followers of Jesus) and collective memories that are held by the various social groups we (and others) belong to.

Psychologists have long recognized that there are different kinds of personal memories we have as individuals. Remembering how to ride a bike is not the same thing as remembering what the capital of France is; and neither is like remembering what you had for dinner last night.

Remembering how to do things with your body—how to breathe deeply, how to swim, how to hit a backhand—is sometimes referred to as "procedural" memory. This is obviously an extremely important form of memory. But since it is of no relevance to my interests in this book, I won't be going into it here. There are, however, two other kinds of memory that are directly relevant, which need to be differentiated from one another.

In 1972 an experimental psychologist named Engel Tulving published a groundbreaking article that argued for a distinction between what he called "episodic" memory and "semantic" memory.[1] Episodic memory is what most of us think about when we talk about "remembering" something from our pasts. This is the kind of memory that involves recalling things that happened to you personally: what you did on your first date, the most recent argument you had with a family member, where you went on vacation last year. There are obviously right and wrong answers to these questions, although much of the time there's no way to check to see if your memories about them are correct. You may have a perfectly clear and vivid memory of where you were when you heard about the attacks on the World Trade Center on September 11, 2001, but in many cases— psychologists have demonstrated—clear memories about such things are flat-out wrong.[2]

Psychologists draw some fine distinctions between different kinds of episodic memories, but as a whole these are recollections of episodes from your own life. Semantic memory, on the other hand, involves factual information about the world, quite apart from whether you have personally experienced it. We can know that the Nile is the largest river in Egypt without ever having taken a boat trip on it, or that Duke won the NCAA basketball championship in 2015 without having seen the game. Most of our knowledge about the world involves information that we are not personally involved with, from mathematical equations (what is the square root of 81?), to geology (what is a tectonic plate?), to history (who was Charlemagne?), to— well, to most of the knowledge we learned either in school or outside of it.

It should be clear that episodic and semantic memories are closely intertwined in many ways. The reason you know the square root of 81 (a piece of semantic knowledge) is because at some point in your past you were taught it by a teacher or a book and were drilled on it and tested on it. That is, it involves episodes from your life. But you almost certainly don't have an episodic memory of when and how any of that happened. You simply have a semantic memory of the fact. On the other hand, you can't really perceive the world you live in and store recollections of these perceptions without semantic knowledge that you remember: What is a number? What is a teacher? What is a test? So the two kinds of memory are closely connected with one another, but also quite different.

One of the striking features of both episodic and semantic memory is that sometimes they are very accurate and other times not. We remember most things reasonably well, but the discomforting reality is that we misremember things all the time. A "false" or "distorted" memory, in the way I will be using these terms in this book, involves a memory that is wrong.[3] Sometimes we misremember things about our own past, as we painfully realize from time to time (more often the older we get!). And sometimes we misremember factual information. If you seem to remember that Barcelona is the capital of Spain, that is a false recollection (some people would just call it a mistake— which of course is absolutely right; but in another sense it is something you are misremembering); and if you remember that your honeymoon was in San Francisco when it was actually in Philadelphia, that would be a false memory as well.

In addition to these kinds of individual memories, we also have shared recollections of the past, shared with others in the sundry social groups to which we belong. "Collective memory" is a term used by sociologists to refer to how various social groups construct, understand, and "remember" the past. In reference to my previous examples, we "remember" Abraham Lincoln in certain ways. If we use the term "memory" to refer only to episodic memories, then obviously none of us remembers Lincoln, since none of us knew him. But memory is more than that. One could say that what we know or think we know about Lincoln is simply a kind of semantic memory that lots of us have. That too would be true. But sociologists argue that the memories of Lincoln are not simply individual recollections of the past. These memories are socially constructed. That is to say, our various social groups have shaped the memory. The societies we live in (all of us live in a wide range of societies, or social groups) determine how we remember the past. These memories are thus not only about what happened, but also about the contexts and the lives of those who cherish and preserve them.

That is why, for example, the Reformation is remembered so differently by fundamentalist Christians and hard-core Roman Catholics; or why the legacy of Ronald Reagan or of Malcom X is remembered so differently among different social groups in our country; or why the Cold War is remembered differently by people in the state of Georgia and people in the country of Georgia.

My point is that there are different kinds of memory. And people remember things differently. Sometimes how they remember things—about their personal pasts, about factual information, about their collective history—is not accurate. Let me stress again: most of the time our memories are pretty good. Otherwise we couldn't function as individuals or as a society. But there are times when we simply don't remember the past accurately. It is worth exploring why we remember things poorly, or wrongly; it is also worth exploring whether such frail or false memories might be helpful for understanding the contexts within which we remember the things we do—and the reasons we remember them in the first place.

Remembering Jesus

What about Jesus? How is he remembered?

Arguably more than anyone else in history, Jesus is remembered in remarkably different ways by different people today, and by different groups of people.

In 2013 a major publishing event occurred. A book about Jesus actually made it to the very top of the *New York Times* bestsellers list. It was not written by an expert on the New Testament, but by a sociologist of religion, Reza Aslan, who is a professor of creative writing at the University of California–Riverside. In his intriguing account, titled *Zealot*, Jesus is portrayed not as the peace-loving and gentle good shepherd of the stained-glass window, but as a Jewish teacher who was particularly zealous for the people of his nation, Israel, and for their recovery of the land that was rightfully theirs.[4] The Promised Land, however, was controlled by the much-despised Romans. Jesus favored a military overthrow of the Roman occupation of the land, and that in fact was his principal message. It was because he was a military insurgent that Jesus was arrested and crucified. Only later did his followers alter his message to one that advocated such teachings as "Love your enemy" and "Turn the other cheek." Jesus himself was a zealot who favored revolution.

Aslan was not the first to remember Jesus in this way. As we will see in the next chapter, such views have been in circulation since the

1770s (although Aslan does not acknowledge his predecessors). Still, his is by far the most popular account of Jesus to take this line. Many people who read his account no doubt found it offensive to their religious sensibilities. Others found it persuasive. And this is how they will now remember Jesus.

Just a couple of months after Aslan's book skyrocketed on the best sellers list, another book about Jesus appeared, this one by Bill O'Reilly, the Fox news commentator (coauthored with Martin Dugard). O'Reilly, too, even more obviously, is not a New Testament scholar. But his portrayal of the founder of Christianity proved to be still more popular than Aslan's. It was wildly popular. It was the single best-selling nonfiction book of 2013. It has sold millions. In one way, *Killing Jesus* portrays Jesus in a way remotely similar to the view of Aslan: Jesus was particularly incensed by the Roman control of the Promised Land.[5] A foreign government had no right to exercise its will over Israel. Particularly aggravating to Jesus, in O'Reilly's view, was the fact that the people of Israel had to pay tribute to the Roman authorities. These were the issues that Jesus was particularly vexed about: excessive political control by a remote political power and too many fiscal demands. Jesus wanted smaller government and lower taxes.[6]

It is easy to see how this view of Jesus might resonate with a wide swath of our population today. Remembering Jesus is not simply an antiquarian exercise. It is about today. Not only does the past impose itself on us when we remember; but also our memories of the past are always affected by our views of the present.

Other authors have seen Jesus in almost precisely the opposite way. Some highly credible biblical scholars who stand in a more liberal political tradition have, somewhat unsurprisingly, portrayed Jesus as an advocate of more liberal political values. Some of the best Jesus scholars of our generation are people who themselves came of age in the 1960s. The Jesus they remember fits in well with the agendas that were dominant then and that continue to resound through the halls of liberal academia today. Some scholars have stressed that Jesus was principally concerned that his disciples abandon their material goods to focus on things that are spiritual. They were to care nothing for personal possessions. They were to share all that was theirs and own nothing themselves, living lives of simplicity and communal sharing. Jesus, then, was an antimaterialist—virtually a proto-Marxist, or at least one who was vehemently opposed to a capitalist system focused on greed and possessions.[7]

Others have stressed the significant role that women played in the life of Jesus—not just those women who are prominently named in the Gospels, such as Mary, the mother of Jesus, or his follower Mary Magdalene—but also other women, often unnamed, who appear in important places, women whom he speaks openly with, whom he reveals himself to, whom he touches in public, whom he welcomes among his group of followers without discriminating against them because of their gender, women who were faithful to him to the end even when the male disciples betrayed, denied, and abandoned him. These women were the ones who truly understood him, and Jesus advocated for their liberation from the harsh constraints of their patriarchal society. Jesus in this sense is remembered as a kind of protofeminist, a forerunner of modern views of liberation.[8]

Probably the majority of modern scholars have remembered Jesus as an apocalyptic prophet who was predicting that the end of the world was near, that God was soon going to intervene in the course of human affairs to destroy the forces of evil wreaking such havoc on earth, creating such enormous amounts of pain, misery, and suffering; this cataclysmic act of God was to arrive very soon, within Jesus's own generation. God would send a cosmic judge of the earth to annihilate everything and everyone that stood opposed to him and his purposes, bringing in a good kingdom on earth in which there would be no more war, hatred, natural disaster, violence, sin, or death. This is a view that I myself have held since I was a graduate student in the early 1980s. But is it an accident that the view became so forcefully expressed by scholars in the nuclear age, when the world was in imminent danger of destruction?[9]

All of these views—and others I have not detailed—have clear historical merit in one way or another. They can all be argued for on academic, historical grounds. But what is more significant for my purpose is that all represent different ways that competent, modern authors recall who Jesus was.[10] These authors all have their followers among their readers, who remember Jesus in different ways, sometimes radically different ways.

This is not to mention how Jesus is remembered in our society at large by nonscholars, some of whom have no time for scholars. For many people, of course, Jesus's main objective was to provide the key to eternal life. Others remember Jesus as a healer of souls who could (and can) provide comfort in times of distress or whose power can heal a body that is weak, crippled, or deformed. Others remember Jesus as one who was principally interested in making his followers successful, who guaranteed large amounts of wealth to people who simply followed his prosperity gospel. Yet others remember Jesus as one who, through his ethical teachings and personal example, showed how we need to sacrifice ourselves and our personal comforts for the sake of helping those in need.

I am not saying that every one of these various memories of who Jesus was, what he did, what he taught, and what he intended is mutually exclusive. Many people hold several of these views at once. But why are there so many memories of Jesus? Can they all be accurate memories? Or are there also lots of distorted memories—memories of Jesus that do not conform to who he really was and really taught? Is someone inventing things? I should think that it is fairly safe to say that *someone* is inventing things. They can't *all* be on target. Jesus did not teach both that the goal in life is to get rich by following his divinely inspired directions for prosperity *and* that we should give up all our worldly goods for the sake of others.

Here, though, is my ultimate point, both for this chapter and for the entire book: this invention of memories of Jesus is not simply a modern phenomenon. It has always been going on. From the very earliest of times. As far back as we have recorded memories of Jesus, we have widely disparate accounts of his words and deeds. And the events of his life. And the events of the lives of those who knew him.

One of the ways to begin exploring how ancient memories of Jesus were invented is by examining later memories of people connected with him. Early Christians recalled Jesus's associates—his family members, disciples, and enemies—in intriguing ways, as evidenced in the tales that survive. By looking at a broad range of such stories we can gain some insights into how Christian memory worked, and see how memory sometimes came to be distorted (quite obviously in many cases). These insights may help us understand better the early Christian memories of Jesus himself, as he was being recalled by his later followers.

Memories of Jesus's Companions

In early Christianity there were lots of memories of the people connected in some way with Jesus. I think it's fair to say that a lot of these were "distorted" memories—that is, memories that were not rooted in history so much as in people's vivid imaginations.

Take the Apostle Peter, Jesus's right-hand man. We have, of course, stories about Peter in the New Testament. But for now, to illustrate my point about early Christian memories, we may consider accounts from outside the New Testament. Some of the most popular stories about Peter come from a second-century book known as the Acts of Peter. Here Peter is portrayed as a great miracle worker, able to heal the sick, cast out demons, and raise the dead. Are these accurate memories?

In one episode, after Peter has healed a multitude of sick people in his home, someone asks him why he will not heal his own daughter, a young and beautiful girl who is paralyzed and lying in a corner. To prove that he is able to heal the child, he speaks to her and tells her in the name of Jesus to become well. Her paralysis disappears and she stands up and walks to him.

He then tells her to return to her corner and become paralyzed again. When she complies, the crowd becomes understandably upset and dismayed. Peter explains to them that the Lord had informed him that if the child was healthy, she would lead others astray, presumably because men would lust after her. In fact, he indicates the reason she became paralyzed in the first place was because an older man had seduced her. But before he could have his wicked way with her, God paralyzed her. Now it is the Lord's will for her to remain paralyzed, even though Peter is fully capable of restoring her to heath. The author of this account does not explicitly say so, but it appears that the readers are supposed to agree with him that this is a good thing.[11]

Sometimes Peter's healing powers are not quite so heart-wrenching. In another episode he is preaching to the crowds about the power of Jesus, and they ask him to perform a miraculous sign so they can believe. He is standing by a body of water, and as he turns around he sees a fishmonger's shop with a smoked tuna fish hanging in the window. He asks the crowd, "If you now see this swimming in the water like a fish, will you be able to believe in him whom I preach?" (Acts of Peter, 13). The crowd enthusiastically responds that they will indeed believe if he can work such a miracle. Peter takes the fish, tosses it in the water, and orders it in the name of Jesus Christ to come alive and swim. It does so, and the crowd converts.

Most of the Acts of Peter is about the conflicts that Peter has with an archheretic known as Simon Magus (this is the same Simon who appears in the New Testament in Acts 8:14–24). Simon Magus is a great miracle worker himself, who through his powerful deeds leads people astray by convincing them that he represents the truth. Much of the Acts of Peter represents miracle contests between Simon and Peter, in which Peter is continually shown to get the better of his heretical opponent. None of the episodes is more breathtaking than the final one.

Simon has announced to the people of the city of Rome that he is the one who is from God, and he will prove it the next day by ascending to heaven in their presence. The people gather together to witness the event, and after delivering a short speech about his power, Simon does indeed ascend and begin to fly over the temples and hills of Rome. Peter, however, the true man of God, is not one to be bested by a charlatan. He calls upon God's power to deprive Simon of his ability to fly in midair, and Simon comes crashing to the ground. He breaks his leg in three places, and the crowds attack him and stone him to death. Everyone then becomes convinced that it is Peter and no other who is the one who represents the true God.

No one on the planet today thinks that Peter really did these things. But many ancient Christians thought he did. These are the ways Peter was widely remembered, as a great miracle worker who performed spectacular deeds to prove that he was empowered by the heavenly Jesus, the Lord of all. But surely these episodes represent distorted memories. It is true that in some of the cases the author of the book may have been the one who actually invented these stories about Peter—that is, they may not have been stories in broad circulation that he himself heard. In that case he was not himself "remembering"

Peter in this way. He was just making stuff up. But—and this is a very big "but"—those who then read the stories and believed them (and we have every reason to think that the people who read them, or heard them read, believed them) had their own memories of Peter shaped by them. And so they do represent distorted memories, even if the author created them himself.

We may now shift from considering one of the good guys of the gospel stories to examine one of the very bad guys, Judas Iscariot. Christians have almost always remembered Judas as the evil disciple, the one who betrayed his master to his death and received a divine punishment for it. In the New Testament, there are two different accounts of Judas's death, one in the Gospel of Matthew, where he is said to have hanged himself (Matt. 27:3–10) and one in the book of Acts, where he is said to have fallen headlong so that his belly ripped open and he spilled his intestines on the ground (Acts 15–19). It is very difficult, maybe impossible, to reconcile these accounts. (Read them for yourself and ask: Who purchased the Field of Blood where Judas died? And why was it called the Field of Blood?) What is interesting is that later Christians had yet other recollections of the events surrounding Judas's death.

One of my favorites is found in a manuscript of a noncanonical gospel known as the Gospel of Nicodemus, an account of Jesus's trial, death, and resurrection allegedly written by the mysterious figure Nicodemus, who shows up in the New Testament only in the Gospel of John (see John 3). In this manuscript, we are told that after betraying Jesus, Judas felt terrible remorse and returned home to hang himself. He finds his wife in the kitchen, roasting a chicken on a spit over a charcoal fire. He tells her that he has done the wicked deed and that he is now going to end it all, because Jesus is soon going to rise from the dead and will then deal with him harshly. Judas's wife replies in disbelief: Jesus cannot rise from the dead any more than this roasting chicken can come back to life. As soon as she utters these words, the chicken rises up on the spit and begins to crow. Judas shrieks and goes off to find a rope to hang himself.

There is another, completely different account, preserved in the writings of a church father named Papias. We will meet Papias again in chapter 3. In the early second century he wrote a five-volume book called the *Expositions of the Sayings of the Lord*. Unfortunately, Christian scribes, for some reason, decided not to copy the book for posterity, so we do not actually have it. But later authors occasionally quoted from the book, so we do know a few of the things Papias said. One of his stories involves the death of Judas, a story that may represent a legendary expansion of the version now found in the New Testament book of Acts.

According to Papias, after Judas betrayed Jesus he was inflicted with a divine punishment. His body swelled up to an enormous size. He became so large that he could not squeeze onto a street that had buildings on either side. Not even his head would fit. His face became so fat that a doctor could not locate his eyes with an optical instrument. His genitals became enormously swollen and emitted pus and worms. He finally died on his own land by pouring his innards out on them. This created such a stench that even in Papias's day, nearly a century later, people could not pass by without holding their noses.

Are these accurate memories? They may be true to the idea that Judas was a very bad man who got what he deserved (as the early Christian storytellers heartily believed), but the specific memories themselves are surely distorted.

One could argue that as bad as Judas Iscariot was, the Roman governor, Pontius Pilate, was worse. Judas may have betrayed Jesus, but Pilate was the one who condemned Jesus to be flogged and then crucified. It is interesting to observe that even while Judas became increasingly vilified in Christian memory, Pilate came to be portrayed in a remarkably positive light. Pilate? Remembered well? Yes indeed.

There are a number of noncanonical texts that are collectively known as the "Pilate Gospels." These would include the Gospel of Nicodemus that I just mentioned, which is sometimes titled the Acts of Pilate (because Pilate plays a pivotal role in the first part of it), along with such apocryphal books as the Letter of Pilate to Herod, the Report of Pilate, and the Handing Over of Pilate. What is striking in these accounts is that as time goes on, Pilate comes to be increasingly exonerated in the death of Jesus.

Early on in the Christian tradition—already by the middle of the second century—it was thought that Pilate had sent a letter to the Roman emperor, Tiberius, to explain the big mistake he had just made in crucifying the Son of God (thus Tertullian, *Apology*, 21–24). A version of such a letter was produced at a later time by a Christian author. This is the fourth- or fifth-century "Report" of Pilate, where he tells the emperor that he was not at fault for the death of Jesus. He was forced to execute him by "the entire multitude of the Jews," even though they could not "convict him of a single crime."[12] Pilate goes on to explain that Jesus did many miracles, healing the blind, cleansing the lepers, and raising the dead. Jesus, in fact, showed himself to be more powerful even than the gods that the Romans themselves worship. The Jews, however, threatened to stir up a rebellion against Pilate, and so he had to crucify the Son of God. But Jesus then had his vengeance: all the synagogues of the unbelieving Jews in Jerusalem were destroyed and the Jews were engulfed in flaming chasms in the earth.

This is a terrifically interesting document that relates a very negative memory of the Jews, though obviously a more positive memory of Pilate. But is either memory accurate?

A later Christian author followed up this remarkable account by indicating how Tiberius responded to Pilate's report. Highly aggravated that Pilate had agreed to crucify the Son of God, Tiberius sends soldiers to bring him back to face trial in Rome. Tiberius begins the judicial proceeding by saying, "How could you dare to do such things, you most impious man, after seeing such great signs accompanying that man? By daring to do this wicked deed you have destroyed the entire world." Pilate responds by saying that it was entirely the fault of the Jews. He was not to blame; they forced him to do it. Tiberius will hear none of this, and tells Pilate that it was clear from the signs Jesus did that he "was the Christ, the King of the Jews." As soon as Tiberius speaks the name of Jesus, all the statues of pagan gods in the courtroom fall to the ground and crumble to dust.

The emperor orders Pilate to be executed. But it becomes clear that Pilate himself deeply regrets what he did, and he insists to his death that his hand was forced by the recalcitrant Jews. More than that, he has come to believe in Christ. Before the executioner wields his sword, Pilate prays to Jesus for forgiveness, and a voice comes from heaven telling him: "All the races and families of the nations will bless you, because under your rule everything spoken about me by the prophets was fulfilled." Pilate, in fact, will appear with Jesus when he returns at the Second Coming to judge the tribes of Israel. When the executioner then chops off Pilate's head, an angel of the Lord descends and takes it up to heaven.

What a remarkable tale. How could Pilate possibly be remembered as a Christian convert especially blessed by Christ? Wasn't he a brutal and ruthless Roman administrator who had no concerns for the sensitivities of the Jewish people and no interest at all in Jesus, whom he ordered to be humiliated, flogged, and tortured to death? Yes, that's who he may have been in history. But it's not who he was in the memory of early Christians. They remembered the past life of Pilate in light of their own present circumstances. They remembered

Pilate as innocent in the death of Jesus. And why was that? For a very simple reason. If Pilate was innocent, who was guilty? It was those godless Jews. These memories are being shaped by the world in which storytellers and those who hear their accounts live, a world of deep, bitter, and growing animosity between Christians and Jews. Christians are recalling the past because of what was happening in their own time. I'm afraid we all do that, to one degree or another.

But did early Christians have frail, faulty, or even false memories also of Jesus? Yes, that too.

Memories of the Birth and Early Life of Jesus

Probably the most popular Gospel from outside the New Testament over the centuries was a book that most people have never heard of today. The title scholars have given it is the *Protevangelium Jacobi*, which means the "Proto-Gospel of James." It is called the "ProtoGospel" because it recounts events related to the life of Jesus that allegedly happened before he was born. It is a book that is principally about Jesus's mother, Mary: her own miraculous birth to a woman, Anna, who had been barren; her upbringing, mainly in the Jewish Temple, where she was watched over by priests and fed daily by an angel from heaven; and her engagement to the rich construction man Joseph, who was very much her senior. It was one of his sons from a previous marriage, James, who is said to have written the account. The reality is that the book was written long after James had been laid in his grave. It is probably from the second century.

Throughout the Middle Ages the book was enormously influential on Christian art, storytelling, and memory. Have you ever noticed how medieval paintings always portray Joseph as an old man but Mary as a very young woman? That comes from the Proto-Gospel. Or possibly you know the old Catholic teaching that Jesus's brothers were not really his brothers but were either his cousins or sons of Joseph from a first wife? The latter view also comes from this book. Or the idea that during the trip of the holy couple to Bethlehem right before Jesus was born Mary rode on a donkey? Once more, the Proto-Gospel. In some ways, for centuries this book affected how Christians remembered the events surrounding Jesus's birth more than the books of the New Testament.

As interesting as all its stories are—and most of them are highly interesting indeed—none is more intriguing to modern readers than the story of Jesus's birth itself. In this account, as Joseph and Mary are nearing Bethlehem, she goes into labor. Joseph hurriedly finds a private place for her to give birth, in a cave. He leaves her there to go off to find a midwife. And then a miracle happens. As he is walking, Joseph suddenly sees time stand still. The birds in the air have stopped moving in midflight; in the field before him workers taking their lunch break have frozen in place, with their hands in a bowl or partway up to their mouths; a shepherd is stopped immobile while reaching out his rod to strike the sheep. But "then suddenly everything returned to its normal course."[13] The world had ground to a halt in honor of the Son of God, who has now become human.

Joseph finds a Hebrew midwife and brings her back to the cave, but it is overshadowed by a brilliant cloud. When it disappears, a blinding light shines from within. Eventually it too fades, and Joseph and the midwife see an infant who walks over to Mary and takes hold of her breast. The midwife is astonished at the miracle and goes off to tell another midwife, named Salome, that a virgin has given birth. Salome, however, is doubtful and indicates that she won't believe it until she herself gives Mary a postpartum inspection to see for herself. Really. They come to the cave, and the first midwife tells Mary, "Brace yourself." Salome performs an internal inspection and becomes an instant believer. Mary has not only conceived as a virgin, she has given birth as a virgin: her hymen is still intact. But because Salome has doubted the power of God, her hand begins to burn as if on fire. She prays to God for mercy and is told to pick up the child so that her hand will be healed. She does so, and glorifies God. Thus we have a rather peculiar but highly memorable—and widely remembered—account of the miraculous events at the incarnation of Christ, the Son of God.

As you might imagine, Christians throughout the ages who recalled the life of Jesus as an infant regaled one another with stories about his miraculous youth. Several of the most intriguing accounts can be found in an early medieval gospel that scholars call the Gospel of Pseudo-Matthew. Like its predecessor and source, the Proto-Gospel of James, Pseudo-Matthew was enormously popular. One of its best-known stories involves the infant Jesus's journey to Egypt with his parents, Joseph and Mary, to escape the wrath of King Herod. This trip is recounted without any detail in the New Testament itself, in the Gospel of Matthew (Matt. 2:13–15). In this later account, on the other hand, allegedly also written by Matthew, some of the entertaining details are provided.

In this version of the story, Jesus is not quite two years old at the time. The trip involves not just him and his parents, but also several servants, along with some rather peculiar animals. Early on in the journey, while the holy family has taken a stop, a group of dragons comes out of a cave and approaches them, much to the fear and consternation of Jesus's parents. But not to Jesus. He stands before the dragons and they begin to worship him, in fulfilment of the prophecy of scripture, "Praise the Lord from the earth, O dragons and all the places of the abyss."[14] Jesus tells his parents not to fear and not to think of him as a young child in need of protection, for, he tells them, "I have always been the perfect man, and am now; and it is necessary for me to tame every kind of wild beast." Soon an entire coterie of animals accompanies the family on their journey: lions and leopards, along with the oxen and donkeys and tame goats.

After the family travels for three days, Mary has grown weary from too much sun. They stop and she sits for a while in the shade of a palm tree. She looks up and sees the top of the tree with its luscious fruit, and she bemoans the fact that it is so far beyond anyone's reach. Joseph is surprised she is so worried about food; their main problem is a lack of water. They have nowhere to replenish their supply. The infant Jesus, sitting in his mother's lap, solves both of their problems. He speaks to the tree, "Bend down, O tree, and refresh my mother from your fruit." The palm tree does as he commands. Everyone eats of its fruit and is refreshed. Jesus then orders the tree to open up the hidden springs that lie at its roots. Springs of fresh, clear, cold, and sweet water flow forth.

To reward the palm tree for its faithful response to his commands, on the next day Jesus informs it that one of its branches will be taken and planted in paradise. An angel of the Lord appears from above, cuts off one of the branches, and takes it on up to heaven. Jesus announces that the same palm tree that has refreshed his family will refresh all the saints in paradise. Here Jesus is remembered as the wondrous miracle-working Son of God—already as an infant.

Another account of Jesus as a young boy comes to us in a book called the Infancy Gospel of Thomas. Even though, in antiquity, this book was not as popular as the Proto-Gospel of James, it is extremely popular today, at least among readers familiar with the apocryphal accounts of Jesus's life. It purports to relate incidents from Jesus's life between ages five and twelve. What is ultimately driving the account is a question that some people still have today, even if they have never heard about the early Christian apocrypha: if Jesus did such fantastic miracles during his public ministry, what was he doing before then? In particular, what was he like as boy?

This account shows what he was like. Modern scholars are divided on whether the Gospel is meant to show that Jesus had unearthly powers and a mischievous streak that kept him from controlling them, or if it is instead meant to show that the powerful events of Jesus's later life were foreshadowed in his prepubescence. Or both. If nothing else, readers today widely agree that the stories remembered here are highly entertaining.

It begins with Jesus as a five-year-old, playing by a stream. He decides to gather some of the muddy water together into a pool; he then orders it to become pure—and it happens instantaneously at his word. He then shapes twelve sparrows out of the mud. A Jewish man walking by, however, sees what he has done and becomes incensed: it is the Sabbath, and Jesus has violated the Law of Moses that forbids work on that day. The man hurries off to tell Jesus's father, Joseph, who comes to the stream and sees Jesus with the mud sparrows. He too is angry and asks Jesus why he has done such a thing. Jesus looks at his father, looks at the sparrows, and then claps his hands and says "Begone!" The sparrows come to life and fly off chirping.

This is a great story. Not only has Jesus shown that he is both the Lord of the Sabbath and the Lord of life, he has also destroyed all evidence of malfeasance. Sparrows? What sparrows?

In the next story we see why some readers detect a mean streak in the boy Jesus. Another child, the son of a Jewish scribe, is playing with him at the stream, and he decides to take a willow branch and scatter the water that Jesus has gathered together and purified. Jesus gets angry. He turns to the boy and tells him that he too will wither like a tree with no water and will never grow root or bear fruit. The child is withered on the spot. His parents come and carry him away, bemoaning his lost youth.

Jesus's reputation with his townsfolk does not improve from one story to the next. In the following account he is walking through his village and another boy who is running past accidentally bumps into his shoulder. Jesus is aggravated and announces, "You will go no further on your way." The boy falls down, dead.

Joseph decides that Jesus needs to be educated. Surely some book learning will do him good. On three occasions he tries to find a teacher for the boy. It never ends well. Jesus humiliates the first teacher by delivering a learned and obscure lecture on the meaning of the first letter of the Greek alphabet, a lecture that no one can figure out. The teacher gives up after one letter. The next teacher fares worse. When Jesus refuses to recite the alphabet with him, in frustration he smacks the boy upside the head. Big mistake. Jesus curses him on the spot and he falls in a dead faint. And so it goes.

Jesus eventually does start to use his powers for good. At one point he is playing with a group of other children on a flat roof. One of them, a boy named Zenon, accidentally trips, falls to the ground, and dies. The other children are frightened and run off. Jesus goes to the edge of the roof and looks down, and as he is looking on, lo and behold, Zenon's parents walk up and see their dead son. Looking up, they see Jesus, and assume that he has been at his tricks again and accuse him of killing their son. But this time Jesus has done nothing wrong. So he leaps off the roof, lands by the body, and orders Zenon to rise from the dead and say whether he has killed him. Zenon is restored to life and announces, "No Lord, you did not throw me down, you have raised me up!"

Jesus begins to use his powers for good, raising those he has killed and healing those he has harmed. Moreover, with his miraculous abilities he proves to be remarkably handy around the home and the carpenter's shop. The account ends with Jesus as a twelve-year-old confounding the Jewish teachers of the law in the Temple of Jerusalem, a story taken from the New Testament Gospel of Luke.

When people think of Jesus today, this is not the Jesus they re-member. Most don't remember anything about Jesus's life before he was baptized as an adult. But throughout history people often re-membered Jesus this way. But it's not because he really did wither his playmates and zap his teachers. These are legendary accounts, "dis-torted" memories. But they are how people recalled Jesus when they thought about his young life.

Memories of Jesus's Life and Death

As you might expect, based on everything we have seen so far, apoc-ryphal stories that fed the Christian imagination and populated the Christian memory about Jesus were not restricted to his birth and childhood. There were plenty of legendary tales of his life, teachings, death, and resurrection.

I often get asked why, in my opinion, Jesus never wrote anything.[15] According to some stories, he did indeed write. There is the famous account of Jesus and the woman taken in adultery found in later man-uscripts of the Gospel of John, chapter 8, and familiar to Bible readers today both because it can still be found in most English translations (even if it is normally bracketed as not being original) and because it is the darling of every Hollywood director who has ever made a movie about Jesus.[16] In that story, both before and after Jesus tells the Jewish leaders who want to execute judgment on the woman, "Let the one without sin among you be the first to cast a stone at her," he stoops down and begins to write on the ground. Unfortunately, we don't know what it was he wrote, even though later interpreters, down till today, have made numerous suggestions: Possibly he wrote a scripture verse about false judgments? Possibly a list of the sins of the woman's accusers? Possibly divine threats against those who oppose him? There are lots of options.

Far less familiar to modern readers is a writing by Jesus in a legendary account known as the Correspondence with Abgar. In this account, which appears to have circulated principally in Syria starting in the early third century, Jesus corresponds with the king of the city of Edessa, a man named Abgar. Abgar first sends Jesus a letter, in which he indicates that he has heard of Jesus's great miracles: he can make the blind see, the lame walk, the lepers clean, and the dead raised. Abgar too is ill, and he would like Jesus to come heal him. As a side benefit, by coming to Syria Jesus can escape from the Jews who are trying to do him harm.

Jesus replies to Abgar's request in the one letter we have that is allegedly from his hand. He praises Abgar for believing him without having laid eyes on him (see John 20:29). Regrettably, however, he cannot come to Edessa. He needs to fulfill the mission that he has undertaken. After that he will be ascending to heaven. Jesus does indicate that after his ascension he will send one of his disciples to heal Abgar.

In a later legend we learn that following Jesus's resurrection his brother Judas Thomas did send a Christian missionary named Addai (or sometimes named Thaddaeus) to Abgar. He healed the king and then converted the city of Edessa to the Christian faith. These two letters and the legend were in circulation for a long time. Where they were known they formed a clear memory of Jesus and his foreign correspondence.

Somewhat more familiar to readers of early Christian apocrypha today are the noncanonical Gospels that report teachings of Jesus that were in circulation in various churches throughout the empire. None is more famous than the Coptic Gospel of Thomas, not to be confused with the Infancy Gospel of Thomas discussed earlier. In chapter 6 I will have a good deal more to say about the Gospel of Thomas and how its author and readers appear to have been remembering Jesus. Here I simply want to point out that these recollections of Jesus's teachings were sometimes far afield from how other Christians in antiquity re-called the words of the Savior. Not to mention most Christians today.

This Gospel was discovered in 1945 along with a number of other early Christian texts (fifty-two altogether) in a collection of leather-bound books near the town of Nag Hammadi, Egypt.[17] Most of these other texts represent views of early Christian Gnostics. Modern schol-ars call these followers of Jesus Gnostic because their version of the Christian faith emphasized "knowledge" (the Greek word is *gnosis*) for salvation. What mattered was not the death and resurrection of Jesus but the secret teachings he delivered, whose meaning explained how the divine realm and this material world came into existence. Those who correctly learned the secret knowledge that could bring escape from the material trappings of this world would find salvation in the world above.

Gnosticism is an incredibly complex set of religions, with differ-ent sects having different mythologies, different sacred writings, dif-ferent ritual practices, and different organizational patterns. Luckily we do not need to discuss the Gnostic religions here.[18] One of the debates about the Gospel of Thomas during the past twenty years or so is over whether, like other books among the so-called Nag Ham-madi library, it should even be considered Gnostic. Most experts today think that the answer is no. But again, that is a debate we do not need to enter into here. At this stage I want to make a more basic point: the way Jesus's teachings were remembered by this author and, presumably, his audience, are strikingly different from the way they were and are remembered by other kinds of Christians.

The Gospel of Thomas consists entirely of sayings of Jesus, 114 of them altogether. Among these sayings there are certainly some—a lot, in fact—that will sound familiar to anyone conversant with the Gospels of Matthew, Mark, and Luke. In a way quite similar to these other Gospels, Jesus delivers the following teachings:

• You see the speck that is in your brother's eye, but you do not see the log that is in your eye. When you take the log out of your eye, then you will see well enough to take the speck out of your brother's eye. (Saying 26)

• If a blind person leads a blind person, they both fall into a pit. (Saying 34)

• "Blessed are the poor, for the kingdom of heaven is yours." (Saying 54)

But he is also remembered saying things that strike most readers as highly puzzling, to say the least. The following examples can illustrate the point:

• His disciples said, "When will you appear to us and when shall we see you?" Jesus said, "When you strip naked without being ashamed and take your clothes and place them under your feet like little children and stamp on them, then you will see the Son of the Living One, and you will not be afraid." (Saying 37)

• If they say to you, "Where have you come from?" tell them, "We have come from the light, from the place where the light came to be on its own, established itself, and was revealed in their image." If they say to you, "Is it you?" say, "We are its children, and we are the chosen of the living Father." If they ask you, "What is the sign of your Father in you?" say to them, "It is movement and repose." (Saying 50)

- When you see your likeness, you rejoice. But when you see your images that came into being before you and that neither die nor become revealed, how much you will bear! (Saying 84)

- Blessed is the lion that the human will eat so that the lion becomes human. And cursed is the human whom the lion will eat, and the lion will become human. (Saying 7)

Or there is the saying that is probably the most perplexing, famous, and possibly offensive to modern sensibilities of them all, the one that ends the collection:

- Simon Peter said to them, "Mary should leave us, for females are not worthy of the life." Jesus said, "Look, I am going to guide her in order to make her male, so that she too may become a living spirit resembling you males. For every female who makes herself male will enter the kingdom of heaven." (Saying 114)

Luckily (at least for me), I do not need to provide an extended interpretation of these particular sayings here. As I have indicated, I will have more to say about the ways Jesus is remembered in this text in chapter 6. For now I simply want to stress that however one interprets these latter sayings, they are very different indeed from those that can be found on Jesus's lips in the canonical Gospels. Those who remembered Jesus saying such things were remembering a different Jesus from the one portrayed in Matthew, Mark, Luke, or John.

In addition to recollections of Jesus's writing and teachings, there are numerous alternative memories of what happened at his death and resurrection. Arguably the most intriguing is the fragmentary account known as the Gospel of Peter. This comes to us in a book that was discovered in a cemetery in Upper Egypt in 1886, in a tomb that archaeologists identified as belonging to a monk. The book contains four different texts—so that it was a small anthology—the first of which, occupying ten pages, is a Gospel that claims to be written by Jesus's closest disciple, Peter. This particular copy of the Gospel—the only copy we have—was probably made in the late sixth century or so, and unfortunately, the scribe who made it was copying only a fragment of a larger Gospel (the rest of which, obviously, is no longer available). The surviving portion of the Gospel presents an account of Jesus's trial, death, and resurrection. Scholars are reasonably unified in thinking that originally the book was composed in the early second century. Whether it depended for its account on the narratives found in the canonical Gospels is much debated.

What is not debated is that this is an unusually fascinating memory of Jesus's passion. One of the most immediately striking features of the account is the heightened responsibility borne by the Jews—both the Jewish leaders and the Jewish people—for the death of Jesus. Much like the later Pilate Gospels, here it is not the Roman governor who is principally at fault, but the recalcitrant Jews who by their unfaithful and reckless behavior have brought the judgment of God down upon their heads. Possibly even more striking are the intriguing deviations from the canonical accounts of Jesus's actual death and resurrection. For example, in this account one of the crucified robbers berates not Jesus but the Roman soldiers who are crucifying Jesus without good cause. The soldiers respond by not breaking his legs so he will die in agony. The assumption here is that death by crucifixion comes by slow asphyxiation: a crucified person can breathe only so long as he can push up on the spike through his feet to relieve the pressure on his lungs. Once the legs are broken, that is not possible. And so by not breaking the criminal's legs, the soldiers prolong his torment.

Another example involves Jesus himself on the cross. We are told that he was "silent as feeling no pain." This has raised numerous interpretive questions since the text was discovered. Is the author indicating that Jesus was silent "as if" he had no pain? In that case, he would evidence a rather stoic attitude toward his own torture, possibly as an example for Christians who themselves might be martyred in days to come. Or is the author suggesting that Jesus was silent precisely as one who *did* feel no pain? That appears to be how the text was read by some Christians in antiquity, who understood it to mean that Jesus did not really have a full flesh-and-blood body like other humans, because he was himself a divine being who only seemed to be a human. His was a phantom appearance, a nonmaterial body, a body without nerve endings. If that's what the text means then it would have portrayed Jesus in terms widely acceptable to some groups of Gnostics and other kinds of Christians who stressed Jesus's full divinity at the expense of his humanity.

By far the most interesting divergence from the canonical Gospels comes at the end of Peter's narrative, where we have an actual description of Jesus's resurrection. We get no such description in the New Testament. In all four of the canonical Gospels Jesus is crucified, dead, and buried, and then on the third day, following the intervening Sabbath, one or more of his women followers come to the tomb to provide his corpse with the proper rites of burial, only to find the tomb empty, the body gone, and the Lord raised from the dead. The resurrection event itself, when Jesus emerged from the tomb as the Lord of life, is not described in the New Testament. It happened some time before the women showed up.

But not so in the Gospel of Peter. Here we are told that (as in Matthew's account) Pilate appointed Roman guards to watch the tomb to prevent Jesus's followers from stealing the body. While the guards are performing their duty, to their amazement they see the heavens split open, two angelic beings descend, the stone in front of the tomb roll away, the angels enter into the tomb, and then three persons emerge. Two of them, presumably the angels, are so tall that their heads reach up to the sky. The one they support on the way out is taller still—his head reaches above the sky. Behind them, out of the tomb, there emerges the cross. A voice comes from heaven and asks, "Have you preached to those who are asleep?" The cross replies, "Yes."

This is an absolutely astounding account. Whether the author wanted his readers to take it as something that literally happened is anyone's guess. How we wish we knew. Whatever its status as a literal description of a historical event, the account is clearly filled with deep symbolism. The angels are gigantic because they are superhuman, and of course superhumans are massively larger than humans. Jesus, as the Son of God, is much larger than angels. The voice of God speaks to the cross to find out (or for others to know) whether the message of salvation brought by the crucifixion has been proclaimed to those who were already dead, dwelling in Sheol or Hades at the time. The cross affirms that indeed, the good news of salvation has reached the underworld.

What a splendid way for early Christians to remember Jesus. He is not remembered as a crucified criminal who was humiliated and tortured to death by enemies more powerful than he. Quite the contrary, he is the powerful Savior who has overcome all the powers that are opposed to God: the powers of Rome, the powers of the devil, the powers of sin and death. His victory is now blazoned both across the pages of a text that proclaims his conquest and in the hearts of those who read and hear what he has done and who he is. Christ is the Lord not only of the living but also of the dead. This is quite a memory of Jesus.

The Very Real Memories of Jesus

No one today would seriously maintain that these memories of Jesus and his followers were historically accurate. These are not accounts of the past that depict events that really happened in the ways they are described. But does that really matter?

It might matter to people whose only concern is to know what really took place in the past. But why should that be a person's only concern? Shouldn't we be concerned also about other things? If we want to read a book, do we really only want to read histories and historically accurate biographies? Are our only human interests tied to what has really happened in the past? Don't we also want to read novels? And short stories? And poetry? Don't imaginative storytellers who piece together complicated plots with intricate but invented characters have something to say to us? Can't "truth" be bigger than the bare-bones question about what happened before now?

As I will be stressing in chapter 8, surely truth can be embodied in other art forms. When we stand in awe before a painting of a biblical scene or of an apocryphal narrative by Giotto, or Caravaggio, or Rembrandt, our first question is never (or at least, *should* never be) whether it is historically accurate. Or whether its depiction of Mary, the mother of Jesus, or of his disciple Peter, or of Jesus himself is really what they must have looked like. Aesthetics obviously can't be reduced to, or dependent on, or even related to historical accuracy. Why should historical accuracy be our only concern in *any* realm of discourse outside, of course, of history itself?

When it comes to how Jesus was portrayed, understood, believed in, thought about, imagined, and remembered throughout the centuries of the early church, starting with the New Testament itself, there is no reason to privilege history as the one and only question of interest. It may be one of our questions—for some of us, a massively important one—but it doesn't need to be the only one. What I have been discussing in this chapter are ways that Jesus was remembered by Christians after he had died. We need always to remember ourselves that memories do not need to be historically accurate to be vivid and meaningful—at least true in our own consciousness. The "distorted" memories of Jesus—by which I mean memories that are not accurate in the strictly historical sense—are just as real to those who hold and share them as "true" memories (that is, *historically* true).

It is in fact a question worth asking whether any of us has any "true" memories of Jesus in the technical sense. How would we know? Historians, of course, can ask what probably happened in the past, for example, in the earthly ministry of Jesus with his disciples. And historians can establish with relative levels of probability that this, that, or the other tradition is likely something that happened or didn't happen. But history is all a matter of such greater or lesser probabilities. When dealing with a figure such as Jesus, these probabilities are established only by critically examining the memories that were recorded by later authors. Another task, though, is to consider the memories themselves and to study them as memories, whether they are rooted in historical realities or instead were invented, either consciously or intentionally, by later storytellers.

In this book I am interested in both tasks. I'm interested in knowing which memories of Jesus are historically probable. Did he really tame a group of dragons? Did he really zap his playmates when they got on his nerves? Did he really bless the lions who eat humans so as to become human? Was he really executed because of "the Jews"? Did he really heal the sick, cast out demons, and raise the dead? Did he really die on the orders of the Roman governor, Pontius Pilate? Or are some of these stories products of frail, faulty, or even false memories? To answer these questions we need to learn more about how people remember, both as individuals (the subject of chapters 3, 4, and 5) and as social groups (the subject of chapters 6 and 7).

Even beyond that, what can we say about the memories themselves, and what can they tell us about the people who held and shared them? What do they tell us about their understandings of Jesus, his importance for their lives, his role in providing salvation? How can they inform us about the communities in which these memories were shared? How were some of these memories generated, shaped, and transmitted by authors who were living in Christian churches with distinctive understandings about who Jesus was and about what it means to follow him? These questions about the Christian collective memory also need to occupy us (in chapter 6).

Before moving into an exploration of these questions we need to pursue further the scholarship that has been devoted to how Jesus was remembered in the earliest days of the Christian faith. This scholarship has almost entirely been undertaken by historical scholars of the New Testament, most of whom have been either uninterested in or not knowledgeable about what we have learned about individual memories from cognitive psychologists or about collective memories from anthropologists and sociologists. For those of us who are interested in knowing about how Jesus was remembered in antiquity in light of what we now can say about memory—both individually and collectively—it is important to see how scholars have addressed the question of how Jesus was remembered by Christians in the years, decades, and centuries after his death. That will be the subject of the next chapter.

CHAPTER 2

The History of Invention

W HEN MEMORY RESEARCHERS SPEAK ABOUT "distorted" memories they do not necessarily mean anything negative by it. They are simply referring to memories of things that did not really happen.[1] Most, probably all, of the memories of Jesus discussed in the previous chapter are distorted in that sense. People brought to mind words and deeds of Jesus that the historical Jesus himself did not actually say and do.

It is relatively easy for most people with a modicum of education and good sense to realize that Jesus did not really tame dragons, wither his bothersome playmates, or bless lions that become human. It is easy to see that these memories were "invented." That does not mean that someone necessarily decided to dupe the world by fabricating a story about Jesus. We remember things that didn't happen all the time, without meaning to be malicious or deceitful. It just happens, regularly. Moreover, stories about important people are invented every day. Even though these stories are not "true" to history, they may intend to convey some other kind of truth, just as fiction generally can convey important truths. Stories get made up wherever and whenever people talk about someone or something they have seen or heard. When those stories are accepted, believed, and transmitted as historical narratives, they then become distorted memories—even if the people who tell them are convinced they are accurate.

Was that happening to the narratives of Jesus's words and deeds—not simply in later times, when the apocryphal Gospels were written, but earlier, in the years and decades before even our canonical Gospels were written?

It is interesting that so many people can instantly recognize distorted memories about Jesus from outside the New Testament but cannot see them inside it. I suppose it is for the same reason that readers of the Bible typically do not see discrepancies in the New Testament Gospels until someone points them out to them. Any critical scholar of the New Testament who teaches a class on the historical Jesus will repeatedly have the same experience. She will spend a class period examining in detail the same story told in two or more of the Gospels and will identify and explain the differences, some of which are flat-out contradictions. After class a student will come up and say, "I've read these Gospels for years, and I've never noticed these discrepancies. Why didn't I see them before?"

It's a great question. Why don't we see things that are right in front of our eyes? One reason psychologists give is that we often do not see something if we are not looking for it.

One of the most famous psychological experiments ever published was undertaken by two rather creative and, well, good-humored psychologists named Daniel Simons and Christopher Chabris. They called their study "Gorillas in Our Midst." It is an experiment about sight-blindness, about not seeing something if you're not expecting to see it.[2]

Simons and Chambris have done the experiment many times, always with the same basic result. The participants are shown a film of about a minute in length in which two groups of people, one wearing white and the other black, are passing a basketball back and forth. The viewers of the film are asked to pay attention to the people passing the ball and to count the number of passes made by the team wearing white.

These directions—to pay attention to a particular feature of the film—are meant to concentrate the viewers' attention. Partway through the film, a woman dressed in a gorilla suit walks onto the scene, faces the camera, thumps her chest, and then walks off. She is onscreen for about nine seconds.

Afterward the participants in the experiment are asked if they saw anything unusual happen in the scene. Here is the astounding result. Only about half of the observers typically have noticed someone in a gorilla suit.

It seems absolutely incredible that people wouldn't see something so obviously bizarre and unexpected. After they have done the experiment, Simons and Chambris tell the unobservant viewers about the gorilla, usually to great disbelief. When they then replay the film, these participants often respond by saying that it must be a different film. Surely I would have seen *that*! It's right there on the screen. Anyone would see that. Right?

Well, wrong. If you're not looking for something, you often won't see it.

Simons and Chambris draw their own conclusion: "we perceive and remember only those objects and details that receive focused attention."[3] If you're focused on people wearing white shirts passing a basketball you may not notice a gorilla beating its chest.

And so to return to my question: is it possible that some people—many people—see "invented" traditions about Jesus, or "distorted" memories of what happened in his life, when they are looking for them, in books from outside the New Testament? But that when the books are inside the New Testament they are not looking for such things and so don't see them?

As it turns out, critical scholars of the New Testament—for as long as there have been critical scholars of the New Testament—have argued that the answer to that question is a resounding yes. This in fact was the answer given by the very first biblical scholar to write an account of Jesus's life not from a religious or theological point of view that affirmed the absolute inspiration of the Bible but from a critical point of view that treated the Gospels as historical sources that, like all historical sources, have to be examined with a keen eye for discrepancies and inventions. The scholar's name was Hermann Samuel Reimarus (1694–1768).

Hermann Samuel Reimarus

Reimarus was very much a scholar of the eighteenth century, and like other thinkers caught up in the intellectual movements of the Enlightenment, he wrestled with new discoveries in the sciences and how they related to older church dogma that insisted that God was active in the world doing miracles—both in the present and back in biblical times. Reimarus was not a scientist, however, but a philosopher, linguist, and biblical scholar. He published some significant work during his lifetime, but he hid his magnum opus from view, opting not to expose it to the public eye for some very obvious reasons. To say that this hidden book would have been controversial would be one of the great understatements in the history of biblical scholarship. The book would have been savagely attacked by other scholars of his day and would almost certainly have lost Reimarus his teaching position, as happened later to other, bolder biblical scholars who chose to pub-

lish their views during the heyday of their careers. As a result of Reimarus's reticence, during his life no one—not even his family—knew
his views about Jesus and the Gospels.

His book then fell into the hands of the great German philosopher G. E. Lessing, who published it posthumously in a series of works
that are now known as the *Wolfenbüttel Fragments,* or just the "Fragments" (called this because they came out piecemeal and because they
deal with a range of interrelated topics; published 1774-78). The Fragments are all about the discrepancies, contradictions, and historical
inaccuracies of the Bible, both Old and New Testament. Any reading
of the Fragments quickly reveals Reimarus's clear, incisive, and powerful mind. With a razor-like critique he dismantles the various biblical accounts, showing their internal contradictions and historical
implausibilities with a zeal and barely suppressed glee that one scarcely
finds even in the present day.

By far the most important Fragment to be published was titled
"The Intention of Jesus and His Teaching."[4] It is here that Reimarus
lays out his understanding of the historical Jesus as a Jewish preacher
who was not and never intended to be a spiritual messiah who died
for the sins of the world and then was raised from the dead. For Reimarus, that view of Jesus was invented by his disciples after his death.
During his life, Jesus was something different altogether. To put it in
the language I am using in this book, the memories of Jesus that have
come down in the history of the church are distorted. They are not
true to the life of the man himself.

Reimarus starts by making a very strong assertion that would have
appeared radical in his day but seems altogether reasonable to anyone
now who wants to consider Jesus from a strictly historical perspective.
When Jesus preached, he would have used words, terms, and concepts
that would have made sense to his Jewish audience in his own historical
setting. He would not have changed the meaning of these ideas in

light of later theological views of Christians. Words meant what they meant in that day and age. They did not mean something different.

Thus, when Jesus talked about a coming kingdom of God, he actually meant "kingdom." That is, he was referring to what Jews normally meant when they talked about a kingdom: an actual political realm that had a king at its head. Jesus did not mean something like "heaven when you die," or "the church that will come after my death." Since in none of his teachings did Jesus ever explain that he was saying one thing but meaning another, he really did mean that there was going to be a kingdom ruled ultimately by God here on earth, a physical, spatial, political realm to which some people would belong and from which other people would be excluded.

So too, when Jesus talked about a messiah, he actually meant "messiah." The messiah for first-century Jews was not some kind of spiritual being who resided with God in heaven. And it certainly was not someone who was to be executed and then raised from the dead. Jews had no concept of any such messiah. When first-century Jews used the term messiah, it referred to the "anointed one" (the literal meaning of the term) of God. And who was that? It was the king of Israel, as indicated clearly in the Old Testament itself. When Jesus talked about a coming messiah, he was referring to a man who was going to be made the king of Israel, through whom God would rule his people in the coming kingdom.

For Reimarus, Jesus thought he himself was that future king. He certainly had no idea of being a ruler who was to sit at the right hand of God on a throne in heaven. He was going to be a real, earthly ruler, in a real, earthly kingdom.

How would that happen? Jesus expected that Jews who heard that Israel would soon be ruled by its own king instead of by the Romans would enthusiastically embrace both the message and the messenger. The masses would rally to his cause. There would be a popular uprising against the hated gentile rulers; the Promised Land would be set free from foreign oppression; Israel would again be made a sovereign state, as it had been in the days of the great king David; and it would be their leader, Jesus himself, who would be made the king.

Jesus's disciples were completely committed to this message and were sent by Jesus into the villages and towns of Israel to rally support (see Luke 9:1–10; 10:1–12). Jesus told the disciples that Jews would be desperately eager to hear this "good news" and would enthusiastically welcome those proclaiming it. In fact, Jesus told the disciples that when they went out on their mission they did not even need to take money or food with them. All would be provided by those who were eagerly awaiting the coming kingdom.

Jesus, then, in the last week of his life, marched to Jerusalem with his band of followers expecting the climactic moment to occur. The inhabitants of Jerusalem flocked out to greet him, and he naturally expected that this would be the beginning of the end of Roman rule. But things did not go as planned. The Jews did not back up their initial support for Jesus. There was no uprising. There was to move to drive out the Romans. Quite the contrary, against all his expectations, rather than being exalted to the throne of Israel, Jesus was arrested, tried, and crucified as a political insurgent opposed to the power of Rome. Rather than becoming the glorious king of God's kingdom on earth, Jesus was unceremoniously stripped, flogged, and crucified for his royal aspirations.

The disciples were completely devastated. How could they not be? They had expected that they themselves would be appointed to positions of power in the new kingdom of Israel that was to come, when their master was made the king. Their lord had now been exposed, humiliated, and executed, and they were without hope.

What were they to do? They had left their homes, their families, and their jobs to follow this false, crucified messiah. They had nothing left. And they remembered fondly how just weeks and months before they had been so warmly welcomed in the villages and towns of Israel by those who were eager to hear the message they proclaimed. The disciples were loath to give all that up. So they hatched a plan.

Reimarus argued that immediately after Jesus's death, the disciples realized they could continue their preaching ministry and still receive the rewards that had been theirs during Jesus's life. They simply had to alter the message that both Jesus and they had been proclaiming. While Jesus was still with them, they had preached about the coming messiah who would establish God's kingdom. They decided to shift that message away from a political messiah to a spiritual one. They formulated a message in which Jesus was not, and never had planned to be, a literal king on the throne of Israel. Jesus had planned to be a spiritual savior. He had planned to die on the cross for the sake of others. God had put his stamp of approval on Jesus's sacrificial death by raising him from the dead. The disciples, right after Jesus's crucifixion, invented the idea of a spiritual messiah whose death and resurrection brought salvation.

But how could they convince anyone that Jesus was a spiritual savior who had been raised from the dead? They obviously had to make their claim plausible. For that to happen, there had to be an empty tomb. So the disciples stole the body of Jesus and reburied it elsewhere. For Reimarus, Jesus was never raised from the dead. The disciples invented that story so they could start a new religion. In this new religion they themselves were to be the leaders.

This, then, is how Christianity began, a religion that Jesus never, ever envisioned. He himself proclaimed a Jewish faith rooted in the historical expectations of Israel. His disciples invented a new, Christian, faith rooted in the idea of a dying and rising spiritual savior.

As you might imagine, when Lessing published "The Intention of Jesus and His Teaching" it caused an enormous uproar. Many readers were outraged. Others were thrown into consternation. Could this account of Jesus's life and teachings be true? Had Christianity been disproved? One contemporary biblical scholar, Johann S. Semler, describes the impact made by the book:

> Many thoughtful and serious young men who had dedicated themselves to the Christian ministry were involved in great perplexity in consequence of their own convictions being thus so fearfully shaken. Many determined to choose another profession for their future labors rather than persevere so long amid increasing uncertainty.[5]

In the modern day, over 230 years after Reimarus's frontal assault on the Gospels and their portrayal of Jesus was published, virtually no one accepts his specific reconstruction of the life of Jesus, although some aspects of it continue to resurface, sometimes in popular books that do not acknowledge their intellectual lineage when rehashing older views.[6]

But on a more general level, throughout the history of scholarship, especially since the nineteenth century, scholars have widely realized that Christians in the early years after Jesus's death were not only altering traditions about Jesus's life and teaching that they inherited, they were also inventing them. We do not need to wait for noncanonical Gospels such as the Infancy Gospel of Thomas, the Gospel of Peter, or the Gospel of Nicodemus for "distorted" memories of Jesus to surface among authors and their readers. (Recall: by "distorted" memories I simply mean any recollections of the past that are not accurate with respect to what really happened.) The evidence that distorted memories were beginning to emerge soon after Jesus's life—or even during his life—can be found in the written accounts that began to appear forty years or so later, that is, in our canonical Gospels. Often these accounts cannot be reconciled with one another.

But any time you have two or more irreconcilable accounts, they cannot all be historically accurate. Someone, then, is changing or inventing the stories.[7]

But who was doing so? A major breakthrough in our understanding of the Gospels occurred nearly a century ago. Some scholars in Germany came to realize that these stories were not simply altered, or even invented, by the Gospel writers themselves. Such things were happening in the years before the Gospels as Christians told and retold accounts of Jesus's life. It was during the oral phase of transmission, as stories about Jesus circulated by word of mouth, that distorted memories of Jesus were sometimes created. The scholars who most decisively developed and elaborated these views are known as the "form critics."

The Form Critics

To make sense of the views put forth by the form critics I need to provide some background on the history of scholarship on the New Testament, starting back in the nineteenth century.[8]

The Scholarly Backdrop

Early in that century it had become widely realized, at least among some critical scholars in Germany, that the Gospels could not all be eyewitness accounts of the life of Jesus and that there were, in fact, serious discrepancies among them.[9] How, then, could one know what actually happened during Jesus's public ministry and at his death and resurrection? The obvious solution was to try to find the earliest of the Gospels, on the assumption that a source closest to the events that it narrates is more likely to be historically accurate.

Was the Gospel of John written by an eyewitness? There were debates throughout the nineteenth century over the status of this book. Many scholars continued to think that it was a firsthand account written by Jesus's disciple John, the son of Zebedee, designated in the Gospel, it was thought, as the "beloved disciple." But many others doubted that it was written by John. Even if it were, it was so different from the other three Gospels that it appeared—as it had done since the very early church—to be a more "spiritual" or theological account of Jesus rather than one strictly interested in the historical record.

The other three Gospels are called the Synoptics. That is because they are so similar in content, telling many of the same stories, often in the same sequence, sometimes in the very same words, that you can lay them out side by side in columns so they can be "seen together" (the literal meaning of the word "synoptic"). It came to be widely thought that these three accounts were less theologically driven, earlier, and more historical than the fourth Gospel. But which of the three was the earliest?

Numerous scholars at the time engaged in an analysis of the "Synoptic problem." This is the problem of explaining why Matthew, Mark, and Luke have so many and such detailed similarities—in places word-for-word agreements—and yet so many differences. The solution that emerged from these analyses indicated that Mark was the first Gospel to be written. It is our shortest account, and there are good reasons for thinking that it was used as a literary source by the authors of Matthew and Luke for many of their stories.[10]

Matthew and Luke appear to have had some other source for their traditions of Jesus that are not found in Mark. These are principally sayings. For example, both Matthew and Luke have the Lord's Prayer and the Beatitudes ("Blessed are the poor . . ."). But since these are not in Mark, they must have gotten them from elsewhere. Eventually it came to be thought that Matthew did not get these traditions from Luke or Luke from Matthew, so they must have derived them from some no-longer-existing source, which scholars then called "Q" (taken from the word for source in German, *Quelle*). Matthew also had other sources for his traditions not found in Mark or Luke, and Luke had other sources for his traditions not found in Mark or Matthew.

What matters for our purposes here is that Mark was eventually recognized to be the earliest Gospel. It also seemed to be the least theologically driven of the four, much more compact and succinct, and therefore, it was judged, the most historical. Once that had been determined, a spate of books began to appear attempting to detail the life of Jesus based principally on the narrative given in Mark, which was judged to be historical.

The problem with Mark is that it is *so* terse that there are huge gaps in the narrative. It is hard to determine what is driving Jesus's action and what his ultimate objective is. To solve that problem scholars writing about Jesus filled in the gaps either with inventive narratives they spun out of their own imagination or with psychological analyses about what must have been motivating Jesus at one point of his life or another.[11]

All of these efforts were rooted in the sense that Mark is the earliest and most historical account without any serious theological overlay (or what I have been calling "distorted memories"). That view was demolished in the early twentieth century by German scholar William Wrede, in a book he called *The Messianic Secret*.[12] Wrede engaged in a deep and perceptive analysis of Mark's Gospel, and showed that one of the overarching organizing principles in the Gospel was not at all historical. It instead represented a theological understanding of Jesus. That was the view that Jesus tried to keep his messianic identity a secret.

Throughout Mark, when someone recognizes that Jesus is the messiah, he tries to hush them up. He heals someone and then instructs him not to tell anyone (1:44). When the demons he exorcises cry out his identity, he orders them to be silent (Mark 3:11–12). His disciples call him the messiah and he enjoins them not to let it be known (Mark 8:29–30). His three closest followers see him transformed into a radiant divine being in their presence and he tells them not to reveal what they have seen until after his resurrection (Mark 9:1–9).

Wrede argued that these injunctions do not make much sense for the historical Jesus himself who, if he was the messiah, would surely have wanted people to know. His commands to silence, therefore, were not historical recollections of what really happened. They were Mark's attempt, or the attempt of the Christian community behind Mark's Gospel, to explain something that was otherwise puzzling. Here was Mark's overarching question: why was Jesus revered as the messiah in the community of his own day if—as they knew—he was not widely acknowledged as the messiah during his lifetime? Mark presented a solution. Jesus must have kept it a secret.

Mark's messianic secret is not, then, a historical datum but a theological explanation of Jesus's identity. For Mark, even though no one appeared to recognize it during his lifetime, Jesus really was the messiah.[13] In turn, that must mean that Mark's Gospel is not a historical account of what actually happened. Like the other Gospels, it too is theologically driven.

If the earliest of our Gospels is not just historical but also theological, what about the traditions about Jesus *before* the Gospels were written? That became the concern of the form critics, scholars especially active in the 1920s, who wanted to shift the focus of attention away from the written Gospels to the traditions lying behind them. The scholar who began this shift was Karl Ludwig Schmidt, who was very soon eclipsed in importance by two of the real stars among twentieth-century biblical scholars, Martin Dibelius and Rudolf Bultmann.[14]

The Early Form Critics

Schmidt wrote a book arguing that when the author of Mark's Gospel produced his account, he was principally responsible for devising the narrative framework for his stories. As Schmidt pointed out, it is possible to read Mark and isolate its stories into units: this is a healing story; that is a story of an exorcism; this other passage is a collection of Jesus's teachings; and so on. But to introduce these various stories, the author has provided a kind of narrative backdrop: for example, he indicates that Jesus went from this place to that place, and while he was approaching this city . . . and then comes the story.

If Mark was responsible for the narrative framework of the stories, where did the stories themselves come from? The form critics maintained that they did not come from authors who were themselves followers of Jesus or who acquired their information directly from eyewitnesses. The stories instead came from oral traditions in circulation in the years prior to the Gospels. The authors of the Gospels—all of them, not just Mark—wrote down stories that had been passed along by word of mouth for years and decades before they wrote. For that reason, when the Gospel writers produced their accounts, they were not simply inventing the stories themselves; but they were also not recording what actually happened based on direct testimony. They were stringing together stories that had long been circulating among the Christian communities. For Dibelius, "stringing together" is precisely what the Gospel writers did. The Gospel stories are "pearls on a string." The authors provided the string, but they inherited the pearls.

Form critics such as Dibelius and Bultmann were principally interested in the pearls, not the string. They wanted to learn more about the kinds of stories that had been circulating orally within the Christian churches. We have access to these stories, of course, only in their written form as they appear in the Gospels. But by examining these stories we can acquire a better understanding of where they came from and how they came to acquire the shape they have.

Even though there were significant differences in how Dibelius and Bultmann approached the task of analysis, they were agreed in their ultimate objectives. They were principally concerned about two features of the oral traditions recorded in the Gospels. They wanted to analyze the "form," or shape that the stories took (that is why they are called form critics) and they wanted to determine the *Sitz im Leben,* or, in English, the "situation in life" that led to the formation of the stories.

As to the forms of the stories, these critics came to see that there are certain *kinds* of stories that recur in the Gospels. And each kind of story has its own distinctive shape. The details that fill out the story will vary. But all the stories of a particular kind will have the same form. For example, if you have a healing story, it works like this: someone is described as having an ailment; he comes up to Jesus; he asks to be healed; Jesus says something to him in reply; he then heals him by a word or touch; and the crowds all marvel. You have the same basic story time and again. Only the details of who it is, what the illness is, what Jesus says, and so on are changed.

Or there are stories of Jesus's controversies: Jesus or his disciples do something (e.g., on the Sabbath); the Jewish leaders object; Jesus responds by showing why they are wrong; and the story ends with Jesus delivering a one-liner that encapsulates his point and humiliates his opponents. Same story, repeatedly.

Dibelius and Bultmann had different ways of categorizing the various forms of the stories, but they agreed that the stories had taken shape because of the way they were told and retold during the years of oral transmission.

When they wanted to discuss the "situation in life" of the stories, the form critics were not asking about a specific story but about the genre, or form, of the story itself. That is to say, what was happening to the Christian community that led them to tell healing stories, or controversy stories, or parables, and so on? And what led them to tell this kind of story in this particular way, with these particular (consistent) features? If you could figure that out, you could begin to write the history of early Christianity, in the crucial years before the Gospels, where you have almost no other written sources to help you know what was happening in the church (except for the letters of Paul, which are not about the history of early Christianity per se but are directed to problems in specific communities).

And so, for example, in what context would stories emerge about Jesus's conflicts with the Pharisees, ending in a clever one-liner? Probably in a context where the Christians themselves were being confronted by non-Christian Jews, over their refusal, for example, to keep the Jewish laws of Sabbath. Since such stories show how Jesus bested the Pharisees on such issues, they would provide a sanction for the behavior of Christians decades later. Or in what context would stories of Jesus healing the sick or raising the dead emerge? Probably in contexts where Christians were trying to prove to outsiders that Jesus was the Son of God who had come in fulfillment of the prophecies of the healing power of the coming messiah. These stories, in other words, are not so much about Jesus as they are about the community that was telling the stories.

If you'll recall, in the first chapter I indicated that when we remember what has happened before now, it is as much about the present as the past. It is the *relevance* of the past that makes us remember it in the present. Although the form critics would not have put it this way, the same applies to the early Christian storytellers in the oral stages of the transmission of the stories about Jesus. They told stories that remembered Jesus's past in light of the community's present. These may have been "distorted" memories in the sense that—for the form critics—they involved words and deeds that did not actually go back to the historical Jesus. But they were valuable memories nonetheless, and no less real to the people who held and shared them than recollections that actually were rooted in the life of the historical Jesus.

As you might imagine, the form critics were highly controversial both in their heyday in the 1920s and in the years to follow.[15] Not all scholars agreed with them. Far from it. It was (and is) often objected that just because a story might prove useful for a later Christian community, this in itself is not evidence that it didn't happen. And many scholars considered the form-critical views too skeptical about our ability to get behind the oral traditions of Jesus to the life of the man himself. Even so, the virtue of the form-critical approach, looking at the matter in hindsight, is that it grappled with a reality we are facing when dealing with our canonical Gospels. As is widely known, the authors of these books were writing between forty and sixty-five years after the death of Jesus. They were not his personal companions. They were not even from his same country.

No one, at least among today's critical scholars, thinks that the Gospel authors simply made up all their stories themselves. But where then did they get them from? Ultimately most of the stories they retold must have come from oral traditions, as followers of Jesus told and retold stories about him—starting while he was alive and then even more after he was dead.[16] These oral traditions were in circulation year after year, and decade after decade, before they were inherited by the authors of our Gospels. The form critics realized this, even if their approach to the oral traditions met with considerable resistance.

Today, nearly a century after Schmidt, Dibelius, and Bultmann did their work, we are still more or less in their same boat, even if it is now motored with newer equipment. Anyone who is interested either in the historical Jesus himself or in the early Christian memories of Jesus has to take very seriously the fact that the surviving accounts of Jesus's life embody recollections of Jesus as these were passed down by word of mouth over all these years.[17]

Weren't the Traditions Memorized?

Many people, when they first consider the reality that the traditions in our Gospels must have circulated orally for decades before being written down, come up with a commonsensical response. Surely the sayings of Jesus, and the accounts of his life, were actually memorized by his followers so they would be preserved accurately. Aren't oral cultures known for being able to preserve their traditions spotlessly? After all, since they didn't have written records to keep their memories alive, people in such cultures must have worked with special diligence to remember what they learned and to pass their stories along seamlessly from one person and one generation to the next. Right?

Unfortunately, decades of intense research have shown that this idea is probably not right at all, as we will see at greater length in chapter 5, when I talk about what anthropologists have learned about oral cultures and how they preserve their traditions. For now I want to focus on a specific question: wouldn't Jesus's followers have memorized his teachings and made sure that the stories about his life were not altered as they were told and retold?

The scholar who is best known for advancing such a view was a Scandinavian specialist in New Testament and early Judaism named Birger Gerhardsson. Gerhardsson's most significant book appeared in 1961, *Memory and Manuscript*.[18] The book was written specifically to attack the views of the form critics, who continued to exercise their influence in his day, more than forty years after their work had begun to appear. The virtue of Gerhardsson's very long study was that it took seriously the reality that Jesus was a first-century Jew, and that to appreciate what it meant to be a Jewish teacher at the time we have to look at historical sources of information.

Gerhardsson was especially interested in what is called rabbinic Judaism. That is the Judaism based on the teachings of the rabbis, as known from later Jewish sources such as the Mishnah and the Talmud.[19] It is known from these lengthy and complicated sacred texts that rabbis developed distinctive teachings about Jewish law, and in fact devised a set of laws that were corollary to the written law of Moses as found in the Hebrew Bible, the Torah. These other laws are sometimes known as the oral law.

Gerhardsson maintained that an ancient rabbi would instruct his students in the oral law not simply by lecturing but also by having them memorize his teachings. Memorization was the very first step in learning, and it happened through constant repetition. That is to say, even before a disciple could learn the interpretation of his rabbi's sayings, he needed to memorize them word for word. Only then, once the teachings were memorized, would the student be allowed to engage in the task of interpretation. In Gerhardsson's summary statement, "The pupil is thus in duty bound to maintain his teacher's exact words. But the teacher is also responsible for seeing that the exact wording is preserved. . . . He must repeat it over and over again, until he has actually passed it on to his pupil or pupils, i.e., until they know the passage in question by heart."[20] Gerhardsson argued that since Jesus was a Jewish teacher, he too must have trained his disciples that way. This is what it meant to be a rabbi.

This is obviously a very appealing view. It situates Jesus in a Jewish historical context that we know about from other sources and it makes sense of the idea that his followers were disciples who would have been eager to commit his teachings to memory. Unfortunately, very few scholars find Gerhardsson's views convincing. In part that is because there is almost no evidence for them.

Critics have noted several major problems.[21] The first is that when applied to Jesus, the pedagogical practices of the rabbinic texts are anachronistic. That is to say—at least to some degree—Gerhardsson is reading back into an earlier period information that we have for only a much later time. As I pointed out, Gerhardsson bases his views on what we know from the Mishnah and the Talmud. The Mishnah is the first surviving body of rabbinic materials, and it is usually dated to about the year 200 CE. The Babylonian Talmud is much later, in about the sixth century. Jesus, of course, lived long before either one, as a teacher active in the '20s of the first century—nearly two hundred years before the Mishnah, the earlier of these texts. Both the Mishnah and the later Talmud do preserve materials from earlier periods, but experts in rabbinic materials do not think that we can take practices written in about the year 200 and assume that they have any relevance for the situation in the year 29. That would be somewhat like taking American legal procedures of the year 2000 and saying that they applied to the 1820s.

Moreover, there is nothing in the tradition to suggest that Jesus was a rabbi in the later technical sense—or that anyone at all was in his day. Rabbinic Judaism began to be a significant feature of the Jewish religion after the destruction of Jerusalem in 70 CE, when the rabbis (who were probably to be connected with the earlier Pharisaic form of Judaism) became prominent among Jewish teachers. Jesus, of course, was living well before that. What happened later is of limited relevance to the situation in his day.

It should also be stressed that, as anyone who reads the Gospels knows, there is not a single word about Jesus having his followers memorize his teachings. He does not have a set "oral law" that he passes along. He does not drill the disciples to make sure they remember his exact words. And so Gerhardsson's views appear to be anachronistic.

An even bigger problem is that we have clear and certain evidence that Jesus's followers were not passing along his teachings, or accounts of his deeds, as they were memorized verbatim. This is one of the complaints that other scholars generally lodge against Gerhardsson—he does not engage in a detailed examination of traditions that are preserved in the Gospels to see if his theory works. What is the evidence that Jesus's teachings were preserved word for word the same? On the contrary, the striking differences in the words and deeds of Jesus as reported in the Gospels is compelling evidence precisely that they were not memorized and passed along without significant change.

I first realized this myself many years ago when I was a graduate student at Princeton Theological Seminary. One semester, Gerhardsson's teacher Harald Riesenfeld was in town giving a lecture. In his talk he argued a position that was in line with the views of his more famous student (he actually had originally given the idea to Gerhardsson): Jesus's words and deeds were passed along as they had been committed to memory. The morning after his lecture I had breakfast with Riesenfeld, and I told him that I was puzzled by something. The accounts of the words and deeds of Jesus in the New Testament are at odds with each other in numerous places. How could they have been memorized?

I gave him an example. In Mark's Gospel, a man named Jairus comes up to Jesus and tells him that his daughter is very sick. He would like Jesus to come and heal her. They head to Jairus's house, but they are unexpectedly delayed. Before they arrive, she dies. Members of Jairus's household come and inform him that there is now no longer any reason for Jesus to come. Jesus tells Jairus not to fear. They continue on to the house, and Jesus proceeds to raise the girl from the dead (Mark 5:21–43). It is a terrific story, very moving and powerful.

The same story is found in the Gospel of Matthew, but with a striking difference. In Matthew's version Jairus comes up to Jesus and informs him that his daughter has already died. He would like Jesus to come raise her from the dead (Matt. 9:18–26).

And so I asked Riesenfeld: how can Matthew's version be right if Mark's is right? Either the girl was already dead when her father came to Jesus, or not. Riesenfeld's response was stunning and has stayed with me till today. Since he was convinced that the stories about Jesus were memorized by his followers, he believed Matthew and Mark were describing two different occasions on which Jesus talked with Jairus and brought his daughter back to life. The first time Jairus came to Jesus before the girl had died. The next time it happened, she had died already. Jesus raised her from the dead twice.

I realized then and there that this theory of disciples remembering precisely the words and deeds of Jesus simply didn't make sense to me.

The final problem with Gerhardsson's view is that it does not take seriously the realities of how traditions of Jesus were being circulated in the early church. The authors of the Gospels were not writing what they had memorized sitting at Jesus's feet. As we will see in chapter 3, the disciples of Jesus did not actually write the Gospels. The disciples were lower-class, illiterate peasants who spoke Aramaic, Jesus's own language. The Gospels, on the other hand, were written by highly educated Greek-speaking Christians forty to sixty-five years later. The stories had been in circulation for decades, not simply among disciples who allegedly memorized Jesus's words and deeds, but also among all sorts of people, most of whom had never laid eyes on an eyewitness or even on anyone else who had. And so, just as there is no evidence that Jesus's followers memorized his teachings, the idea that everyone throughout Christendom telling stories about

Jesus had memorized them is beyond belief. This model for under-standing where the Gospel traditions came from simply doesn't ap-pear to work.

Were the Traditions "Controlled"?

A more recent theory of how the traditions about Jesus were passed along by word of mouth in the early church in the years and decades before the Gospels were written has been put forth by an author named Kenneth Bailey, whose views have been championed by sev-eral scholars, including the New Testament expert James Dunn.[22] Bailey is not himself a specialist in the New Testament. He is a Chris-tian who has spent decades as a teacher in the Middle East. On the basis of his extensive experience, he has written books about how modern Middle Eastern culture can illuminate the life and teachings of Jesus from the New Testament.[23]

Most important for our purposes here is an article he wrote in 1991 called "Informal Controlled Oral Tradition and the Synoptic Gospels."[24] In this article Bailey argues that the early communities of the followers of Jesus were very similar to villagers in the Middle East today, who have traditions they pass along in informal contexts in which they take measures to ensure that the traditions are preserved accurately.

Bailey relates, from personal experience, a kind of village meeting called the *haflat samar*. This is an evening gathering in which villagers come together to tell stories, proverbs, riddles, poems, and accounts of important figures in its community. At these gatherings there are no official storytellers. Anyone who has grown up in the community and has long heard the traditions is permitted to speak.

The key point that Bailey wants to make is that when a speaker tells one of the community's traditions, the others who are listening exercise a kind of informal control over the recitation by correcting the person if he gets something wrong. Some traditions, Bailey indicates, have to be retold exactly the same way every time. These would include such things as poems and proverbs. If someone gets even one word wrong or out of place, others publicly correct him, to his shame. Other kinds of tradition can be more flexible—for example, accounts of people from the past or historical events in the community. In these cases, it is more important to get the gist and the details straight. The stories are not told word for word the same every time. But if something is incorrect, the listeners will let the speaker know, in no uncertain terms. Other kinds of information passed along in the *haflat samar* are controlled even less—for example, recent events or news about neighboring villages.

Bailey argues that this is comparable to what must have happened in the early church. In his view, in the land of Palestine in the years after Jesus's death, eyewitnesses were the only ones allowed to tell the teachings and deeds of Jesus. The parables and important one-line sayings of Jesus, and his other discourses, were preserved intact. Whenever Christians in the community came together, the eyewitness would recount the traditions. If he got something wrong, one or more other members of the group would publicly correct him. This fear of being embarrassed before the group ensured that the traditions were passed along without serious change. The reason was that Christians wanted to make sure that they remembered exactly what Jesus said and did. As Bailey puts it, "In light of the reality described above, the assumption that the early Christians were not interested in history becomes untenable."[25] For Bailey, they were indeed interested in what actually happened in history. Just as modern storytellers in the Middle East are today.

Despite the obvious attractiveness of this theory to explain the circulation of the early Gospel traditions, there are numerous problems with it. For one thing, on the very basic level, one might wonder what evidence Bailey cites to show that early Christians came together to recount their community tradition in the manner of the *haflat samar*. In fact, he doesn't cite any at all. So far as I know there is no evidence. Certainly there were no villages made up of Christians in the first century. But maybe the local churches operated in this way? If they did so, none of our sources mentions it, including our only sources for the earliest church: the book of Acts, the letters of Paul, or even the Gospels themselves.

Moreover, what would make anyone think that the only people telling stories about Jesus—even in Palestine in the first century— were eyewitnesses who observed what Jesus said and did? Again there is no evidence that this was the case, and a little common sense shows just how implausible it is. Are we to imagine that eyewitnesses fanned out and rooted themselves in every village of Palestine where some- one told stories of Jesus? Not only is that inherently implausible, but also, according to the New Testament book of Acts, the disciples of Jesus stayed for the most part in Jerusalem once the church had begun after Jesus's death.

Even if eyewitness did settle in all the villages of Palestine, how would that relate to our broader concern, which is how the Gospel writers got their information? The Gospel writers were not from Pal- estine. We don't know what cities they lived in, but they were in Greek-speaking areas of the Roman Empire. What are the chances that in their churches only eyewitnesses were telling the stories?

Think concretely for a second about a specific church that we actually know about. We are arguably better informed about the Christian community in Corinth than any other church in the first century, because Paul wrote two lengthy letters to it that describe its local situation. The Corinthian church was not established by an eye- witness to the life of Jesus, but by the Apostle Paul.[26] Paul never knew Jesus during his life. Paul himself did know several eyewitnesses. He tells us that three years after he converted he spent two weeks in Jerusalem with Peter (Gal. 1:18–19). Strikingly, he swears that he didn't see any other apostle at the time except Jesus's brother James. And he was there for only two weeks. We don't know what they were talking about. We also don't know if Paul talked with any other eyewitnesses before establishing the church in Corinth.[27]

But assume Paul got information about Jesus's words and deeds during those two weeks with Peter and James. He later converted former pagans in Corinth to become followers of Jesus. Presumably he told them stories about Jesus. They presumably told others, who converted. These told others, who converted. Paul was there for this time, directing the affairs of the church. But then he went away to start a church in some other city. After he left, the people certainly continued telling their stories. As did their converts. Evidently a Christian teacher named Apollos eventually came to town and participated in the growing community (1 Cor. 3:6). But he too was not a disciple of Jesus during his ministry. So he too was not an eyewitness. He appears to have converted more people, who presumably converted more people, who converted more people.

And so imagine that we are in the church of Corinth in, say, the year 55 CE, twenty-five years or so after Jesus's death. When the church gets together, who is telling the stories about Jesus? I think we can assume that the answer is: just about everyone. Paul's two letters back to the church, 1 and 2 Corinthians, say nothing about a *haflat samar*. And among the people he refers to in the letters, he never mentions an eyewitness. The Christians do get together at least once a week for worship and to celebrate a meal commemorating Jesus's death and resurrection. When they meet together, they are certainly telling one another the stories they have heard about Jesus. These stories may be told formally in the worship service. But they also are told informally, as Christians encourage one another, build one another up, urge one another to keep and grow in the faith. Possibly when someone tells a story, someone else corrects him. In fact, that seems more than likely: it almost always happens when one person tells a story that someone else also knows.

Does this group context for telling the stories ensure that they are accurate? Actually, modern psychological studies suggest that just the opposite is normally the case. Cognitive psychologists have studied the phenomenon of "group memory" and have reached several very important conclusions that might be surprising. One is that when a group "collectively remembers" something they have all heard or experienced, the "whole" is less than the sum of the "parts." That is to say, if you have ten individuals who have all experienced an event, and you interview the ten separately, you will learn a good deal about what happened when you piece all the information together. But if you interview them precisely as a group, you will get less information.

That may be counterintuitive, but it has been demonstrated time and again. Some researchers have wondered if that's because of what you might call a "tug-of-war" mentality. If you are individually playing tug-of-war, you will probably strain to your utmost as you yank on the rope. But if you are in a group of ten, you will pull less hard, since it seems that your effort is not as important. Possibly when people remember as a group, the same thing happens. They don't work as hard, so less is remembered.[28]

But there are bigger problems with group memories. They are more often frail and faulty than individual memories—just the opposite of what you might expect. It is nonetheless the case, for well-documented reasons. For one thing, if one person—say, a dominant personality—injects into the conversation an incorrect recollection or "distorted memory" that others in the group do not remember, they tend to take the other person's word for it. As one recent study has shown, "The misinformation implanted by one person comes to be shared by the group as a whole. In other words, a collective memory could become formed around misinformation."[29]

From that point on, as more members of a group recount this distorted memory, the other members of the group—even if they either distinctly think that the memory is wrong or don't remember it—feel considerable social pressure to agree with everyone else. One interesting experiment set out to test how commonly that happened, and found that 65 percent of the participants actually changed their views because of social pressure exerted on them (not necessarily consciously) by the group as a whole. About 40 percent of these errors were "persistent," that is, they became "permanent" memories of those who actually did not at first have them. The conclusion of this study is striking: "Humans may be predisposed to trust the judgment of the group, even when it stands in opposition to their own original beliefs."[30]

It seems that the idea of a group ensuring the accuracy of traditions is not psychologically defensible. But what about Bailey's *haflat samar* analogy? Doesn't it show that at least in the Middle East group memories are preserved intact? Unfortunately, the answer is no. A very perceptive New Testament scholar, Theodore Weeden, took the examples of "accurate" Middle Eastern traditions that Bailey himself cited in his article, and showed decisively that in fact they were not preserved with anything like verbatim, or even general, accuracy. Even in these instances the "accurate" memories were changed radically as they were told and retold over the years. Some of the different retellings of the story were so full of discrepancies and variations that it is hard to believe they were actually the same story.

Bailey, for example, tells of stories that he heard about a nineteenth-century missionary in Egypt named John Hogg. Hogg's daughter, Rena, had written a biography of her father in 1914. Bailey indicates that he had heard oral accounts about Hogg in the 1950s and '60s—and so forty to fifty years after Rena had written them—and that the versions he heard were "the same stories." In fact, he claimed, about 90 percent of the time they were actually in "the same words."

Weeden had the bright idea of comparing Bailey's version of the stories with the written account in the 1914 biography. Were the stories the same? Not even close. The stories were vastly different. The episodes were radically changed. The events were altered. The words were not at all the same. Weeden shows this in detail.[31]

So are Middle Eastern habits of preserving tradition evidence that the tales of Jesus were told in antiquity without serious alteration? Here is Weeden's conclusion with respect to one of the stories of the missionary John Hogg: there was "no evidence that the indispensable, non-variables of the methodology of informal controlled oral tradition . . . were maintained in the course of telling the story over the forty years between the time Rena Hogg reported it and the time that Bailey heard it." Such stories were not being passed along by "informal controlled oral tradition but rather *contra* Bailey [by] informal *uncontrolled* oral tradition." There was no social control.[32]

As a coup de grâce Weeden takes another story that Bailey cites about Hogg and notes that when Rena herself told the story in her biography, she did so—as she herself says—to show how "fact and fancy mingle . . . in lore" and that it occurs in "many versions." It is, in fact, a "bogus story." That is hardly evidence of a controlled tradition.

And so Bailey's position, as attractive as it may appear at first glance, does not appear to hold water. But wouldn't it be different in the case of Jesus? Wouldn't the presence of eyewitnesses in the first century ensure that the stories about Jesus were not being significantly changed? That Christians were being reminded and were remembering his words and deeds as they really were? I will deal with the problem with eyewitness testimony—is it always reliable?—in the next chapter, including the issue of whether the Gospels are directly based on eyewitness testimony. For now I'd like to explore a bit further how the stories about Jesus were circulating before the Gospels were written.

How the Traditions Circulated

If during the forty to sixty-five years separating Jesus's life and the earliest surviving Gospels, his sayings and deeds were not memorized by his followers and then passed down, verbatim, through the church, and if they were not circulated accurately within informally controlled settings, how were they being told and retold?

One obvious point to stress, which has not occurred to everybody, is this: stories about Jesus were circulating even during his lifetime. Moreover, even then they were not being told only by eyewitnesses. When someone who saw Jesus do or say something then and told someone else who wasn't there, it is impossible to believe that this other person was forbidden from sharing the news with someone else. Life just doesn't work that way. Think about any public person you know: the president of the United States, a movie star, a famous author, or even just a popular university professor. People tell stories about them. And other people repeat the stories. Then other people repeat the stories. And the stories obviously are told in different words every time. Thus the stories change. Moreover, stories get made up. You don't have to take my word for it. Ask any public figure. It is true that the people about whom the stories are told might hear a wild version and correct it. But there is no guarantee that everyone will hear the correction so that from then on they tell the story correctly. On the contrary, non-eyewitnesses continue to tell the story. And yet other stories.

This happens even when people are alive and there are plenty of eyewitnesses who can correct things. If the president has a meeting with his cabinet and word leaks out about what was said there, and it gets reported in the news, and someone in Kansas tells his next-door neighbor about it, then that person tells her husband. Is there an eyewitness in her living room (someone from the president's cabinet) to make sure that she tells the story correctly?

People were telling stories about Jesus while he was living, but even more after he had died, mainly because after his death he attracted many, many more followers than he had while he was living. Contrary to what you might unreflectively assume, a lot of the eyewitnesses to Jesus (most of them?) never did become his followers. For evidence, consider the stories of Jesus's passion in the New Testament. I'm not saying these accounts are accurate (see chapter 4), but just think about what they are saying. At Jesus's trial a large crowd was watching the event. How many in the crowd were his followers? The men disciples had all fled. So if there were dozens of eyewitnesses there (hundreds?), at best only a handful of women were near and dear to him.

To be sure, after his death probably most of the people actually talking about him and remembering his life were the people who cared. Recall what we saw in the previous chapter: we remember the past because of what we are experiencing in the present. Most dwellers in Jerusalem at the time of Jesus's death in, say, the year 30 CE, had no interest in Jesus. Why would they? The people talking about him were the ones who had followed him earlier. These people, or at least some of them, came to believe he had been raised from the dead. They told others, who also came to believe that God had done a great miracle and exalted Jesus up to heaven. They told others, who told others, who told others.

We don't know for a fact that the New Testament Gospels were the first written accounts of Jesus's life. As I have said before, probably the majority of scholars think that there was a document we call Q that provided two of our Gospels with many of their sayings of Jesus; and possibly there were other written accounts floating around. But the vast majority of people telling stories about Jesus were not writing them down or even reading them. For one thing, the vast majority of people in that time and place simply couldn't read, let alone write.

It is very difficult to establish literacy rates in antiquity, but the best estimate is put forward by a scholar of ancient Judaism, Catherine Hezser, who has produced a massive and authoritative study called *Jewish Literacy in Roman Palestine.* In her expert judgment, based on all sorts of evidence she adduces, something like 97 percent of the people in Palestine in Jesus's day could not read or write. And more could do the former than the latter.[33]

The stories about Jesus, then, were not principally circulating in written but in oral form. How quickly can information travel in that medium?

There was a fascinating study done about ten years ago that relates to that question. Two psychologists, Kent Harber and Dov Cohen, wanted to see how rapidly emotionally charged stories could circulate.[34] For their experiment, they took 33 college students to a local morgue. There they were told about bodies that had been given to science; they were shown a brain; some of them were taken into a room to see a cadaver.

The students did not know this was an experiment in social communication. Some days later, they were interviewed by their professors and asked how many people they had told about their experience. Those people were then tracked down and asked how many people they had told. Those people were then tracked down and asked how many they had told. What happened was this: 97 percent of the students who went to the morgue told one or more people about it; 82 percent of those people told someone else; and 48 percent of those people told someone else. The totals are very interesting: within three days, the adventures of these 33 students had been told to 881 people. Word of a social experience can spread remarkably fast. As the two researchers later concluded, "Social sharing would seem fully adequate to spread of information within a small collective, including populations that lack written language or other media for mass communication."[35]

In other words, a story does not have to be written in the newspaper or broadcast on the evening news or even on modern social media to get around very widely and very quickly. Moreover, the vast majority of the people telling the story—just within three days—are people who were not eyewitnesses and did not get their information from eyewitnesses. What do you suppose happens to stories when they are told, remembered, retold, and then remembered again, just within three days? Or three years? Or, as in the case of Jesus, forty to sixty-five years? How many changes would be made in them?

One important issue, of course, involves the storytellers themselves. Who were actually telling the stories about Jesus? To deal with that question it is important to think about the context within which the stories of Jesus were being told. I began to answer that question earlier when I mentioned the case of the church in Corinth, which was not founded by an eyewitness, but by Paul. How many churches *were* established by eyewitnesses? Was the church in Rome? Philippi? Thessalonica? Ephesus? Lystra? Derbe? Crete? Antioch? Tarsus? Evidently none of the above, at least if we are to trust the New Testament on this score. How were these churches started? In some cases we know with relative certainty: a number of them were founded by Paul (e.g., Philippi and Thessalonica). Others were started by other, unnamed missionaries who were not eyewitnesses (e.g., Antioch; Acts 11:19–21). Others we simply don't know about. The church in Rome, for example, was definitely not started by Paul, since he indicates in his letter to the Roman Christians that he had never been there (Rom. 1:13). Moreover, when he sends greetings to a very large number of people in the congregation, he doesn't mention Peter as being there—or any other eyewitness. He does mention two apostles in Rome, a man named Andronicus and a woman named Junia (Rom. 16:7). Possibly they started the church? If so, Paul doesn't say so. And there is nothing to indicate that either one had been an eyewitness to the life of Jesus or a companion of an eyewitness.

The same is true of other missionaries we know about, for example Apollos (1 Cor. 1:12; 3:6). He was an apostle who was visiting other churches—at least in Corinth—although it is hard to know if he actually started other churches. But again he was not a personal companion of Jesus during his life. The same can be said of the apparent founder of the church at Colossae, Epaphras (Col. 1:7), and the unnamed opponents of Paul in the region of Galatia who preach a Gospel message contrary to Paul's (Gal. 1). Just about the only missionary we know about who was a companion of Jesus during his ministry is the Apostle Peter. Paul indicates that Peter was the missionary to the Jews just as he, Paul, was the missionary to the gentiles (Gal. 2:7–8).[36] That makes it all the more odd that we don't have any firm indication that Peter established churches, especially outside of Palestine.[37]

Churches were principally being established in gentile territory. In Paul's churches, the vast majority of converts were former pagans, those who had worshipped many gods: the gods of Rome, the gods of their own localities, the gods of their families, the gods of all sorts of description and function (we know this for his churches in Thessalonica and Corinth; see 1 Thess. 1:9–10 and 1 Cor. 12:2).

How were these missionaries supposed to convert such people away from religious traditions that they had grown up with and that were deeply imbued within them? Or, for that matter, how was a missionary supposed to convert a Jew dedicated to keeping the Jewish law as part of the "covenant" that God had made with his people? How was a missionary to convince someone to change his or her religious beliefs and accept Jesus as the only Son of the only God?

They obviously could not convert anyone simply by saying "believe in Jesus." Jesus *who*? No one is going to become a follower of a person they know absolutely nothing about. And so Christian missionaries were obviously, and necessarily, telling stories about Jesus. How else would someone decide to believe in him? Any potential convert had to know who Jesus was. What he did that was so special. What he taught that was so compelling. How he died. Why he died. What happened after he died. The stories had to be told. Otherwise there would be no converts. And the people telling the stories in virtually every case we know about were not people who accompanied Jesus during his public ministry.

It was not only these missionaries who were converting others, however. The converts themselves were converting people. Take another hypothetical but completely plausible situation: suppose I live in the town of Colossae in, say, the year 50 CE. The missionary Epaphras comes to town and I meet him at his place of business. I'm a highly religious man, but I'm always interested in new ideas. Epaphras begins to tell me about the Son of God, who did miraculous deeds in Galilee: he healed the sick, and cast out demons, and raised the dead. At the end of his life, he was betrayed by his own people and crucified by the governor, Pontius Pilate. But then God raised him from the dead.

At first I might think that Epaphras is making it up. Or that he's a bit looney. But then I talk to other people whom Epaphras has convinced. They also are full of stories, both about the amazing things Jesus did and the fact that people actually saw him alive after his death. They also tell about other miracles that are happening, even now, in the powerful name of Jesus.

I eventually become convinced. I give up my pagan gods: the gods of Rome, the gods of Colossae, the gods of my family. I confess that I believe in only the Jewish God, who created all things and sent his Son into the world to die for my sins and be raised from the dead. I decide to get baptized to join the body of Christ. Then I start coming together with the small group of like-minded people, the followers of Jesus, every week to talk about our faith and the Lord we worship.

Do I refuse to tell anyone about Jesus because I'm not an eyewitness? Of course not. I tell my wife, and our children, and my neighbors. This is the most important thing that has ever happened in my life. It's not simply the change of an opinion. It is a radical, revolutionary new way of looking at the entire world: who I am, where I came from, what the world is, how it came into being, what I am supposed to think, what I am supposed to believe, how I am supposed to act, what I am supposed to do. My faith in Jesus has turned my entire world upside down. *Of course* I'm going to tell people. And I'll urge, or even require, some of them—my wife and children, and my slaves, and anyone else in my household—to come with me to the weekly services to meet others like me who are followers of Jesus. Some of them will convert. When my wife converts, she'll be like me. She'll tell others: her mother, her sisters, our next-door neighbor.

Suppose the woman next door converts. She starts coming to our weekly gatherings. She convinces her husband to come. Six months later he converts. He takes a business trip to Smyrna. He tells his business associates about Jesus. They learn there is a community of people who follow Jesus in their town. They decided to go. They convert. They tell their families. Some of them convert.

And so it goes. In the midst of all this, what are the contexts within which stories of Jesus are being told? They are being told by evangelists, whether official missionaries or your spouse or the man next door. The stories have to be told, and retold, retold again, repeatedly, to convince people that Jesus really was the miracle-working Son of God who died for the sins of the world but was then raised from the dead. The stories are also being told by the converts among themselves, both in casual contexts—at work, on a day off, in the evening—and in more structured contexts, as in the weekly meetings. The stories are being told as leaders of the community teach the converts more information about Jesus and his life and death and what it means to believe in him. The stories are being told during the worship services when people reverence, and pray to, and reflect on, and adore Jesus and God his Father. The stories are being told as people are preparing to be baptized once they have been convinced of the truth about Jesus. They are being told by leaders, and by most other members of the community, when they exhort each other to be strong in the faith and to remember the life and teachings of Jesus when outsiders mock or even persecute them; when they are deciding how to live and how to behave and how to treat others; when they come to prayer, asking him to provide food when resources are scarce, or to heal once again, or to cast out a demon, or even to raise the dead.

Stories about Jesus are being told in evangelism, in instruction before baptism, in teaching, in worship services, in casual conversations, in mutual exhortation and encouragement, in the church gatherings, in the homes, in discussions with neighbors, and in all sorts of contexts. They are not being told only by eyewitnesses or even by Palestinian Jews from about the same time and place as Jesus. They are being told mainly by people who have never been to Palestine, don't speak the language of Palestine, have never known anyone from Palestine—let alone anyone from Palestine who happened to have met Jesus.

This is the reality of the oral traditions of Jesus. These are the contexts within which the stories were being told. These are the people who were telling the tales.

What happens to stories when they are told in these sorts of context by these sorts of people? Anyone who thinks the stories don't get changed, and changed radically, and even invented in the process of telling and retelling, simply does not know, or has never thought about, what happens to stories in oral circulation, as they are handed down by word of mouth, day after day, week after week, month after month, year after year, and decade after decade.

But is that actually the case in predominantly *oral* cultures, such as in the first century? Didn't people in oral cultures have better memories? Didn't they make sure that traditions they passed along remained the same? That is a question I will deal with directly in chapter 5. In the meantime, a more pressing, and rather nagging, question keeps coming back to mind—at least to my mind and probably to yours. What *about* the eyewitnesses? It is one thing to say there were no eyewitnesses in Colossae in the days of Epaphras and his converts. But what does that have to do with the Gospels? Aren't these somehow *authorized* accounts? Aren't they written by the actual companions of Jesus or at least by people who were given their stories by companions of Jesus? And if so—quite apart from what might be being said about Jesus in Corinth, or Philippi, or Ephesus—can't we trust that these particular accounts are not merely memories of Jesus but are accurate and "true" memories of Jesus?

Those are the questions I will address in the next chapter.

CHAPTER 3

Eyewitness Testimonies and
Our Surviving Gospels

IN THE HISTORY OF MEMORY STUDIES an important event occurred
in 1902.[1] In Berlin, a well-known criminologist named von Liszt was
delivering a lecture when an argument broke out. One student stood
up and shouted that he wanted to show how the topic was related to
Christian ethics. Another got up and yelled that he would not put up
with that. The first one replied that he had been insulted. A fight
ensued and a gun was drawn. Professor von Liszt tried to separate the
two when the gun went off.

The rest of the students were aghast. But Professor von Liszt informed them that the event had been staged.

He chose a group of the students to write down an exact account
of what they had just seen. The next day, other students were instructed to write down what they recalled, others a week later. The
results of these written reports were surprising and eye-opening. This
was one of the first empirical studies of eyewitness testimony.

Professor von Liszt broke down the sequence of events, which had been carefully planned in advance, into a number of stages. He then calculated how accurately the students reported the sequence, step by step. The *most* accurate accounts were in error in 26 percent of the details reported. Others were in error in as many as 80 percent.

As you might expect, research on the reliability of eyewitness testimony has developed significantly over the years since this first rather crude attempt to establish whether it can be trusted to be reliable. Scholarship in the field has avalanched in recent decades. But the findings are consistent in one particularly important respect. A report is not necessarily accurate because it is delivered by an eyewitness. On the contrary, eyewitnesses are notoriously inaccurate.

There have been many books written about whether the Gospels were written by eyewitnesses or by authors relying on eyewitnesses. Some of these books are written by very smart people. It is very odd indeed that many of them do not appear to be particularly concerned with knowing what experts have told us about eyewitness testimony.[2]

This chapter is focused on two questions. Are the Gospels based on stories about Jesus that had been passed around, changed, and possibly invented by Christian storytellers for decades before being written down, or were they written by eyewitnesses? If they were written by eyewitnesses, would that guarantee their essential accuracy? We will deal with the second question first.

Research on Eyewitness Testimony

Psychological studies of eyewitness testimony began to proliferate in the 1980s, in part because of two important phenomena related to criminal investigations. The first is that people started recalling ugly, painful, and criminal instances of sexual abuse when they were children.[3] These recollections typically surfaced during the process of therapy, especially under hypnosis. Both those who suddenly remembered these instances and the therapists treating them often maintained that these repressed memories explained why the patients had experienced subsequent psychological damage. Some of these reports involved incest committed by relatives, especially parents; others involved abuse by other adults—for example, in child care centers. As reports of such memories began to proliferate, some psychologists started to wonder if they could all be true. Some were obviously real memories of real events. But was it possible that others were not true memories at all, but false memories that had been unconsciously implanted during the process of therapy? It turns out that the answer is a resounding yes, which creates enormous complexities and problems for all parties: the victim or alleged victim, the therapist, the accused adults, and the judges and juries of the legal system.

The other phenomenon involved the use of DNA evidence to overturn criminal convictions. Once DNA became a reliable indicator of an accused person's direct involvement in serious crimes, such as murder or rape, a large number of previous convictions were brought back for reconsideration. Numerous convictions were overturned. As Harvard psychologist Daniel Schacter has recently indicated, in about 75 percent of these reversed judgments, the person charged with the crime was convicted solely on the basis of eyewitness testimony.[4] What is one to make of such findings? In the words of a seminal article in the field, "Reports by eyewitnesses are among the most important types of evidence in criminal as well as in civil law cases. . . . It is therefore disturbing that such testimony is often inaccurate or even entirely wrong."[5]

This particular indictment emerged out of a study unrelated to DNA evidence. It involves an interesting but tragic case. On October 4, 1992, an El-Al Boeing 707 cargo plane that had just taken off from Schiphol Airport in Amsterdam lost power in two engines. The

89

pilot tried to return to the airport but couldn't make it. The plane crashed into an eleven-story apartment building in the Amsterdam suburb of Bijlmermeer. The four crew members and thirty-nine people in the building were killed. The crash was, understandably, the leading news story in the Netherlands for days.

Ten months later, in August 1993, Dutch psychology professor Hans Crombag and two colleagues gave a survey to 193 university professors, staff, and students in the country. Among the questions was the following: "Did you see the television film of the moment the plane hit the apartment building?" In their responses 107 of those surveyed (55 percent) said yes, they had seen the film. Sometime later the researchers gave a similar survey with the same question to 93 law school students. In this instance, 62 (66 percent) of the respondents indicated that they had seen the film. There was just one problem. There was no film.

These striking results obviously puzzled the researchers, in part because basic common sense should have told anyone that there could not have been a film. Remember, this is 1992, before cell phone cameras. The only way to have a film of the event would have been for a television camera crew to have trained a camera on this particular apartment building in a suburb of Amsterdam at this exact time, in expectation of an imminent crash. And yet, between half and two thirds of the people surveyed—most of them graduate students and professors—indicated they had seen the nonexistent film. Why would they think they had seen something that didn't exist?

Even more puzzling were the detailed answers that some of those interviewed said about what they actually saw on the film—for example, whether the plane crashed into the building horizontally or vertically and whether the fire caused by the plane started at impact or only later. None of that information could have been known from a film, because there was no film. So why did these people remember not only seeing the crash but also details about how it happened and what happened immediately afterward?

Obviously they were imagining it, based on logical inferences (the fire must have started right away) and on what they had been told by others (the plane crashed into the building as the plane was heading straight down). The psychologists argued that these people's imaginations became so vivid, and were repeated so many times, that they eventually did not realize they were imagining something. They really thought they were remembering it. In fact they did remember it. But it was a false memory. Not just a false memory one of them had. A false memory *most* of them had.

The researchers concluded, "It is difficult for us to distinguish between what we have actually witnessed, and what commonsense inference tells us that must also have been the case." In fact, commonsense inference, along with information we get by hearsay from others, together "conspire in distorting an eyewitness's memory." Indeed, "this is particularly easy when, as in our studies, the event is of a highly dramatic nature, which almost by necessity evokes strong and detailed visual imagery."[6]

The witnesses to the life of Jesus certainly were recalling events "of a highly dramatic nature"—Jesus walking on the water, calming the storm with a word, casting out a demon, raising a young girl back to life. Moreover, these stories certainly evoked "strong and detailed visual imagery." Even if such stories were told by eyewitnesses, could we trust that they were necessarily accurate memories?

As I have intimated, the psychological research on such matters is not restricted to a German criminologist in 1902 or to three Dutch psychologists ninety-one years later. The research is abundant and all points in the same direction. People remember all sorts of things, some of them in vivid detail, even though they never happened at all.[7]

One of the most peculiar pieces of evidence comes to us from an entirely unexpected realm, the study of UFO abductions. As it turns out, there are a lot of people in the United States who claim they have been abducted by aliens. No one knows how many, since there is no way to count them. One of the best-known researchers is John E. Mack, a psychiatrist who teaches at Harvard Medical School, who has investigated the cases of more than a hundred abductees.[8] The fullest and most compelling study is by Susan Clancy, whose Ph.D. is in psychology and whose book is called *Abducted: How People Come to Believe They Were Kidnapped by Aliens.*[9]

Clancy herself does not believe that aliens exist or that there is any kind of objective reality (i.e., a real abduction) behind these people's belief that they were abducted. But people out there "know" they have been. One of the many important points that Clancy makes in her psychological analysis is that these "memories" of abduction are socially constructed. That is to say, the culture we live in and experience makes it possible for people to think aliens have temporarily carted them off. Clancy notes that there were virtually no abduction narratives prior to 1962—that is, before alien invasions started to be featured in movies and on television.

A major portion of her study, then, is about the power of suggestion, and about how once a "possibility" has been implanted in someone's head, it sometimes becomes a "memory" that has generated its own reality. If someone has a mental framework that allows for the existence of aliens, and comes to think that alien abductions happen, it is possible to imagine that he has experienced an abduction himself. And once that is imagined, if it is imagined vividly and frequently enough, it becomes a part of the person's mental apparatus. As Clancy puts it, "In situations where the perceptual clarity of an imagined event is high—where we have provided contextual details by vividly imagining the event—we have a lot of trouble distinguishing between products of reality and those of fantasy."[10] She further argues, in congruence with other memory experts, that when a vivid imagining of an event is discussed or described "in the presence of authority figures who encourage belief in and confirm the authenticity of the memories that emerge," the memories are cemented that much more strongly in the brain.[11]

It is not simply wild imaginations that can lead to false memories. On the much more banal level, even those of us who do not think we've been taken up into spaceships by aliens can generate recollections of things that did not actually happen by thinking, or being urged to think, they did. This is another firm finding of modern psychology based on interesting sets of experiments.

One recent study involved participants who watched an eighteen-minute film showing the adventures of two boys at a summer camp.[12] Afterward an interviewer asked the participants questions about the film, requiring them to give a response. Some of the questions, however, were about episodes that were not in the film. When participants said so, the interviewer insisted that they come up with an answer to the question anyway, something other than "I don't know" or "I didn't see that." Eight weeks later the participants were again interviewed about the film. At that point 50 percent of them "remembered" the episode they previously had said they had not seen.

The researchers explained that when the participants had been forced to imagine something that was not in the film, they had necessarily done so within the constraints of their own "idiosyncratic knowledge and beliefs." That is, the way they answered the question was the most plausible way they, personally, could imagine. Since that plausible construction of something they had not seen fit in so naturally with their own views and ways of thinking about things, they later remembered it as something they had actually observed. "Over time, these forcibly fabricated events eventually became an integral part of the participants' enduring memory for the witnessed event."[13]

This finding was borne out by one of the most interesting recent experiments undertaken outside the laboratory. Three psychologists at Wesleyan University—John Seamon, Morgan Philbin, and Liza Harrison—wanted to see if *imagining* a bizarre experience could later lead to a *memory* of it. They titled the results of their study, "Do You Remember Proposing Marriage to the Pepsi Machine?"[14]

The study involved forty students who were taken to a variety of locations around campus. In each location they were instructed either to perform an action, to imagine performing it for ten seconds, to watch the experimenter performing the action, or to imagine the experimenter performing it. The actions were either normal or bizarre. For example, if they were in the library, they were asked to look up a word in a dictionary; or they were asked to pat the dictionary and ask how it was doing. Elsewhere they were asked to check the Pepsi machine for change or to go down on one knee and propose marriage to it.

Two weeks later the participants were interviewed and asked if the action had been imagined or performed. The conclusions were clear. Whether the action was normal or bizarre, participants who imagined it often remembered doing it: "We found that imagining familiar or bizarre actions during a campus walk can lead to the subsequent false recollection of having performed these actions."[15] In this instance the researchers found that imagining the action vividly, but just one time, could produce the false memory. Moreover, imagining someone else performing the action led to just as many false memories as imagining doing it oneself.

To sum up the situation, consider the words of one of the world's leading experts on false memory, Daniel Schacter: "Numerous experiments have demonstrated ways in which imagining events can lead to the development of false memories for those events."[16]

Does such research have any bearing on the memories about Jesus, a great teacher and miracle worker, by eyewitnesses or by those who later were told stories by eyewitnesses—or even those told stories by people who were not eyewitnesses? Can imagining that a great religious leader said and did something make someone remember that he really did say and do these things? It might be interesting to address that question by looking at another famous Jewish teacher. For my example I have chosen a person from the modern period known as the Baal Shem Tov. He was the eighteenth-century founder of Hasidic Judaism.

Memories of the Baal Shem Tov

The name Baal Shem Tov is Hebrew for "Master of the Good Name." It was bestowed on various Jewish holy men who were thought to have special, mystical insight into the nature and reality of God (who was called, reverentially, "the good name"). Such a person was a "master" of the name because he knew how to use it to perform miracles. Even though the designation was given to others, "the" Baal Shem Tov refers to a Jewish teacher named Israel ben Eliezer (ca. 1700–1760 CE), who was known for his compelling teachings and mystical powers. The designation is often shortened into an acronym, so sometimes he is simply called "the Besht."[17]

Even though he was not just like Jesus—very, very far from it—the Besht was remembered in some intriguingly similar ways. He was thought to be a charismatic figure adored by his followers to whom he taught his own distinctive version of the Jewish faith; he was said to have had direct encounters with God; he was allegedly able to heal the sick, cast out demons, control the weather, predict the future, and even raise the dead. He was also assigned other miracle-working powers not normally associated with Jesus: he could become invisible, fly through the air, and provide protection against the spells of sorcerers. As was the case with Jesus, the miraculous deeds and persuasive teachings of the Besht were written a generation after his death, and these accounts were alleged to have been based on the accurate reports of eyewitnesses.

Their messages were not particularly similar. The Besht was a proponent of pious ecstasy and insisted that God was present in all things. His goal in life, and the goal to which he urged his followers, was to attain a kind of unity with God through intense concentration and by abandoning all thought of oneself. He was personally highly enthusiastic; his devotion was especially intent. But it is very difficult to know the specifics of what he taught. The problem is that his two chief disciples recorded very different accounts of his words. As one of the most recent and complete studies, by Jewish historian Moshe Rosman, has indicated, "If we understand that each man regarded the Besht's teaching as raw material to be selected, shaped, and utilized in the service of his own vision, then the differences between them cease to confound. But then we must also admit that their transmissions of the Besht's sayings are not simply that." In fact, he concludes, "It seems impossible to move beyond what tradition made of the Besht's teaching to arrive at an articulate and nuanced explication of what that teaching was."[18] Yes indeed. Many have argued something similar with respect to the Christian accounts of Jesus.

Our principal source of information about the Besht comes in a series of anecdotes about his life written fifty-four years after his death and titled *In Praise of the Baal Shem Tov* (in Hebrew, *Shivhei ha-Besht*). The book was published in 1814 in Poland. Its author was Rabbi Dov Ber, who, as it turns out, was the son-in-law of a man who had been the personal scribe and secretary for the Besht, a rabbi called Alexander the Shohet (= butcher). The book contains 251 short tales about the Besht. Fifteen of these are said to have come directly from Alexander; the rest come from other sources, including the rabbi of the author's own community who had heard them from his own teacher.

Throughout the tales the Besht heals the sick, exorcises dybbuks (restless souls of the dead who possess other people), and helps barren women conceive. He can ascend to heaven and miraculously shorten a journey. He is often shown to be superior to others he encounters: rabbinic scholars, medical doctors, and sorcerers. While those outside the Hasidic tradition might consider these stories simply to be pious fictions, legendary accounts based on hearsay started by gullible devotees, the author Dov Ber himself claims they are rooted in reliable sources and relate historical realities. As he reflects, "I was careful to write down all the awesome things that I heard from truthful people. In each case I wrote down from whom I heard it. Thank God, who endowed me with memory, I neither added nor omitted anything. Every word is true and I did not change a word."[19]

Judge for yourself. Here are summaries of seven of the stories.

- Story 31. Dov Ber claims he heard this directly from his father-in-law (the Besht's personal scribe). A scholar named Rabbi David came and stayed in the house of the Besht. In the middle of the night the rabbi awoke and to his horror saw a bright light underneath the oven. He thought that there was a fire. When he went to put it out with the contents of his chamber pot, he saw that it was the Besht, apparently in a trancelike state. Above him was a bright light shining like a rainbow. Rabbi David fainted. The next day he insisted and the Besht "revealed himself" to him—that is, he revealed his true nature.

- Story 98. This one also came from Dov Ber's father-in-law. The Besht was living in the inn of a village that was experiencing a drought because a spell had been cast on it by a witch. The Besht prayed, and the rains came. The demon who empowered the witch told her what had happened. The witch sent the demon to attack the Besht, but the demon could not get within four steps of him. The Besht ordered the demon to attack instead a gentile woman sitting in a nearby house, and then the Besht imprisoned the demon in the forest. Later the Besht was walking by the forest and went in to see the demon sitting in its prison there. The Besht laughed and told his companions the story.

- Story 106. This one is told by another rabbi. The Besht and another rabbi and their servants were traveling in the dead of winter and realized that they wouldn't be able to make it home before they froze to death. The Besht ordered a stop. He then touched a tree with his finger and the tree caught fire. They warmed themselves sufficiently and went on their way.

- Story 220. The Besht was having a meal with some of his followers when suddenly he raised his arms and moved them as if he were swimming, saying, "Fool! Do this and you will be saved." An hour later a man came to the door and told them that he had just fallen into a river but didn't know how to swim. But then the thought came to him to try to move his arms in a certain way, and he swam to safety.

- Story 223. At the birth of a boy the Besht began to weep. He told the child's father that when the boy had his bar mitzvah he would be drawn into the river. Sure enough, years later, on the special day, after the bar mitzvah ceremony, everyone went to the river to cool down from the hot summer sun. The boy was kept at home, but he sneaked off to enjoy some fun. When his father found out he grabbed the boy, took him back, and locked him in his room. Then a creature with a head and two hands came up out of the river, slapped his hands on the water, and declared in disgust that "The one who is mine is not here."

- Story 237. One of Dov Ber's teachers had a strong desire "to learn the language of the animals, birds, and palm trees." The Besht "revealed to him the essential profundity of the secrets of this knowledge," so that he could hear the Besht with one ear and understand the conversations of the birds, animals, and other beasts with the other.

- Story 244. The Besht promised a certain man that he would have children, but none was forthcoming. When the man had become old, he continued to ask the Besht, and miraculously the man's wife bore a son. But the boy died in a matter of days. The man complained to the Besht that he promised him progeny, but now the boy was dead. The Besht told him that the boy would come back to life. But it didn't happen. After the customary number of days, the Besht instructed the man to prepare for the ritual of circumcision. He acquired the services of those who could perform the rite, and took the dead child to the synagogue. They cut his foreskin. Nothing happened. But then when the Besht said a blessing over him, the boy's breath returned to him, and blood gushed out of the incision.

There are many, many tales such as these throughout the account. And what is my point? Do I think the Besht actually had supernatural powers to do these things, to be transformed into a divine, glowing presence, to cast out and imprison demons, to ignite trees with his finger, to raise the dead, and all the rest? No, personally, I don't believe it. But are the stories based ultimately on eyewitness reports? Writing some fifty-four years after the events the author claims they were indeed based on eyewitness testimony. Does that make them reliable? Even if devoted followers of the Besht say yes, virtually everyone else realizes that these allegedly eyewitness reports are anything but historical.

What then about the Gospels of the New Testament? If they are based on eyewitnesses are they necessarily accurate? Do they in every instance represent accurate memories? Given what we have seen in this chapter, I think the answer has to be no. They are not *necessarily* reliable. And, of course, they are not necessarily unreliable either! All of them have to be examined historically to see whether and how far they preserve accurate memories of Jesus and distorted memories. But before we proceed to do that, what can we say about the relationship of these canonical accounts to eyewitness memories?

Jesus and the Eyewitnesses

The most recent full investigation of this question is a large book by a conservative British scholar named Richard Bauckham. His book *Jesus and the Eyewitnesses* tries to establish that the accounts of Jesus found in the Gospels of the New Testament can be directly linked to eyewitness reports and that therefore they can be trusted to be reliable and accurate.[20]

Bauckham states his thesis early in the book: "the Gospels . . . embody the testimony of the eyewitnesses, not of course without editing and interpretation, but in a way that is substantially faithful to how the eyewitnesses themselves told it, since the Evangelists were in more or less direct contact with the eyewitnesses, not removed from them by a long process of anonymous transmission of the traditions."[21] Later he indicates that eyewitnesses "remained the living and active guarantors of the traditions" (p. 290). Note his word "guarantors." Bauckham thinks that, at the end of the day, the Gospel narratives about Jesus— even those in the Gospel of John (which, in his view, was actually written by a personal companion of Jesus)—are highly reliable reports of what he said and did.

Outside the ranks of conservative evangelical Christians, very few if any biblical scholars have found Bauckham's case persuasive. It founders on numerous grounds, not the least of which is its steadfast refusal to take seriously scholarship on eyewitness testimony under-taken for more than a century by such experts as legal scholars who see the real-life importance of the question. As a result, possibly the most remarkable feature of Bauckham's book—devoted exclusively to the question of eyewitnesses—is its optimistic view of eyewit-nesses: the driving and underlying assumption throughout is that if a report derives from an eyewitness, we can more or less rely on it.

The book is also not persuasive that the Gospels are either eyewit-ness reports themselves (e.g., John) or reports directly based on eye-witness testimony.[22] We have already seen some of the problems with that view, and will see more throughout the rest of this chapter. It is crucial to remember that those who were involved with Jesus in his ministry were lower-class Aramaic-speaking Jews in rural Palestine. They were not literate. They were not educated.[23] They were poor. They did not have the time, money, inclination, or wherewithal to travel around the world. Jesus never left Palestine. He spent almost his entire life in Galilee before making a trip to Jerusalem in the last week of his life. The same can almost certainly be said about virtually all of his followers. And about those who saw and heard him during his public ministry.

The Gospel writers, on the other hand, lived in other parts of the world, probably major cities scattered throughout the empire. Their language was Greek, not Aramaic. They never indicate that they interviewed eyewitnesses (I'll say more on this in a moment). They almost certainly did not go to Palestine to make inquiries among the people who knew Jesus during his lifetime—for example, through interpreters. They inherited the stories they heard in Greek. These stories had been in circulation for years and decades before they themselves heard them. There had been stories, of course, during Jesus's lifetime, tales of his activities, sayings, and death. These would have been told in Aramaic, in Palestine. Some of those stories came to be translated into Greek and circulated in Christian communities in that form. Other stories were almost certainly constructed originally in Greek (as I will show in a later chapter). The unknown authors of these Gospels may well have been raised on these stories as Christians from their youth. Or possibly they converted as adults and heard the stories as recent converts. When they wrote their accounts, they obviously put their own spin on the stories. But the vast majority of the stories themselves had been circulated by word of mouth for forty or fifty years, or more, before these authors put them together into their extended narratives.[24]

The stories were being told, probably daily, for decades, in places such as Rome, Corinth, Thessalonica, Philippi, Ephesus, Galatia, Alexandria, and so forth. As we saw in chapter 2, in none of these places, as far as we know, was there an eyewitness to the life of Jesus who could vouch for the stories (not that an eyewitness would "guarantee" their accuracy). The closest thing we have to a surviving author who was an eyewitness to the life of Jesus is the Apostle Paul,[25] who, before engaging in his missionary work, met two of the apostles

(Gal. 1:18–20; at a later date he also met with the disciple John; Gal. 2:9).

It is a pity that we do not know what the three of them talked about. Given the context in which he discusses the encounter, it appears that the top item on Paul's own agenda was his decision to preach the death and resurrection of Jesus to gentiles. Possibly he wanted the leaders of the church of Jerusalem to be on board for his mission. Since he had already converted to the faith before this meeting he must have known some of the basics about Jesus, especially, of course, the fact that Jesus was crucified and the Christian belief that he had been raised from the dead. This was always at the heart and soul of Paul's Gospel message: the death and resurrection of the messiah Jesus (1 Cor. 15:3–5). But it does seem almost inconceivable that Paul would have met with Jesus's chief disciple and a member of his family and not discussed *something* about Jesus's life: who he was, what he had done, what he had taught, what had happened in that fateful last week, days, and hours.

Still, one of the most striking features of Paul's surviving letters is just how little he actually tells us about Jesus's life prior to his death There are thirteen letters in the New Testament that claim to be written by Paul. Scholars are widely convinced that seven of them, at least, actually go back to Paul. There are debates about the authorship of the other six.[26] But suppose you were to mine these letters—take all thirteen of them—for the information they provide about the things Jesus said, did, and experienced between the time he was born and the time he died. How many stories of Jesus would you discover?

I occasionally give this as an assignment for my undergraduate students. They are often surprised to find that for a full list, they don't need a 5 x 7 card. Here is what Paul tells us:

Jesus was born of a woman. (Gal. 4:4; this may not seem like a particularly helpful datum, since one might wonder what the option might be. But since Paul believes that Christ was the incarnation of a preexistent divine being [see Phil. 2:6–8] it makes sense that he also wants to emphasize that he "came to the world in the usual way.")

- He was born as a Jew. (Gal. 4:4)

- He was descended from the line of King David. (Rom. 1:3)

- He had brothers (1 Cor. 9:5), one of whom was named James. (Gal. 1:19)

- He had twelve disciples. (1 Cor. 15:5)

- He conducted his ministry among Jews. (Rom. 15:8)

- He had a last meal with his disciples on the night he was turned over to the authorities. (1 Cor. 11:23)

- Paul knows two things Jesus said at this last supper. (1 Cor. 11:23–25)

- Paul knows two other teachings of Jesus: that Christians should not get divorced (1 Cor. 7:10) and that they should pay their preacher. (1 Cor. 9:14)

- Jesus appeared before Pontius Pilate. (1 Tim. 6:13; this datum is found only in a letter Paul probably did not himself write)

- Jesus died of crucifixion. (1 Cor. 2:2)

- Those responsible for his death were Judeans. (1 Thess. 2:14–15)

That's pretty much all that Paul tells us. And he is the one author who has any known connection with an eyewitness. It is useful to see that Paul at least knows this much. But think of all the things that Paul doesn't mention: that Jesus was born in Bethlehem, to a virgin; that he was baptized by John the Baptist; that he was tempted in the wilderness; that he preached about the coming kingdom of God; that he told parables; that he cast out demons; that he did any miracles of any kind; that he delivered any other teachings of any kind; that he had controversies with other Jewish teachers; that he was transfigured; that he traveled to Jerusalem in the last week of his life; that he made the triumphal entry; that he cleansed the Temple; that he was arrested in the Garden of Gethsemane; that . . . well, it's obviously a very long and significant list. To make a complete list, all you would have to do is cite virtually any story in the Gospels, and it would be something Paul doesn't tell us.

It is a very interesting question to ask just why Paul does not give us more information about Jesus. Is it because he did not think Jesus's earthly life was important? How could it not be important? Is it because he thought his readers already knew all that information? If so, why doesn't he remind them of it, just as he regularly reminds them of all sorts of other things he taught them when he was among them? Is it because he simply had no occasion to mention the events of Jesus's life? Paul certainly seems to have occasions—plenty of them—as he talks in his letters about issues that were directly germane to things Jesus said and did (when he talks about miracles that he himself performed; when he tells people to pay their taxes; when he delivers his own ethical teachings; or when he indicates that Jesus had to die and be raised). So why doesn't he appeal to Jesus's own authority for such things? Is it because he actually doesn't know much more about Jesus's life than what he tells us? How could he not know much more? These are genuine questions that, at the end of the day, are not very easy to resolve.[27]

What is clear is that even though Paul is our one direct link to an eyewitness report, he doesn't give us much information about Jesus. So the fact that he had that link does not help us much.

What about the Gospels? Were they written by eyewitnesses or by those who knew eyewitnesses?

The Gospels and Eyewitness Testimony

The first thing to emphasize about Matthew, Mark, Luke, and John is that all four are completely anonymous. The authors never indicate who they are. They never name themselves. They never give any direct, personal identification of any kind whatsoever.

This is unambiguously the case for Matthew and Mark. Their accounts are given entirely in the third person, narrating what Jesus and others connected with him did, said, and experienced. Even the passage in Matthew's Gospel in which the disciple Matthew is called by Jesus to be his follower is narrated in the third person, about someone other than the author, with no indication that he is talking about himself (Matt. 9:9–13). Moreover, as we will see, there is no clear and certain evidence that anyone thought this book was written by Matthew (or Mark by Mark, and so too for the others) for a century after it was placed in circulation.[28]

The Gospels of Luke and John are slightly different in that both their authors speak at the beginning, and in John, also at the end, using the first-person pronoun. Unfortunately, the authors do not say who that first person is—in fact, they give virtually no clue who they are, with one exception (as we will see). The way they use the first-person pronoun clearly shows that, whoever they were, they were not eyewitnesses to what they narrate.

Both accounts are widely misunderstood by casual readers. Luke begins his narrative by writing in the first-person plural and moving to the first-person singular. In the following translation I have italicized the key terms:

> Since many have undertaken to compile a narrative about the things that have been fulfilled among *us*, just as they were delivered over to *us* from the beginning by eyewitness and ministers of the word, it seemed good also to *me*, as one who has followed closely for a long time, to write an orderly account for *you*, most excellent Theophilus. (1:1–3)

Here Luke (as I'll call him; we don't know his real name) is dedicating his account of Jesus's life to an unknown person named Theophilus. The two uses of the first-person plural ("among us" and "to us") are both references to the broader community of Jesus's followers. The stories about Jesus that the author is about to narrate were circulated by those who were eyewitnesses and by those who proclaimed the word. It is important to note that Luke decidedly does not say that he himself interviewed eyewitnesses or bases his account on what he directly learned from eyewitnesses. He simply says that the stories of Jesus were transmitted in the years before he wrote first by eyewitnesses and then by those who proclaimed the Christian Gospel. That obviously is true enough: the stories of Jesus were first told by people who knew him. If Luke had wanted to indicate that his principal sources of information for these stories were interviews he had conducted with the actual disciples of Jesus, why would he not say so? That would have improved his claim that unlike the narratives of his predecessors, his account was orderly and accurate.

The Gospel of John also utilizes the first-person plural in its opening passage. This is the famous "Prologue" (1:1–18) that describes Christ as the preexistent Word of God who created the world and then came into the world as a man of flesh: "And he became flesh and he dwelled among us, and we have seen his glory. . . . And from his fullness we have all received—grace upon grace. For the law was given through Moses, but grace and truth came through Jesus Christ" (1:14, 16–18).[29] At first glance it might seem that the author is saying that he himself, personally, saw Jesus's glory—that is, that he was a personal companion of Jesus. But on closer reading it is clear that this is not at all what he means. The "us" is again the community of Jesus's later followers, who have received the grace of God that has exceeded what was given by the Law of Moses. "All of us" have beheld Christ's glory by seeing who he really is and by obtaining the grace that he alone brings.

At the end of the Gospel of John the author again reverts to a first-person plural, in another verse that is widely misunderstood. After describing Jesus's resurrection appearance to Peter, in which Jesus tells Peter that the "beloved disciple" might still be alive when Jesus returns in glory, the author says, about that beloved one, "This is the disciple who is testifying about these things and who wrote these things, and we know that his testimony is true" (21:24). For some reason I have never been able to understand, readers frequently take this verse to mean that the beloved disciple is claiming to have written the Gospel of John. But that's not the case at all. The author cannot be that disciple himself because he clearly differentiates between himself ("we") and the beloved disciple ("his" testimony), the one who testifies about these things and wrote them down.

Doesn't that mean, though, that the author is claiming to base his account on a written report by the beloved disciple? Yes indeed, that is what he is saying. One of his sources of information, he says, was an account written by a disciple especially beloved of Jesus. He doesn't tell us who that disciple is, but as we will see later, Christians said that it was none other than John, the son of Zebedee. Whether the historical John of Zebedee, a peasant fisherman from rural Galilee, who was known to be illiterate, could have produced a written report about Jesus's life is another question altogether. Acts 4:13 says John was literally "unlettered" (Greek, *agrammatos*)—that is, he did not know his alphabet.

In short, the Gospel writers are all anonymous. None of them gives us any concrete information about their identity. So when did they come to be known as Matthew, Mark, Luke, and John? I will argue they were not called by those names until near the end of the second Christian century, a hundred years or so after these books had been in circulation. That obviously matters if we are interested in knowing how closely they were connected to eyewitness testimony.

The Gospels in the Earliest Church

I begin that discussion by considering the earliest references to the books, which occur in a group of authors who were writing, for the most part, immediately after the New Testament period. These are the "Apostolic Fathers." That term is not meant to indicate that these authors themselves were apostles, but that, in scholarly opinion starting hundreds of years ago (though no longer), they were companions of the apostles. Theirs are among our earliest noncanonical writings.[30]

In the various Apostolic Fathers there are numerous quotations of the Gospels of the New Testament, especially Matthew and Luke. What is striking about these quotations is that in none of them does any of these authors ascribe a name to the books they are quoting. Isn't that a bit odd? If they wanted to assign "authority" to the quotation, why wouldn't they indicate who wrote it?

Almost certainly the first Apostolic Father is the book of 1 Clement, a letter from the church of Rome to the church of Corinth written in about 95 CE (and so, before some of the last books of the New

Testament) and traditionally claimed to have been composed by the third bishop of Rome, Clement. Scholars today widely reject that claim, but for our purposes here it does not much matter. Just to give an example of how the Gospels are generally treated in the Apostolic Fathers, I quote one passage from 1 Clement:

> We should especially remember the words the Lord Jesus spoke when teaching about gentleness and patience. For he said: "Show mercy, that you may be shown mercy; forgive, that it may be forgiven you. As you do, so it will be done to you; as you give, so it will be given to you; as you judge, so you will be judged; as you show kindness, so will kindness be shown to you; the amount you dispense will be the amount you receive." (1 Clem. 13:1–2)

This is an interesting passage, and fairly typical, because it conflates a number of passages from the Gospels, containing lines from Matthew 5:7; 6:14–15; 7:1–2, and 12; Luke 6:31 and 36–38. But the author does not name the Gospels he has taken the texts from and certainly doesn't attribute them to eyewitnesses. Instead, he simply indicates that this is something Jesus said.

The same is true of other Apostolic Fathers. In the first chapter of the intriguing book known as the Didache, which contains a set of ethical and practical instructions to the Christian churches, the anonymous writer quotes from Mark 12; Matthew 5 and 7; and Luke 8. But he never names these Gospels. Later he cites the Lord's Prayer, virtually as it is found in Matthew 6; again he does not indicate his source.

So too, as a third example, Ignatius of Antioch clearly knows Matthew's story of the star of Bethlehem (Ignatius, Eph. 19) and Matthew's story of Jesus's baptism, which was undergone "in order to fulfill all righteousness" (Smyr. 1). But he doesn't mention that the account was written by Matthew. Similarly, Polycarp of Smyrna quotes Matthew chapters 5, 7, and 26 and Luke 6, but he never names a Gospel.

This is true of all our references to the Gospels prior to the end of the second century. The Gospels are known, read, and cited as authorities. But they are never named or associated with an eyewitness to the life of Jesus. There is one possible exception: the fragmentary references to the Gospels of Matthew and Mark in the writings of the church father Papias.

The Witness of Papias

My readers will need to forgive me if I cover something here that I already talked about in my earlier book *Jesus Interrupted*. But I cannot very well give a reasonably full coverage of the names of our canonical Gospels and bypass the complicated issues surrounding the witness of Papias. Papias is often taken as evidence that at least two of the Gospels, Matthew and Mark, were called by those names already several decades after they were in circulation.

Papias was a Christian author who is normally thought to have been writing in about 120 or 130 CE. As we have seen, his major work was a five-volume discussion of the teachings of Jesus called *Exposition of the Sayings of the Lord*.[31] It is much to be regretted that we no longer have this book. We don't know exactly why later scribes chose not to copy it, but it is commonly thought that the book was either uninspiring, naïve, or theologically questionable. Later church fathers who talk about Papias and his book are not overly enthusiastic. The "father of church history," the fourth-century Eusebius of Caesarea, indicates that, in his opinion, Papias was "a man of exceedingly small intelligence" (*Church History*, 3.39).

Our only access to Papias and his views are in quotations of his book in later church fathers, starting with the important author Irenaeus in about 185 CE, and including Eusebius himself. Some of these quotations are fascinating and have been the subject of intense investigation among critical scholars for a very long time. Of relevance to us here is what he says both about the Gospels and about the connection he claims to have had to eyewitnesses to the life of Jesus.

In one of the most famous passages quoted by Eusebius, Papias indicates that instead of reading about Jesus and his disciples in books, he preferred hearing a "living voice." He explains that whenever knowledgeable people came to visit his church, he asked them what they knew. Specifically he spoke with people who had been "companions" of those whom he calls "elders" who had earlier been associates with the disciples of Jesus. And so Papias is not himself an eyewitness to Jesus's life and does not know eyewitnesses. Writing many years later (as much as a century after Jesus's death), he indicates that he knew people who knew people who knew people who were with Jesus during his life. So it's not like having firsthand information, or anything close to it. But it's extremely interesting and enough to make a scholar sit up and take notice!

Richard Bauckham is especially enthusiastic about Papias's testimony, in part because he believes that Papias encountered these people long before he was writing, possibly as early as 80 CE—that is, during the time when the Gospels themselves were being composed. Bauckham does not ask whether Papias's memory of encounters he had many decades earlier was accurate. But as that is our interest here, it will be important to raise the questions ourselves.

Two passages from Papias are especially important, as Bauckham and others have taken them to be solid evidence that the Gospels were already given their names during the first century. At first glance one can see why they might think so. Papias mentions Gospels written by Mark and by Matthew. His comments deserve to be quoted here in full. First on a Gospel written by Mark.

> This is what the elder used to say, "when Mark was the inter-preter [or: translator] of Peter he wrote down accurately every-thing that he recalled of the Lord's words and deeds—but not in order. For he neither heard the Lord nor accompanied him; but later, as I indicated, he accompanied Peter, who used to adapt his teachings for the needs at hand, not arranging, as it were, an orderly composition of the Lord's sayings. And so Mark did nothing wrong by writing some of the matters as he remembered them. For he was intent on just one purpose: not to leave out anything that he heard or to include any falsehood among them." (Eusebius, *Church History*, 3.39)

Thus, according to Papias, someone named Mark was Peter's in-terpreter or translator (from Aramaic?) and he wrote down what Peter had to say about Jesus's words and deeds. He did not, however, produce an orderly composition. Still, he did record everything he ever heard Peter say and he did so with scrupulous accuracy. We will see that these claims are highly problematic, but first consider what Papias says also about a Gospel by Matthew.

> And so Matthew composed the sayings in the Hebrew tongue, and each one interpreted [or translated] them to the best of his ability. (Eusebius, *Church History,* 3.39)

There are numerous reasons for questioning whether these passag-es—as quoted by Eusebius—provide us solid evidence that the New Testament Gospels were given their names in the late first or early second century.

First, it is somewhat curious and certainly interesting that Eusebius chose not to include any quotations from Papias about Luke or John. Why would that be? Were Papias's views about these two books not significant? Were they unusual? Were they contrary to Eusebius's own views? We'll never know.

Second, it is important to stress that in none of the surviving quotations of Papias does he actually quote either Matthew or Mark. That is to say, he does not give a teaching of Jesus, or a summary of something he did, and then indicate that he found it in one of these Gospels. That is unfortunate, because it means we have no way of knowing for certain that when he refers to a Gospel written by Mark he has in mind the Gospel we today call the Gospel of Mark. In fact there are reasons for doubting it, as I will show in a minute.

Before doing so, I want to point out that if Papias did have our first two Gospels in mind, there are good grounds for thinking that he did not consider them authoritative accounts of Jesus's life. Not only does he explicitly say that he did not find written accounts all that useful, especially in comparison with the "living voice," that is, with the interviews he undertook of people who knew others who had been companions of the apostles of Jesus. But we also have one story that Papias tells that overlaps with an account found in Matthew, and it is clear that he does not consider Matthew's version to represent the Gospel truth.

You may remember that in the first chapter I described the death of Judas as found in Papias. This was the passage that indicated that Judas, after his foul deed of betrayal, himself became extremely foul. He swelled up to enormous size, so that he could not even walk down a street; his genitals became swollen and disgusting; and he burst forth (did he "explode"?) and spilled his intestines on the ground, creating a stench that was still incredible a century later. Matthew's Gospel—the one we have in the New Testament—also describes the death of Judas. But it is not like this at all. According to Matthew, Judas hanged himself (Matt. 27:5). If Papias saw Matthew's Gospel as an eyewitness authority to the life of Jesus and those around him, why didn't he accept its version of Judas's death?

This raises an even bigger and more fundamental question. When Papias talks about a Gospel written by Mark and another by Matthew, is he actually talking about the Gospels that *we* know about by these names? At first this seems to be a weird question, but in fact what Papias says about the two books he references (Matthew and Mark) suggests he is referring to books different from the ones we have.

That is easy to show with Matthew. Papias says two things about the "Matthew" he is familiar with: it consists only of sayings of Jesus and it was composed in Hebrew. Neither is true of our Matthew, which does have sayings of Jesus, but is mainly composed of stories *about* Jesus. Moreover, it was not composed in Hebrew but in Greek, as virtually every critical scholar on the planet agrees.[32] It is possible, of course, that like other early Christian scholars, Papias thought Matthew was originally composed in Hebrew when it was not. But it is also possible that these later writers thought Matthew was written in Hebrew because they knew about Papias's comment and thought he was referring to our Gospel. But he appears not to be: Matthew is not simply a collection of Jesus's sayings.

If Papias was not talking about our Matthew, was he talking about our Mark? It is widely acknowledged that he considered "his" Mark to be problematic because of its disorderly arrangement: that's why he says that the preaching of Peter was not given "in order." But that somewhat negative remark in itself is odd, because he doesn't make the same comment about Matthew, even though the narrative outline of our Matthew is pretty much the same as of our Mark—with additional materials added. Apart from that, Papias indicates that

Mark's Gospel gives an exhaustive account of everything Peter preached and that it gives it without changing a thing. The reality is that there is no way that anyone could think that the Gospel of Mark in our Bibles today gives a full account of Peter's knowledge of Jesus. Our Gospel of Mark takes about two hours to read. Are we to think that after spending months (years?) with Jesus, Peter had no more than two hours' worth of memories?

Of course it may be that Papias is exaggerating for effect. But even so, since he does not appear to be referring to the book we call Matthew, why should we think that he is referring to the book we call Mark? Despite repeated attempts over the centuries by readers to show that Mark's Gospel is "Peter's perspective," the reality is that if you simply read it without any preconceptions, there is nothing about the book that would make you think, "Oh, this is how Peter saw it all." Quite the contrary—not only does Peter come off as a bumbling, foot-in-the-mouth, and unfaithful follower of Jesus in Mark (see Mark 8:27–32; 9:5–6; 14:27–31), but also there are all sorts of stories—the vast majority—that have nothing to do with Peter or that betray anything like a Petrine voice.

There is, though, a still further and even more compelling reason for doubting that we can trust Papias on the authorship of the Gospels. It is that that we cannot really trust him on much of anything. That may sound harsh, but remember that even the early Christians did not appreciate his work very much and the one comment we have about him personally from an educated church father is that he was remarkably unintelligent.

It is striking that some modern authors want to latch on to Papias for his claims that Matthew and Mark wrote Gospels, assuming, as Bauckham does, that he must be historically accurate, when they completely overlook the *other* things Papias says, things that even these authors admit are not and cannot be accurate. If Papias is not reliable about anything else he says, why does anyone think he is reliable about our Gospels of Matthew and Mark? The reason is obvious. It is because readers *want* him to be accurate about Matthew and Mark, even though they know that otherwise you can't rely on him for a second.

Does anyone think that Judas really bloated up larger than a house, emitted worms from his genitals, and then burst on his own land, creating a stench that lasted a century? No, not really. But it's one of the two Gospel traditions that Papias narrates. Here is the only other one; it is the only saying of Jesus that is preserved from the writing of Papias. Papias claims that it comes from those who knew the elders who knew what the disciple John the son of Zebedee said that Jesus taught:

> Thus the elders who saw John, the disciple of the Lord, remembered hearing him say how the Lord used to teach about those times, saying:
>
> > "The days are coming when vines will come forth, each with ten thousand boughs; and on a single bough will be ten thousand branches. And indeed, on a single branch will be ten thousand shoots and on every shoot ten thousand clusters; and in ever cluster will be ten thousand grapes, and every grape, when pressed, will yield twenty-five measures of wine. And when any of the saints grabs hold of a cluster, another will cry out, 'I am better, take me, bless the lord through me.'" (Eusebius, *Church History*, 3.39.1)

Really? Jesus taught that? Does anyone really think so? No one I know. But does Papias think Jesus said this? Yes, he absolutely does. Here is what Papias himself says about the traditions of Jesus he records in his five-volume book, in Bauckham's own translation: "I will not hesitate to set down for you along with my interpretations everything I carefully learned from the elders and carefully remembered, guaranteeing their truth." So can we rest assured about the truth of what Papias says, since he can provide guarantees based on his careful memory? It doesn't look like it. The only traditions about Jesus we have from his pen are clearly not accurate. Why should we think that what he says about Matthew and Mark are accurate? My hunch is that the only reason readers have done so is because they would like him to be accurate when he says things they agree with, even when they know he is not accurate when he says things they disagree with.

However one evaluates the overall trustworthiness of Papias, he does not provide us with clear evidence that the books that eventually became the first two Gospels of the New Testament were called Matthew and Mark in his time.

The Gospels Toward the End of the Second Century

The situation with respect to the names of the Gospels does not immediately change after the writings of the Apostolic Fathers. The most important author from the middle of the second century is the eventual martyr Justin, a philosopher-turned-Christian who ran a kind of Christian philosophical school in Rome. We have three works from Justin's hand: two "apologies"—that is, reasoned defenses of the Christian faith against the charges of its intellectual detractors—and a "dialogue" that he allegedly had with a rabbi named Trypho about the truth claims of Christianity over against Judaism.

In these books Justin quotes Matthew, Mark, and Luke on numerous occasions, and possibly the Gospel of John twice, but he never calls them by name. Instead he calls them "memoirs of the apostles." It is not clear what that is supposed to mean—whether they are books written by apostles, or books that contain the memoirs the apostles had passed along to others, or something else. Part of the confusion is that when Justin quotes the Synoptic Gospels, he blends passages from one book with another, so that it is very hard to parse out which Gospel he has in mind. So jumbled are his quotations that many scholars think he is not actually quoting our Gospels at all, but a kind of "harmony" of the Gospels that took the three Synoptics and created one mega-Gospel out of them, possibly with one or more other Gospels.[33] If that's the case, it would suggest that even in Rome, the most influential church already by this time, the Gospels—as a collection of four and only four books—had not reached any kind of authoritative status. The same conclusion is suggested for other parts of Christendom. Justin's student, a man named Tatian, created a Gospel harmony of all four of the canonical accounts, again possibly with other Gospel traditions; this is the famous Diatessaron, which no longer survives intact but which was used for centuries in the Syrian church instead of the four "separate" Gospels. Again, there is no evidence that Tatian knew these Gospels by the names they now bear.

It is not until nearer the end of the second century that anyone of record quotes our four Gospels and calls them Matthew, Mark, Luke, and John. That first happens in the writings of Irenaeus, whose five-volume work *Against the Heresies,* written in about 185 CE, was an attempt to describe and attack various heretical factions within the Christian church of his day. Irenaeus had been associated with the same circles that Justin frequented in Rome, and had acquired a good deal of his understanding of the faith there, in that major ecclesiastical and intellectual center. It was after he moved to Gaul (modern France) and became the bishop of Lyons there that Irenaeus wrote his most famous book, which still survives. In the course of his work he quotes our four Gospels abundantly. What is most striking for our purposes here is that he actually refers to the Gospels by name.

There were, of course, numerous Gospels in circulation in the late second century. Irenaeus is particularly keen to insist that only four of the then-available Gospels could be accepted as authoritative. His reasoning may not seem overly persuasive to modern readers. In Irenaeus's view there have to be four Gospels, no more and no fewer. Some heretical groups, he tells us, err in accepting only one or another of the Gospels. This leads them to the unbalanced view of Jesus at the heart of their heresy. For a full and orthodox understanding, the four Gospels have to be read and accepted as a unit as authoritative. And the reason is this: the gospel of Christ was spread to the four corners of the earth by the four winds of heaven, and so there need to be four Gospels: Matthew, Mark, Luke, and John (*Against Heresies,* 3.11.7). Here there is no ambiguity: Irenaeus quotes these books in numerous places and gives them their names.

It is striking that at about the same time another source also indicates that there are four authoritative Gospels. This is the famous Muratorian Fragment, a document discovered in the seventeenth century by an Italian scholar named Muratori (hence its name).[34] It is only a fragment because the beginning is lost, much to our chagrin. What survives is a list of the books that its anonymous and unknown author considers to be the Christian scriptures. The fragment begins at the very end of a sentence that is referring to a book of scripture. It then says that the "third book of the Gospel is Luke." It goes on to describe Luke in such a way as to make it obvious that it is talking about the Gospel we now have. It then speaks of the fourth Gospel, which it calls John. Again, the list is clearly describing our John.

Since these are the third and fourth Gospels, and there are no more in its list (it moves to Acts and the epistles from there), it is obvious that its first two books were also Gospels, and no one doubts what they were. Here too then we have an author who has four Gospels and understands them to be, presumably, Matthew and Mark and, explicitly, Luke and John. The date and place of the Muratorian Fragment is debated among scholars, but, based on a couple of comments found in the fragment itself the majority believes that it was produced at about the time of Irenaeus, at the end of the second century, and that it was written in Rome.[35]

This is remarkable. Before this time and place, nowhere are the Gospels said to be four in number and nowhere are they named as Matthew, Mark, Luke, and John. Justin, living in Rome just thirty years earlier, did not number or name the Gospels. But now, near the end of the second century, in sources connected with Rome, they are both numbered and named. How do we explain that?

Here is another point to consider. In our surviving manuscripts of the Gospels they are always called by the same names, with titles such as "According to Matthew," "According to Mark," "According to Luke," "According to John"—never by any other names (although the way the titles are phrased do differ). Some scholars have argued that this is evidence that the Gospels were *always* named these things, from the beginning. That is not necessarily the case, however. It needs to be pointed out that we don't start getting manuscripts with Gospel titles in them until about the year 200 CE. The few fragments of the Gospels that survive from before that time never include the beginning of the texts (e.g., the first verses of Matthew or Mark, etc.), so we don't know if those earlier fragments had titles on their Gospels. More important, if these Gospels had gone by their now-familiar names from the outset, or even from the beginning of the second century, it is very hard indeed to explain why the church fathers who quoted them never called them by name. They quoted them as if they had no specific author attached to them.

There is one other reason for thinking that the Gospels did not originally circulate with the titles "According to Matthew," "According to Mark," and so on. Anyone who calls a book the Gospel "According to [someone]," is doing so to differentiate it from *other* Gospels. This one is Matthew's version. And that one is John's, etc. It is only when you have a collection of the Gospels that you need to begin to differentiate among them to indicate which is which. That's what these titles do. Obviously the authors themselves did not give them these titles: no one titles their book "According to . . . Me." Whoever did give the Gospels these titles was someone who had a collection of them and wanted to identify which was which.

Why then were they eventually called by the names we have today? To solve this puzzle, two further points need to be stressed. The first one I have already covered: these books were all written anonymously. By that I do not mean that the very first audience who read Mark did not know who its author was. My assumption is that each of these books was written for a tightly knit Christian community in one city or another by one of its members. The people who first read the book almost certainly knew who wrote it. But suppose this Gospel was written in Rome. There were lots of churches in Rome, and all the Christians there almost certainly did not know one another. For more than two hundred years churches met in private homes, not in specially designated buildings; so the churches necessarily had to be small—two or three dozen people at most, I should think. In a city such as Rome, who knows how many churches might be spread throughout the city? It was a big place.

If someone—say his name was Silvanus—wrote a Gospel that his own small community read, someone from another church in town may have wanted a copy. A copy was made and taken to this other house-church. Some (most?) people in this other church probably wouldn't know the author. Then it went to another church. Then a Christian from Ephesus visited town and learned that there was a written account of Jesus's life. She wanted a copy to take back to her church, had one made, and took it. It is almost certain that no one knew the author. Then a copy went to Antioch. And one to Corinth. And to Lystra. And to . . . lots of places. There was no name attached to the book to begin with. Why would there be? The author was writing an account of Jesus's life based on stories he had heard. He wasn't composing a work of fiction in his own name. Within months most of the people reading the book would not know its author. So far as we can tell, no one really cared who the author was. There was evidently no discussion of the matter for many, many decades. What people were interested in was the content of the book: here is a written account of the things Jesus did and said.

By the middle of the second century there were lots of books like this, a variety of Gospels in circulation. Some of them did have names attached to them. For example, there was a Gospel that claimed to be written by Peter (the one mentioned in chapter 1, which has a giant Jesus walking out of the tomb with a talking cross emerging behind him). Another that claimed to be written by Thomas (with all those sayings of Jesus). Yet a third that claimed to be written by James. Another by Philip. And lots of others. But the four that were most in favor in some of the churches—especially in Rome—didn't have any names attached to them.

That would have raised a key question, though: why should any authority be attached to these particular accounts of Jesus's life and teachings instead of the others that actually have apostles' names associated with them?

The reason many readers considered these anonymous books authoritative is because they portrayed Jesus in a way that was seen to be widely acceptable. These were the books people read the most (or rather heard the most, since most people couldn't read). These were the books that teachers taught from. These were the books that preachers preached from. There came a time when it was necessary both to differentiate them from one another and to ascribe authority to them by claiming that unlike the other accounts in circulation they really had been written by people who would know about Jesus and who gave an authoritative account of his life.

So far as we know from our evidence, that happened by 185 CE. At that time, two sources, Irenaeus and the Muratorian Fragment, independently of one another, speak of there being four authoritative Gospels. One of them explicitly names Luke and John (its references to Matthew and Mark being lost) and the other explicitly names Matthew, Mark, Luke, and John. Strikingly, both sources are closely connected with the church in Rome. After that time, everyone in the orthodox Christian communities agrees that these are the four authors of the four Gospels. How do we explain these facts?

I would like to put forward a hypothesis that can, in my opinion, account for all the data. By the time of Justin, one of the leading teachers in Rome, the Gospels were not named in Christendom's most important church, Rome, or anywhere else. If they were, he and/or his predecessors would surely have mentioned it. But they *were* known by name in Rome some thirty years later by both Irenaeus and the Muratorian Fragment. I would propose that sometime during those intervening years, between Justin and Irenaeus, some kind of authoritative and influential edition of the four Gospels was published and circulated in Rome. This was an edition that contained the four Gospels and only these four Gospels. In the manuscript itself the Gospels were named: "According to Matthew," "According to Mark," "According to Luke," and "According to John." This would explain why the books were not known by these titles before, but were afterward.

These ascriptions made perfect sense to people who read the books, for reasons I will explain in a moment. This edition of the Gospels was rapidly copied and recopied and became common property. Since Rome was the theological and practical center of Christendom at the time, and since it had so many people—Christians included—coming to and from the city, this edition of the Gospels spread quickly throughout the worldwide church. Scribes who copied these books started giving them their titles. Everyone familiar with these Gospels within a couple of decades was accepting the idea that they were written by Matthew, Mark, Luke, and John.

Those are the apostolic names that came to be associated with these books all over the Christian map. That is how the Gospels came to be titled everywhere. That is how the Gospels came to be referred to, from that time down to today.

Why Matthew, Mark, Luke, and John?

The final, big question is why these four names were chosen. They are the names of two of the disciples of Jesus and two of the companions of important apostles. Matthew was named after the tax collector who became Jesus's follower in the first Gospel (Matt. 9:9–13). John was named after Jesus's disciple the son of Zebedee, assumed to be the "beloved disciple" mentioned in the fourth Gospel (John 21:20, 24). Mark is named after a person popularly connected with Peter (1 Pet. 5:13). Luke is named after a traveling companion of Paul (Col. 4:14). But why these four in particular?

In fact, there were clear and compelling reasons. Matthew was an obvious choice. Since the days of Papias, it had been thought that Jesus's disciple Matthew had written a "Hebrew" Gospel. It came to be thought that this book must have been it. (Never mind that Papias was talking only about a list of Jesus's sayings and that our Matthew was not written in Hebrew. Early Christians as a rule didn't know that.) The call of Matthew the tax collector is found only in this first Gospel (9:9–14), and so obviously (at least it was obvious to some people) this Gospel was especially focused on Matthew.[36] Moreover, the first Gospel has always been seen as the most "Jewish" of the Gospels; if Matthew wrote a Gospel in Hebrew, it was for Jews or for Jewish followers of Jesus. That would be this Gospel. Whoever named the first Gospel wanted it to be attributed to a follower of Jesus, so Matthew was an obvious choice.

The reasons for naming the fourth Gospel John are less straight-forward but somewhat more intriguing. In many ways the disciple who is closest to Jesus in this Gospel is not Peter but the mysterious "disciple whom Jesus loved" (e.g., John 13:23; 20:2). Who was this beloved disciple? He is never called by name. But the author indicates that he wrote down what he knew about Jesus (21:24–25). Some readers (wrongly) read the reference to him in 19:35—where he sees water and blood coming out of Jesus's side at his crucifixion—to be the author's reference to himself, spoken in the third person. So the author was thought to be someone particularly close to Jesus. Which of Jesus's close disciples would it be?

In the other Gospels, Jesus's closest disciples—the "inner three"— were Peter, James, and John (e.g., Mark 5:37; 9:2–13). But the be-loved disciple of John's Gospel could not be Peter, because he is mentioned in episodes alongside Peter (e.g., 20:1–10). Moreover, it was widely known that James the son of Zebedee had been martyred early in the history of the church, before any of the Gospels was writ-ten (Acts 12:2). That leaves John, the son of Zebedee, who is other-wise not called by name in the Gospel. Even though he is elsewhere said to be illiterate (Acts 4:13) he came to be considered the beloved disciple who wrote the fourth Gospel.

The authorship of the third Gospel, Luke, is also relatively un-problematic, but for completely other reasons. The author of that book also wrote the book of Acts (read the first few verses of each book and you'll see why this has always been obvious to most people). Acts is not about the life, death, and resurrection of Jesus, but about the spread of Christianity in the years after Jesus's ascension. The main character for most of Acts is the Apostle Paul, whose missionary endeavors form the subject of a good bit of the book.

Acts is told in the third person, except in four passages dealing with Paul's travels, where the author moves into a first-person narrative, indicating what "we" were doing (16:10–17; 20:5–15; 21:1–18; and 27:1–28:16). That was taken to suggest that the author of Acts—and therefore of the third Gospel—must have been a traveling companion of Paul. Moreover, this author's ultimate concern is with the spread of the Christian message among gentiles. That must mean, it was reasoned, that he too was a gentile. So the only question is whether we know of a gentile traveling companion of Paul. Yes we do: Luke, the "beloved physician" named in Colossians 4:14. Thus Luke was the author of the third Gospel.[37]

That leaves the Gospel of Mark. One can see why the Gospel of Luke would not have been named after one of Jesus's own disciples. But what about Mark? Here too there was a compelling logic. For one thing, since the days of Papias, it was thought that Peter's version of Jesus's life had been written by one of his companions named Mark. Here was a Gospel that needed an author assigned to it. There was every reason in the world to want to assign it to the authority of Peter. Remember, the edition of the four Gospels in which they were first named, following my hypothesis, originated in Rome. Traditionally, the founders of the Roman church were said to be Peter and Paul. The third Gospel is Paul's version. The second must be Peter's. Thus it makes sense that the Gospels were assigned to the authority of Peter and Paul, written by their close companions Mark and Luke. These are the Roman Gospels in particular.

The main reason there may have been reluctance to assign this book directly to Peter (the "Gospel of Peter") was because there already was a Gospel of Peter in circulation that was seen by some

Christians as heretical and that was known to authors such as Justin Martyr in Rome.[38] It is the Gospel I mentioned in chapter 1, with a Jesus who does not appear to suffer and who comes forth from his tomb as a very nonhuman giant. It was easiest then to assign Peter's real account to the figure that had been known for many years to have written down his recollections of Jesus's words and deeds, Mark.

That Mark and Luke were considered to be the Gospels of Peter and Paul is clearly seen in other writings from about this time. Just about two decades after Irenaeus, the church father Tertullian stressed, "That which Mark produced is stated to be Peter's, whose interpreter Mark was. Luke's narrative also they usually attribute to Paul. It is permissible for the works which disciples published to be regarded as belonging to their masters." Tertullian, of course, would have no way of knowing who actually wrote these two Gospels. He is simply repeating the tradition he learned when he converted, that Mark represents Peter's views and Luke Paul's. By his time this was the accepted view, and it continued to be the accepted view until the modern era.[39]

And so we have the four Gospels, two assigned to disciples of Jesus and two to the close companions of the two founders of the Roman church, Peter and Paul.

The Real Authors of the Gospels

The reality is that these persons were almost certainly not the authors of these Gospels, which were first circulated without any names attached. The assignment of apostolic authors to the accounts came only a century or so after they were written.

It is highly unfortunate that we don't know who really wrote these accounts. Still, even without knowing their names, we can say a few things about them. Unlike the lower-class, Aramaic-speaking, illiterate peasants who were numbered among Jesus's followers, the authors of the four Gospels were highly educated, fully literate, Greek-speaking Christians of a later generation who lived outside of Palestine. There are eternal and unsolvable debates about where they were living. Was Mark in Rome? Matthew in Antioch? John in Ephesus? Luke in . . . where? No one knows—for Luke or for any of the others.

What can be said with relative certainty is that each of them had sources of information for their accounts of Jesus's life, death, and resurrection. Some of their sources may have been written. Matthew and Luke, as we have seen, appear to have used the Gospel of Mark for many of their stories, along with the collection of sayings that scholars have called Q. Did they have other written sources? Possibly. Oral sources? Almost certainly. What about Mark and John? They too may have had written sources for some of their stories. The stronger case can be made for John, but it is conceivable for Mark as well.[40]

It is possible that the Gospel writers themselves may have made up some of their accounts; but that does not appear to be the case with most of their stories, since, for example, many of the stories are attested by more than one of them. Many of the stories they inherited may have come directly to them from oral sources. And ultimately, of course, nearly *all* of the stories about Jesus in the Gospels came from the oral tradition. That is true even if there were earlier written texts that provided information to the canonical Gospel writers. In that case, even these texts were based on stories that had been in circulation year after year and probably decade after decade before being written.

All the stories about Jesus to be found in the Gospels—whether the canonical four or those outside the New Testament—represent ways that he was "remembered" by early Christian storytellers. Even if the authors made up some of their stories, those invented accounts were later told and retold and so entered into the Christian memory.

Some of the later Christian memories of Jesus probably were first placed in circulation by eyewitnesses. The fact that they go back to eyewitnesses, however, does not mean they are necessarily "accurate" memories, in the sense that they are memories of things that really happened. They *may* be that. Or not. Other memories were generated by later Christians. These represent "invented" traditions. In almost all cases these would become distorted memories.

Memory is obviously a key category when dealing not just with eyewitness reports but also with stories that are in circulation, whether ultimately tied to an eyewitness or not. For that reason, if we are to understand more fully what these ancient recollections of Jesus are and whether they conform to the reality of what he said, did, and experienced, it is important for us to know more about memory. That will be the focus of the next four chapters. In these chapters we will be interested not simply in the historical question of which memories are accurate (i.e., that indicate what Jesus actually did say and do) but also the equally important question of what the other memories of Jesus can tell us about the people who recalled him in these ways, and the contexts they were living in that made such recollections relevant to their lives.

CHAPTER 4

Distorted Memories
and the Death of Jesus

Some people have absolutely incredible memories. In his 2011 bestselling book *Moonwalking with Einstein*, freelance writer Joshua Foer describes how he went from being a normal human to become a memory cyborg, in his successful quest to win the 2006 USA Memory Championship. Much of his book describes how memory masters do it, techniques that Foer claims any of us could use to do astounding mental feats. Apparently only those of us who have never tried—that is, most of us—think it is impossible.

Even those who use tried and true methods of memory, which go back to the ancient Greeks, obviously have an enormous range of abilities. The thirty-two "grand masters of memory" in the world are able to memorize a sequence of a thousand random digits in less than an hour; they can memorize the sequence of 520 shuffled cards—that's ten decks—also in an hour; or one shuffled deck in ten minutes. Try it sometime. Without memory tricks there's no way to do it.

Most of us, of course, don't spend our days memorizing random numerals or decks of cards. And most of us have reasonable but not fantastic memories. In our daily lives, we forget stuff all the time. Why is that? It is a crucial question for anyone interested in knowing about how memory may have worked in the early church, during all those years when stories about Jesus were being circulated among people orally, before any of our Gospels were written.

The Study of Memory: In the Beginning

Psychologists have studied memory for more than 130 years, trying to figure out what memory actually is, what different kinds of memory we have, and how it is we remember the past at all. Today the study of memory can be found in all sorts of fields: neuroscience, which examines how the brain works; sociology, which studies how social groups remember their shared past; cultural anthropology, which looks into how oral cultures preserve their traditions; literary studies, which explore how memory functions in great works of literature (think Proust); and history, which in a sense is all about memory and its relationship to the past. But the most extensive explorations are in psychology.

A German psychologist named Hermann Ebbinghaus (1850–1909) was the first to ask and explore pointed questions about memory. Ebbinghaus approached the question by experiments, conducted on himself, involving rote memorization. Because he wanted to study memory in a pure form, his experiments were intentionally unrelated to everyday life. Ebbinghaus created twenty-three hundred three-letter nonsense syllables, such as DAX, GUF, and NOK. Then he tried to memorize them.

After he mastered a number of these invented syllables, he tested himself. He waited a while, and tested himself again. Then he waited a while longer, and tested himself again. Ebbinghaus was essentially interested in learning how long information can be retained in memory. Or to put it otherwise: how long it takes us to forget.

Based on these experiments Ebbinghaus drew a significant conclusion that has, somewhat remarkably, stood the test of time. Most forgetting happens very quickly. At least when it came to his recollection of nonsense syllables, Ebbinghaus forgot more than half of them after an hour. But an hour later he had not forgotten the other half. Instead, a full day later, in addition to the original half he forgot, he forgot only another 10 percent. An entire month later, only 14 percent more. Ebbinghaus thus showed that the rate of forgetting significantly drops off after a passage of time; as a result, you can chart this rate of forgetting on a kind of statistical curve that eventually flattens out. After a while, you pretty much keep on remembering what you remembered six months ago.

In 1885, Ebbinghaus published his results in a groundbreaking book called *On Memory* (in German, *Über das Gedächtnis*). Subsequent experiments confirmed many of Ebbinghaus's findings.[1] But eventually researchers wondered what memorizing nonsense has to do with how we actually remember things in our lives. How does it relate to remembering factual information (Where is the Golden Gate Bridge?), or personal experiences (What did I really do the night of my high school graduation?), or even bodily skills (How do I do the breaststroke?)? How does memory work more broadly? Are there different kinds of memory for these different kinds of knowledge?

The commonsensical answer to that last question is yes, as I mentioned already in chapter 1 (but mention again here in case you don't remember): remembering how to do something is different from remembering factual information. Both are different from remembering what happened in your personal past. Each kind of memory is interesting and, of course, massively important for our lives. But in this

133

book my interest is principally with the specific kind of memory that involves recalling information and experiences from the past, either by personally being involved or by learning about them from others.

Remembering, 1932

When most of us try to conceptualize what it means to remember something that happens to us, we probably have some kind of vague notion that it's like taking a picture with your I-phone. You snap a picture of the moment with your brain, and it's back there somewhere tucked away until you retrieve it. Researchers for more than eighty years have realized that this is not how memory actually works. The major breakthrough came in the research of a British psychologist, F. C. Bartlett, as published in his famous book *Remembering*.[2]

Bartlett decided to examine memory not in some kind of "pure" form removed from the realities of life (as in memorizing nonsense syllables) but precisely in view of how we recall things we personally experience. On the basis of a large number of studies, Bartlett showed that memories are not snapshots stored in some location in the brain to be retrieved later. The brain doesn't work like that. Instead, when we experience something, bits and pieces of its memory are storied in different parts of the brain. Later, when we try to retrieve the memory, these bits and pieces are reassembled. The problem is that when we reassemble the pieces, there are some, often lots of them, that are missing. To complete the memory we unconsciously fill in the gaps, for example, with analogous recollections from similar experiences.

Suppose you are trying to remember what the doctor's office looked like on your last visit. You saw, heard, smelled, and generally experienced things there. When you try to remember the experience, you piece it all together as well as you can; but your brain fills in the bits you don't actually remember by recalling what you *typically* would find (and have found) in doctors' offices, such as a reception desk; chairs; tables; a corner for children to play; magazines; a TV overhead showing health videos. Now, it may be that the last time you were in the doctor's office the TV was turned off, but you remember it being on. That's because your memory is filling in the gaps with what you would be accustomed to seeing. The problem is that there is precisely no way to know when your mind is filling in the gaps and when it has retrieved the information from this or that part of the brain.

At every point of this memory process something can go wrong: at the point at which you perceive something (your doctor's office: you may not notice everything, for example); when you store it (as your mind decides which parts to stick away to access later: it may do a very partial job of that); and when you retrieve it (as your mind pieces it all back together: it may be missing lots of pieces and to make the memory seamless it fills in the gaps with other recollections).

The net result of Bartlett's experiments is that when we remember something, we are not simply pulling up an entire recollection of the past from some part of our brain. We are actually *constructing* the memory from bits and pieces here and there, sometimes with more and sometimes with less filler. In the process of this construction project, which we are undertaking virtually all the time, errors can happen. There can be massive omissions, alterations, and inventions of memory.

In Bartlett's own words:

Remembering then is not a matter of literally reduplicating the past. . . . In fact, if we consider evidence rather than presupposition, remembering appears to be far more decisively an affair of construction rather than one of mere reproduction.

Remembering is not the re-excitation of innumerable fixed, lifeless, and fragmentary traces. It is an imaginative re-construction, or construction, built out of the relation of our attitude towards a whole active mass of organized past reactions or experience, and to a little outstanding detail which commonly appears in image or in language form. It is thus hardly ever really exact, even in the most elementary cases of rote recapitulation.[3]

Of *particular* importance to our concerns here are some of the more interesting experiments that Bartlett performed. On numerous occasions he tested something he called "repeated reproduction." In this experiment a subject was given something in printed form—it could be a very short story (say, several paragraphs long), a passage that was arguing a certain point, or even a simple drawing. The subject was allowed to study the piece and then after, say, fifteen minutes, was asked to reproduce it as accurately as possible. Then, still later, he was asked to produce it again. And later still, again.

What Bartlett consistently found was that if the person was asked to reproduce the object soon after looking at it, and at frequent intervals, then however it was recalled and replicated the first time was usually how it was replicated in later recollections, even if the first recollection was in error. It was the erroneous repetition, rather than the real object, that came to be fixed in the mind. On the other hand, if the subject did not reproduce the object right away, but much later, and if the recollections were not in relatively quick and frequent sequence, then the reproductions changed significantly, time after time, with innumerable omissions, simplifications, and transformations occurring "almost indefinitely."[4] In either event, whether the object was recollected immediately and frequently or only later and infrequently, the experiment showed that "accuracy of reproduction, in a literal sense, is the rare exception and not the rule."[5]

These findings may be relevant when thinking how figures from the past are remembered by people who knew them. People's perceptions will necessarily be partial (you simply can't observe everything) or in error (you misperceive some things); what they store in memory will be partial and sometimes in error, as will be what they construct when trying to retrieve the memory. If they tell and retell what they experienced soon after the event and frequently thereafter, their first recollection will tend to be how they tell it every time. If they do not tell it for a while, and retell it only infrequently, every retelling may be different.

Of even greater importance for understanding the transmission of tradition in early Christianity—during the period when all stories of Jesus were being passed along not in written Gospels, but by word of mouth—is another set of experiments that Bartlett did involving something he called "serial reproduction." In this experiment, rather than a person observing something and then repeatedly trying to reproduce it, one person makes the observation and relates it to another, who relates it to another, who relates it again to another, and so on. The object that is observed can again be a short story, or a descriptive prose passage, or even a picture. As Bartlett conducted the experiment, Subject A would, for example, read a very short passage twice. After an interval of doing something else for fifteen to thirty minutes the person would be asked to recall the passage in writing. Subject B would be shown the account as A wrote it, read it twice, do something else for fifteen to thirty minutes, then write down what he remembered of it. And so it would go through, say, ten subjects.

In this case the alterations made during the serial recollection of the material tend to be very serious and get worse with each recollection, so much so that if you look at the original story (or description, etc.) itself, and the reproduction of it by the tenth subject, you would be hard pressed indeed to say that what she was reproducing was the story you had read. The differences tend to move in the same direction. Material gets omitted, from one reproduction to another; the accounts tend to become increasingly coherent, as links between thoughts are provided that were not in the original; and details get changed all over the map. As Bartlett summarizes:

> It is now perfectly clear that serial reproduction normally brings about startling and radical alterations in the material dealt with. Epithets are changed into their opposites; incidents and events are transposed; names and numbers rarely survive intact for more than a few reproductions; opinions and conclusions are reversed—nearly every possible variation seems as if it can take place, even in a relatively short series.[6]

Bartlett goes on to point out that the results that emerged in these controlled experiments, with unusually intelligent and highly educated undergraduates at Cambridge University, would almost certainly be far worse in the real world with average people, who were not the elite students at one of the greatest universities in the English-speaking world. What, one might wonder, would happen to serial reproductions of, say, sermons of Jesus, or accounts of his life? One should not urge that these would not change much given the presence of eyewitnesses to guarantee their accuracy, in light of what we have already seen in chapter 3. Nor should anyone think that a predominantly "oral culture" such as found in the early Roman Empire would effectively preserve traditions without changing them, for reasons we will see in chapter 5. For now I want simply to emphasize the point first demonstrated by Bartlett more than eighty years ago: "The one overwhelming impression produced by this more 'realistic' type of memory experiment [i.e., as opposed to remembering nonsense syllables] is that human remembering is normally exceedingly subject to error."[7]

Remembering in the Meantime

As you might imagine from what I have said already, there has been a massive amount of research on memory in all sorts of fields since the days of Bartlett, some of it highly relevant to the questions I am trying to address about how Jesus was being remembered in the decades between his life and the time our Gospels were written. Psychologists now know significantly more about what memory is and how it works than Bartlett could ever have imagined. But some of his over-arching discoveries and basic theses have been completely borne out, if significantly nuanced, in the decades since. As Endel Tulving, the prominent psychologist we met in chapter 1, summarized the matter, "A good part of the activity of memory consists not in reproduction, or even in reconstruction, but in sheer construction. And constructed memories do not always correspond to reality."[8]

What is even more striking is that when we are dealing with problems of memory, it is not simply that we forget things over time or don't quite remember things correctly. Sometimes we actually have "distorted memories," that is, recollections—often quite vivid—of things that did not happen. One of the fairly recent discoveries in the field is that distorted memories can be implanted in people's minds, for example, by hearing distorted information about a past event and then remembering it as part of the event. That can happen even with respect to events of one's own personal history. Psychologists have long known this is true of children: adults can be made to think that as a child they were once lost in a shopping mall, or that they accidentally but disastrously overturned a punch bowl at a wedding. Now it is known that distorted memories can be inadvertently planted or created in adults as well, as Daniel Schacter and others have strongly argued.[9] In addition, as leading expert Elizabeth Loftus has forcefully stated, "once activated, the manufactured memories are indistinguishable from factual memories."[10]

Many people will agree that this sort of thing happens on occasion, but as a rule we are reluctant to think it happens a lot, or at least (for most of us!) that it happens a lot to us in particular. We especially tend to think that our most vivid memories—precisely because they are vivid—are the most reliable. That turns out not to be true either.

About forty years ago some psychologists did think it was true. A very famous article published by psychologists Roger Brown and James Kulik in 1977 argued that when we experience a highly unexpected, emotional, and consequential event we have a special memory mechanism that stores it indelibly on the brain. It is almost as if the mind says, "Take a picture of this!" And it does so. Brown and Kulik called these "flashbulb memories." When you recall such memories, they claimed, your mind says "Now print!" and the memory flashes back, as clear as day and as accurately as when you first experienced it.[11]

That certainly seems true to our experience. Probably every one of us remembers where we were when we heard about the attacks on the World Trade Center on September 11, 2001. We remember where we heard the news, how we heard it, whom we were with when we heard it, how we first reacted to it, and so on. It's a flashbulb memory. If such memories exist, and they are accurate, that might be worthwhile knowing when thinking about memories of Jesus. What could be more "flashbulb" (in the days before flashbulbs) than seeing a man walk on water, or feed the multitudes with a few loaves, or heal a man born blind, or rise from the dead?

There has been intense research on flashbulb memories since Brown and Kulik first proposed the phenomenon, however, and their original view appears to be wrong. Yes, such memories are highly vivid. But just because a memory is especially vivid does not mean that it is especially accurate. Many of us have a hard time believing that, at least when it comes to our own vivid memories. But it's true, and has been shown repeatedly.

Psychologists can be very clever about how they go about showing such things. A classic study, which set the stage for much research to come, was done nine years after Brown and Kulik's initial publication. It was undertaken by psychologists Ulric Neisser and Nicole Harsch, who were perceptive enough to realize that a personal and national disaster could be important for realizing how memory works.[12] The day after the space shuttle *Challenger* exploded on January 28, 1986, they gave 106 students in a psychology class at Emory University a questionnaire asking about their personal circumstances when they heard the news. A year and a half later, in the fall of 1988, they tracked down forty-four of these students and gave them the same questionnaire. A half year later, in spring 1989, they interviewed forty of these forty-four about the event.

The findings were startling but very telling. To begin with, 75 percent of those who took the second questionnaire were certain they had never taken the first one. That was obviously wrong. In terms of what was being asked, there were questions about where they were when they heard the news, what time of day it was, what they were doing at the time, whom they learned it from, and so on— seven questions altogether. Twenty-five percent of the participants got every single answer wrong on the second questionnaire, even though their memories were vivid and they were highly confident in their answers. Another 50 percent got only two of the seven questions correct. Only three of the forty-four got all the answers right the second time, and even in those cases there were mistakes in some of the details. When the participants' confidence in their answers was ranked in relation to their accuracy there was "no relation between confidence and accuracy at all" in forty-two of the forty-four instances.[13]

You might think—or at least I did—that after the second questionnaire, when the students were shown the original answers they had filled out just a day after the explosion, they would realize they had since then misremembered and they would revive their original memories. This decidedly did not happen. Instead, when confronted with evidence of what really took place, they consistently denied it and said that their present memories were the correct ones. In the words of the researchers, "No one who had given an incorrect account in the interview even pretended that they now recalled what was stated on the original record. As far as we can tell, the original memories are just gone."[14]

This is a sobering point indeed. All of us have vivid memories of the past. These are the memories we trust the most. We are absolutely *certain* it happened the way we remember: why else would it be vivid? The answer is that it might be vivid because we have replayed the event in our memory time and time again in the same, wrong, way. So now that's how we remember it. Vividly.

The final conclusion that Neisser and Harsch draw is worth stressing: "Our data leave no doubt that vivid and confident flashbulb recollections can be mistaken. When this happens the original memories seem to have disappeared entirely."[15] Or as a very recent study, by psychologists Jennifer Talarico and David Rubin, has shown, "[Flashbulb memories] are distinguished from ordinary memories by their vividness and the confidence with which they are held. There is little evidence that they are reliably different from ordinary autobiographical memories in accuracy, consistency, or longevity."[16]

This may be important when thinking about the eyewitnesses recollections of what they saw Jesus do. If what Jesus did was spectacular, and some of his followers later had vivid memories of his activities, would that guarantee that their memories (say, twenty years later) were accurate?

Remembering the Gist?

Let me make a point that may not be clear from what I have said so far about the psychology of memory. In stressing the fact—which appears to be a fact—that memories are always constructed and therefore prone to error, even when they are quite vivid, I am decidedly *not* saying that all of our memories are faulty or wrong. Most of the time we remember pretty well, at least in broad outline. Presumably, so too did eyewitnesses to the life of Jesus. As did the person who heard a story from an eyewitness may well have remembered in broad outline what he was told. And the person who heard a story from a neighbor whose cousin was married to a man whose father told him a story that he heard from a business associate whose wife once knew someone who was married to an eyewitness. Probably in the latter case—which, as far-fetched as it sounds, may be pretty close to how most people were hearing stories about Jesus—a lot more would have been changed than in the case of an eyewitness telling someone the day after he saw something happen. But my basic point here is that despite the faults of memory, we do obviously remember a lot of things, and the fundamental memories themselves can often be right.

This is a commonplace in the psychological study of memory. We tend to remember the "gist" of an experience pretty well, even if the details get messed up. You may not remember correctly (despite what you think) where, when, with whom, or how you heard about the *Challenger* explosion, or the results of the O. J. Simpson trial, or even (this is harder to believe, but it appears to be true) the attacks of 9/11. But you do remember that you heard about the events, and you remember that they happened.

As we will see, this is an important point, because there are gist memories of Jesus recorded in the New Testament Gospels that are almost certainly accurate. At the same time, there are a lot of details—and in fact entire episodes—that are almost certainly not accurate. These are "memories" of things that didn't actually happen. They are distorted memories.

Still, many of the broad outlines that are narrated in the Gospels certainly did happen. Much of the gist is correct. One big question, then, is just how broad does a memory have to be in order to be considered a gist memory? Different scholars may have different views about that.

John Dean as a Test Case

A famous example can demonstrate my point. There is a much-cited study done of both detailed and gist memories of a person who claimed to have, and was generally conceded to have, a very good memory: John Dean, White House counsel to Richard Nixon from July 1970 to April 1973.

During the Watergate hearings Dean testified in detail about dozens of specific conversations he had during the White House cover-up. In the course of the hearings he was asked how he could possibly remember such things. He claimed to have a good memory in general. But he also indicated that he had used later newspaper clippings about events in the White House to refresh his memory and to place himself back in the context of the events that were described. It was after he publicly described his conversations with Nixon that the White House tapes were discovered. With this new evidence of what was actually said on each occasion, one could look carefully at what Dean had earlier remembered as having been said, to see if he recalled both the gist and the details correctly.

That's exactly what the previously mentioned Ulric Neisser did, in an intriguing article called "John Dean's Memory: A Case Study." Neisser examined two specific conversations that took place in the Oval Office, one on September 15, 1972, and the other on March 21, 1973, by comparing the transcript of Dean's testimony with the actual recordings of the conversations. The findings were striking.[17] Even when he was not elevating his own role and position (as he did), Dean got things wrong. Lots of things wrong. Even big things.

For example, the hearing that involved the September 15 conversation occurred nine months later. The contrast between what Dean claimed was said and what really was said was sharp and striking. In Neisser's words:

> Comparison with the transcript shows that hardly a word of Dean's account is true. Nixon did not say *any* of the things attributed to him here. . . . Nor had Dean himself said the things he later describes himself as saying. . . . His account is plausible but entirely incorrect. . . . Dean cannot be said to have reported the "gist" of the opening remarks; no count of idea units or comparison of structure would produce a score much above zero.[18]

It should be stressed the Neisser does not think Dean was lying about what happened in the conversation to make himself look good: the conversation that really happened and the one he described as happening were both highly incriminating. So why is there a difference between what he said was said and what was really said? Neisser argues that it is all about "filling in the gaps," the problem I mentioned earlier with respect to F. C. Bartlett. Dean was pulling from different parts of his brain the traces of what had occurred on the occasion, and his mind, unconsciously, filled in the gaps. Thus he "remembered" what was said when he walked into the Oval Office based on the kinds of things that typically were said when he walked into the Oval Office. In fact, whereas they may have been said on other occasions, they weren't on this one. Or he might have recalled how his conversations with Nixon typically began and thought that that was the case here as well, even though it was not. Moreover, almost certainly, whether intentionally or subconsciously, he was doing what all of us do a lot of the time: he was inflating his own role in and position in the conversation: "What his testimony really describes is not the September 15 meeting itself but his fantasy of it: the meeting as it should have been, so to speak. . . . By June, this fantasy had become the way Dean remembered the meeting."[19]

Neisser sums up his findings like this: "It is clear that Dean's account of the opening of the September 15 conversation is wrong both as to the words used and their gist. Moreover, cross-examination did not reveal his errors as clearly as one might have hoped. . . . Dean came across as a man who has a good memory for gist with an occasional literal word stuck in, like a raisin in a pudding. He was not such a man."[20]

And so, whether Dean had a decent gist memory probably depends on how broadly one defines "gist." He knew he had a conversation with Nixon. He knew what the topics were. Nonetheless, he appears not to have known what was actually said, either by Nixon or himself.

In this instance we are talking about an extraordinarily intelligent and educated man with a fine memory, trying to recall conversations from nine months before. What would happen if we were dealing with more ordinary people with average memories, trying to recall what someone said maybe two years ago? Or twenty? Or forty? Try it for yourself: pick a conversation that you had two years ago with someone—a teacher, a pastor, a boss. Do you remember it word for word? Even if you *think* you do (sometimes we think we do!) is there any actual evidence that you do? It is important to emphasize what experts have actually learned about memories, and distorted memories. Leading memory expert Elizabeth Loftus and her colleague Katherine Ketcham reflect on this issue: "Are we aware of our mind's distortions of our past experiences? In most cases, the answer is no. As time goes by and the memories gradually change, we become convinced that we saw or said or did what we remember."[21]

These comments are dealing with just our own personal memories. What about a report, by someone else, of a conversation that a third person had, written long afterward? What are the chances that it will be accurate, word for word? Or even better, what about a report written by someone who had heard about the conversation from someone who was friends with a man whose brother's wife had a cousin who happened to be there—a report written, say, several decades after the fact? Is it likely to record the exact words? In fact, is it likely to remember precisely even the gist? Or the topics?

Jesus's Sermon on the Mount in Matthew chapters 5–7 was recorded about fifty years after he would have delivered the sermon. But can we assume he delivered it? If he did so, did he speak the specific words now found in the sermon (all three chapters of them) while sitting on a mountain addressing the crowds? On that occasion did he really say, "Blessed are the poor in spirit, for theirs is the Kingdom of Heaven," and "Beware of false prophets, who come to you in sheep's clothing but inwardly are ravenous wolves," and "Everyone who hears these words of mine and does them will be like a wise man who built his house on a rock"? Or did he say things sort of *like* that on the occasion? Or did he say something sort of like that on some *other* occasion—any occasion at all? Which is the gist and which is the detail?[22]

Or what about episodes from Jesus's life, recorded, say, forty years later? Was Jesus crucified between two robbers who mocked him before he died six hours later? Are those details correct? Or is the gist correct? But what is the gist? Is it that Jesus was crucified with two robbers? Is it that Jesus was crucified? Is it that Jesus died?

Gist Memories of Jesus's Death

One of my purposes in this book is to examine later traditions about Jesus recorded in our Gospels, written between forty and sixty-five years after his death, to see if any of them include distorted memories, either in whole or in part. In this chapter I will focus on traditions involving the death of Jesus; in the next chapter, after exploring the question of whether oral cultures are likely to remember the past more accurately than literary ones, I will explore traditions involving the earlier life and ministry of Jesus. I want to begin with stories surrounding Jesus's last days and hours because these were the most remembered parts of his life. This can be seen simply by considering the amount of space devoted to this period in the Gospels. The Gospel of Mark devotes ten chapters to Jesus's public ministry in Galilee, and fully six to his last week, days, and hours in Jerusalem. The Gospel of John covers the more than a two-year public ministry of Jesus in eleven chapters, but the final week of his life in ten.

Nearly all critical scholars would agree that some gist memories of Jesus's last week, as recorded in the Gospels, are almost certainly accurate.[23] These memories are recorded independently in different sources and do not appear to be remembered in any prejudicial way— for example, because they represent episodes of Jesus's life that Christians particularly would have *wanted* to say happened for their own, later, benefit. Moreover, there is nothing inherently implausible about them. Among these memories would be the following:[24]

- In the last week of Jesus's life, he and a group of his followers left Galilee to go to Jerusalem for the annual Passover festival.

- When they arrived, Jesus engaged in some kind of disruptive activity in the Temple to protest what was being done there by those selling sacrificial animals and exchanging money.

- Jesus spent the week in Jerusalem preaching his message about the coming Kingdom of God. Possibly he started to attract people to his message.

- The ruling authorities—either Jewish, or Roman, or both— feared that Jesus's message could lead to trouble (possibly an uprising during the incendiary time of the festival?) and decided to have him arrested.

- One of Jesus's disciples, Judas Iscariot, cooperated with these authorities.

- After it was dark, following a final meal, probably for the Passover, with his followers, Jesus was arrested in a garden in the presence of his disciples.

- He spent the night in custody.

- The next morning he was brought before the governor, Pontius Pilate, on the charge that he was calling himself king of the Jews.

- Pilate found him guilty of the charge and ordered him to be executed.

- Jesus was immediately taken off and crucified, along with two other criminals.

On one level, this is a lot of information, and it is somewhat comforting to know that at least this much gist memory appears to be historical. But most of us are not satisfied with simply a broad outline. We want to know more. For example, when Jesus was found guilty of a capital offense, what were the reasons? Was he really calling himself the king of the Jews? What did that mean? Was he a violent revolutionary who wanted to raise an army against Rome and install himself as a king? Was he a threat to the social order by promoting equality instead of social hierarchy, and saw himself as a kind of metaphorical king? Was he preaching an apocalyptic message of the coming destruction of the ruling powers that would result in a new kingdom in which he would rule? Something else? Does it matter?

For most of us, it matters. And we are incurably interested in more of the details about all the events surrounding Jesus's last days and hours. When he came to Jerusalem for the Passover, did he ride into the city on a donkey as Jewish people lined the streets hailing him as the coming messiah (i.e., on Palm Sunday)? When he caused a disturbance in the Temple, did he shut down the entire Temple cult? When he was arrested in the garden, did his followers draw swords and try to defend him? When he was put on trial before Pontius Pilate, did Pilate declare him innocent, but order him to be executed only because the Jewish authorities forced him to do so? Did Pilate offer to set Jesus free, only to have the Jewish crowd insist that he release for them instead a man named Barabbas, who was scheduled for execution for insurrection? When Jesus was crucified, did the curtain in the Temple rip in half?

These are just some of the questions we have. We may have many more: when dealing with the memories recorded in the Gospels, we ultimately would like to know about each and every detail. Are they accurate? In what follows I do not plan to cover all the details. That would require several very large volumes. I have instead decided to pick a number of important episodes—the ones just mentioned—that I think embody either wholesale distorted memories or distorted details of a memory that is true in gist.

An Illustration of the Method: Jesus's Trial Before Pilate

The biggest question we have to deal with at the outset is also the most obvious one. How do we know if a memory of Jesus as recorded in the Gospels is accurate, by which I mean that it is something that in fact did not actually take place? My analyses in this chapter and the next will be based on a premise that it is indeed possible to uncover a distorted recollection of Jesus's life, and that it can be done in one of two ways. On one hand, there are some memories of the same event from the life of Jesus that are at odds with one another. This happens, for example, when different Gospels tell different versions of the same incident. It is true that sometimes different versions of an event are simply looking at the same thing in a different way. But sometimes the differences are stark enough—or even contradictory—that it is clear that they both, or all, can't be true to what actually happened. When that is the case, then one or more of the descriptions cannot be historically accurate and represent somebody's distorted memory.[25] On the other hand, there are some descriptions of past events that are simply implausible—utterly beyond what seems likely. These, of course, have to be argued, and explained, on a case-by-case basis. Still, there are such descriptions in our accounts, both of Jesus's life and of his death. Since these are historically implausible episodes, they too would appear to represent distorted memories. These distorted memories are important, I will argue, not only for knowing as best we can what really happened in Jesus's life (although certainly that), but also for knowing what his later followers thought was really important about his life, presumably because their own present contexts were influencing how they remembered him in the ways they did.

I will try to illustrate both ways of detecting distorted memories by picking a single example that contains both features: some aspects of the description differ from one Gospel account to the other, and several other aspects are simply implausible. The example involves Jesus's trial before Pilate, as described in all four of our canonical Gospels.

As I have indicated, most critical scholars would agree that in very broad outline, the Gospel accounts represent a true gist memory. During a Passover festival Jesus was brought before the governor of Judea, Pontius Pilate, found guilty for calling himself king of the Jews, and ordered to be crucified. That in broad outline this is probably a true memory of the event is suggested by various factors: it is beyond reasonable doubt that Jesus was crucified; crucifixion was a Roman form of execution; the Romans appear to have reserved the right of capital punishment to themselves; the governor would have been the one responsible for issuing an order of execution; we know that Pontius Pilate was the governor at the time; and we know that typically the governor was in Jerusalem during the Passover feast.[26] If you add it all up, the gist memory seems completely plausible.

What is striking is how differently the four Gospels narrate Jesus's trial. I will not go into all the details here, but will focus on two features of the accounts: the portrayal of Pilate on one hand and the portrayal of the Jewish leaders and/or crowds on the other. In our earliest Gospel, Mark (15:2–15), Jesus is brought by the Jewish authorities to Pilate, who asks him if he is the king of the Jews. Jesus replies in two words in Greek, "*su legeis*" (you say so). The Jewish leaders level many charges against Jesus, but to Pilate's amazement, Jesus does not reply to them. We are told that it was Pilate's custom to release one prisoner to the Jewish crowd in honor of the Passover holiday. He asks if they would like him to release Jesus. Stirred up by the Jewish priests, they ask instead for the murderer and insurrectionist Barabbas. Pilate asks what he should do to Jesus. The crowd demands his execution. Pilate asks why he should do that, but the crowd is insistent. So he releases Barabbas to them but orders Jesus crucified.

This is a succinct and straightforward account. It is interesting to see how it gets changed by the later Gospel writers. We have already seen the enormous changes made in later, noncanonical accounts such as the Gospel of Peter (see chapter 1); but there are large changes already within the New Testament versions. The Gospel of Matthew almost certainly used Mark for its narrative, and in this account there are some significant differences, only two of which need to concern us here (see Matt. 27:11–26). First, in Matthew's version, during the trial, Pilate's wife sends him a message asking him to do nothing to Jesus because he is innocent. Second, and more striking, when Pilate realizes that the crowd is going to riot if he does not accede to their demands, he calls for water and washes his hands, declaring that he is innocent of Jesus's blood. The crowd then cries out, "His blood be upon us and our children" (Matt. 21:25). Clearly Matthew wants to emphasize even more than Mark that Pilate is not the one who wanted Jesus killed; it is the Jewish leaders and crowds that do (again, compare our noncanonical versions!).

This emphasis comes to be even more pronounced in the Gospel of Luke (Luke 23:1–25), which also used Mark as its source. In this version, right off the bat, Pilate formally declares that he can find no crime in anything Jesus has done. But the chief priests and Jewish crowds continue to bring charges against him. Pilate then learns that Herod, king of Jesus's territory, Galilee, is in town for the Passover. He orders Jesus to be taken off to be tried by Herod. Herod questions Jesus but ends up sending him back to Pilate, apparently not finding anything to charge him with either. When Jesus returns to Pilate, Pilate again declares him to be innocent, two more times. But the Jewish crowd prevails, and so Pilate delivers Jesus "up to their will" (23:25). Here it is crystal clear who is ultimately at fault for the death of Jesus. It is not the Roman governor or the empire he represents. They have found Jesus innocent. It is instead the Jewish authorities and the people they lead.

In some ways that message is magnified even more in our latest canonical account of John (John 18:28–19:16). John probably did not have access to the accounts of the Synoptics, but in very broad outline his version is similar: Jesus is brought to Pilate by the Jewish authorities, is questioned, and then ordered to be crucified. Beyond such basics, however, the account in John is very different indeed.

In John's version the Jewish leaders bring Jesus to Pilate's official place of business, called the praetorium, but they refuse to go inside because they do not want to be ritually defiled, which would make it impossible for them to eat the Passover meal that evening. John never indicates why going into the praetorium would defile these Jews, but their refusal to enter involves two very odd differences from the other Gospels. For one thing, in Matthew, Mark, and Luke, the Passover meal had already been eaten, the night before. In these earlier Gospels, Jesus appears before Pilate on the day after the Passover meal; but in John it is, instead, the morning before the meal. Thus John's account cannot represent an accurate memory if the Synoptic version is historically correct. The other oddity is that since the Jewish leaders will not go in to Pilate but simply send Jesus in, Pilate is put in the somewhat peculiar situation of having to go in and out of his own place of judgment to talk to the accusers and the accused. First he talks to Jesus alone, then he goes out to talk to the Jewish leaders; then he goes in; and then he goes out; and so on. Pilate goes in and out six times.

Another difference in John's account is that Jesus and Pilate have several extended conversations. Jesus is not silent before the accusations, as in the other accounts. Instead, he uses the charges brought against him to speak to Pilate about himself, his identity, his kingdom, and the truth. As in Luke, Pilate tries to release Jesus three times, but "the Jews" will not hear of it: they insist that Jesus be executed. Pilate finally brings Jesus outside and shows him to the Jews and tells them to "behold your king." The Jews urge him to crucify Jesus. Pilate asks whether they really want him to crucify their king, and the Jewish chief priests reply, "We have no king but Caesar." Pilate then "handed him over to them to be crucified" (19:16).

This is a stunning sentence. When it says "to them," whom does it mean? The closest (grammatical) antecedent is "the chief priests." In this account, Pilate not only gives Jesus over to the *will* of the Jewish leaders and the people they represent, as in Luke 23:25. He also gives him over "to them" to be crucified. The Jewish authorities are literally responsible for Jesus's death.

As we have seen, one indicator that an account may preserve a distorted memory is when it differs from another version of the same event in ways that cannot readily be reconciled. We should recall what we saw in chapter 1: when we remember the past, it is because of our present. What we experience in the present affects not only *what* we remember about the past but also *how* we remember it. In light of that reality, what can we say about the "present" of the Gospel writers, producing their accounts of Jesus's trial some four or six decades after the facts? Is it possible that this present led them to distort the memories of what happened at Jesus's trial (whether consciously or unconsciously)? This is an important question to ask, since in our study of memory we are interested not only in the question of whether recollections of the past are historically accurate, but equally with what these recollections can tell us about the people having them and what they found important about the past when they "represented" it to themselves in their mental images of what happened.

One thing we can say for certain is that in the context within which the Gospel writers were producing their work, some forty to sixty-five years after Jesus's death, there were very real and serious tensions between the followers of Jesus—whether they were Jewish or gentile—and non-Christian Jews. Most Jews, of course, rejected the claim that Jesus was the messiah. Those few who did come to believe that Jesus was the messiah were insistent that this belief was absolutely right. Their opponents insisted that these views were wrong. Over time, these different opinions led to considerable animosity and ill feeling. Christians had difficulty understanding why non-Christian Jews didn't see the truth, why they rejected their own messiah. They started claiming that Jews had always rejected their messiah. Eventually they claimed that it was because Jews rejected him that Jesus was turned over to the Roman authorities for punishment. Soon they maintained that in fact the reason Jesus died was because of the recalcitrant Jews. Eventually they argued that in fact the Jews had killed Jesus.

That was a distorted memory. The Jews did not kill Jesus. The Romans killed Jesus. That, of course, does not mean that anyone can blame all the Romans. (It is striking that throughout history Christians have charged "the Jews" with killing Jesus, but they have never charged "the Italians" for doing so.) It was the Roman governor, Pontius Pilate, who ordered him crucified.

In addition, much of the detail of these accounts appears to involve distorted memories. I have already pointed out that John's recollection of when the event occurred cannot be reconciled with that in the Synoptics. One of them is necessarily a distorted memory. Even more interesting, why is it that with the passing of time Pilate is shown to be increasingly innocent in Jesus's death? The attempts to show his innocence differ from one Gospel to the next, but as you line them up chronologically, Pilate becomes more and more exculpated in the decision that Jesus had to die. Historically it would have been Pilate's own decision, pure and simple, probably on the basis of a very brief trial in which he decided that Jesus was a troublemaker.[27] Later, some Christians began to claim that he washed his hands of the affair and declared Jesus not guilty. Somewhat later, he was explicitly said to have declared Jesus innocent three times. Yet later he was recorded as handing Jesus over to Jewish chief priests themselves for execution. It is likely that these are not things that actually happened. They are distorted *memories* of what happened by later Christians in the throes of controversies with Jews over whether Jesus was really the messiah. The memories are important for us, then, in showing the highly fraught context within which Jesus was being remembered by his later followers. They were not simply recalling facts of history; they were remembering the past in ways that were highly relevant to their present.

The other way to isolate distorted memories is to consider their inherent plausibility. I will later be arguing that the entire Barabbas episode probably represents a distorted memory. Here I want to mention just three other aspects of the accounts that seem highly implausible.

The first is that when Jesus is brought to Pilate, Pilate asks the crowd whether he should find him guilty or not, and if guilty, what he should do with him. How are we to imagine that this is historical? What self-respecting judge would ask the people in the courtroom what they would like him to decide and what the sentence should then be? None that I know of. Is there any record of any Roman official ever conducting a trial in this way? No. (We do have some records of court proceedings.) Was Pilate the kind of person who would simply do what his subjects wanted him to do? No. Is it likely that this is actually what happened? Well, probably no.

For the second implausibility, I'll refer only to the Gospel of John. Is it really plausible that the powerful Roman governor would be running back and forth between the accusers and the accused so as not to offend their religious sensibilities? Not really. Can one think of a reason that the author of John's Gospel would *want* to set the scene like this, even though it's not plausible? Yes indeed. In John's Gospel, the Jewish leaders do not want to enter the praetorium because it would prevent them from eating the Passover meal that evening. They desperately want to eat the Passover lamb. They also desperately want Jesus killed. But for the Gospel of John, who is Jesus? In John's Gospel, and only in John's Gospel, Jesus is called the Passover lamb (see John 1:29—"Behold the Lamb of God who takes away the sins of the world). This is an account written to emphasize the incredible irony that the Jewish leaders reject precisely what they most want. Not only do they reject their own messiah, they also reject their own Passover lamb, while wanting to eat the lamb that evening. The memory is thus not just about what happened once in the life of Jesus. It also reflects the antagonism Christian storytellers had toward their Jewish opponents who maintained their Jewish practices and customs yet rejected the claim that Jesus was the one sent from God for the salvation of the world.

The third implausibility is again provided by the memory of the event in John's Gospel. If John is right that Pilate repeatedly went outside to talk to the Jewish accusers to find out what the charges were, and then went inside to query Jesus about it in private, and that Jesus used these opportunities to launch into speeches about his person and identity—how exactly does John know what Jesus said on the occasion? It was just Jesus and Pilate talking, alone. Immediately afterward, Jesus was led off to be crucified. So he didn't tell anyone. It is beyond belief that years later Pilate recounted the episode to interested Christian interviewers. So where did the words of Jesus recorded on the occasion come from? Someone must have invented them. They surely represent distorted memories. At the same time, these are valuable "recollections" of Jesus's words, recollections that make sense in light of later Christian understandings of Jesus: it is he, not Pilate (or even Caesar), who is the ultimate ruler; it is he who is the king—even if his kingdom "is not of this world."

Now that I have established how one can go about determining what are probably fairly accurate gist memories and what appear to be distorted memories, I can take five other episodes in the Gospel passion narratives and explain, in relatively short order, why I think they represent distorted memories, memories that may not be accurate to what actually transpired in history, but are important nonetheless for what they can tell us of those who remembered Jesus in these ways and told their stories to others.

The Triumphal Entry

There seems to be no reason to doubt that Jesus spent the last week of his life in Jerusalem, looking ahead to the celebration of the Passover feast. Passover was by far the busiest time of the year in Jerusalem, when the city would swell many times its normal size as Jewish pilgrims from around the world would come to enjoy the feast in the capital city. They would normally arrive a week early to prepare for the big day.

The festival was, and is, celebrated to commemorate the exodus of the children of Israel from their slavery in Egypt during the days of Moses, more than a millennium before the birth of Jesus. The historical basis for the feast is given in the book of Exodus. There we are told that the people of Israel had been in Egypt for centuries and had been enslaved there. God, though, heard their cries of despair and sent a great leader, Moses, who through his miracle-working power brought the Israelites—well over a million of them—out from their slavery and eventually brought them to the Promised Land.[28] Jewish people throughout the world have celebrated this great exodus event, in some respects the founding event for the people of Israel, once a year at Passover. Since the festive meal in the days of Jesus was to involve eating a sacrificed lamb, the only place on earth to celebrate it properly was in Jerusalem, as it was only there, in the Temple, that animal sacrifices could be made to God. And so those who had the time and money to do so would come to Jerusalem for the feast.

It would be a mistake, though, to think that most Jews in Palestine were celebrating this feast out of purely antiquarian interests, to recall what God had once done many centuries before in freeing his people from the bondage of a foreign oppressor. In the first century, Israel was once again subject to another power, this time not Egypt, but Rome. Many Jews surely anticipated that as God had acted on behalf of his people in the past, so he would do once more in the future, liberating his oppressed people from the tyranny of a foreign power.

The Roman rulers of Palestine understood full well that this time of year was especially incendiary. Not only were there large crowds of Jews in Jerusalem, but also some of these crowds were eager to drive the Romans out of the Promised Land, or to have God do so. The Roman governor, in this case Pontius Pilate, normally stayed at his palatial residence on the Mediterranean coast in Caesarea. But Passover was one time of the year when he would come to stay in Jerusalem, along with his troops, whom he would station around the city to quell any problems that arose, to squelch any riots before they got out of hand.

That is the historical reality of Passover in about the year 30 CE, when Jesus and a group of his followers came to the city along with thousands of other pilgrims for the festival. That reality itself should call into question the memory of how Jesus arrived in town, in the episode known throughout Christian history as the triumphal entry.

In our earliest version, found now in Mark 11, as Jesus and his disciples draw near to the walls of Jerusalem, he sends two of them into a village to procure for him a colt on which he can ride into town. They do so, and Jesus comes into Jerusalem to the acclamation of the gathered crowds. Some throw garments on the road for him to ride over; others cut leafy branches from the fields. The throng of people both before and behind him acclaim Jesus to be the new king who has come to restore the kingdom of David to his people: "And they were crying out, 'Hosanna! Blessed is the one who comes in the name of the Lord. Blessed is the Kingdom of our father David that is coming! Hosanna in the highest'" (Mark 11:9–10).

Matthew has an intriguing variation of this memory of Jesus's entry into Jerusalem. According to Matthew, Jesus's ride into town was a fulfillment of scripture: "This took place in order to fulfill what was spoken by the prophet, who said, 'Speak to the daughter of Zion, behold the king is coming to you, humble and seated on a donkey, and upon a colt, the foal of an ass'" (Matt. 21:5). This is a quotation of the Jewish scripture (see Isa. 62:11; Zech. 9:9). According to Matthew, Jesus fulfilled the scripture in an oddly literal way. As is commonly known, in ancient Hebrew poetry, poetic lines were coupled not by rhyming schemes, as with some English poetry, but by various kinds of conceptual parallelisms. In a two-line sequence (a couplet) the first line might say something, and the next line might say the same thing in other words; or it might repeat part of the first line with an additional thought; or it might express the opposite side of the same coin. There were several ways by which such poetry could work. But it was poetry, not straightforward descriptive prose.

The line from Zechariah about one "seated on a donkey, and upon a colt, the foal of an ass" was the first kind of parallelism I just mentioned, where the second part (a colt, the foal of an ass) is saying the same thing as the first part (a donkey), only in other words. Matthew apparently didn't understand how the parallelism worked. He took it literally. For him, Scripture predicted that there was to be both a donkey and a colt. As a result, in his version, Jesus tells his disciples to secure two animals. They do so. And Jesus rides into down straddling them. It is, needless to say, a very peculiar memory of the event.

But is the event itself an accurate memory? Was there really a triumphal entry?

The very broadest gist of this memory is no doubt true. Jesus must have come into Jerusalem one way or another. But the Gospels' description of the event is highly implausible, and precisely for the reasons I started with. The Roman authorities were particularly keen to prevent any disturbances during the days leading up to Passover, arguably the most incendiary time of the entire calendar year. In the Gospel accounts, the Jewish crowds cry out that Jesus is the one who is about to bring the kingdom of David to his people. How can a Davidic kingdom be set up in Jerusalem? Only if the current rulers are thrown out. Who would be the leader of that Davidic kingdom? Obviously a Davidic king. The crowds in these Gospel accounts are acclaiming Jesus to be the coming messiah who will overthrow the Roman forces who are occupying the city and the land.

Roman soldiers would have been stationed around the city. How can we believe that this wild celebration of their future conqueror would not make them sit up, take notice, and act accordingly? If the throngs were really proclaiming Jesus as the coming messiah in his glorious and heralded entry into the city, how is it that he was not arrested on the spot and taken out of the way, precisely to prevent some kind of riot or mob uprising? I find it completely implausible. I think this must be a distorted memory.

Why would later Christian storytellers remember an event like this, in a way that probably didn't actually happen? The reason is not hard to find. We need to recall that in the decades after Jesus's death, before the Gospels were written, Christians were often in an antagonistic relationship with non-Christian Jews, often blaming the Jews for being a fickle people who rejected their own God and who never understood his plan to save the world. The story of Jesus's triumphal entry embodies that view. Here the Jewish crowds are portrayed as ecstatic that their future king, the messiah, has arrived, and they proclaim him blessed on his coming into the holy city. They expect that he will now establish God's kingdom on earth, with his throne in Jerusalem.

But it is precisely these same people who, several days later, reject Jesus, calling for his crucifixion. Why did the Jewish people turn on Jesus? For these storytellers it is because the Jewish people have always turned on God and his prophets. They are an unfaithful people, ultimately opposed to God rather than on his side. And they are a fickle people, hot at one time and cold at another, acclaiming God's messiah at one moment and then calling for his blood the next. Jesus wasn't the king that Jews were expecting. When he came into Jerusalem, he did not start a rebellion to have himself installed as king. He preached against a sinful people, telling them to repent, and against their leaders, arousing their anger. And so—not understanding God's plan of salvation—the Jews of Jerusalem (according to this way of remembering the events) flat out rejected Jesus for not being the messiah they wanted, and they demanded his crucifixion. For Christian storytellers, that is how Jews have always treated God and his prophets. This memory of Jesus, then, is as much about the conflicts that later Christians were having with their Jewish opponents who rejected Jesus as it is about what actually happened in Jesus's life itself.

The Cleansing of the Temple

The Gospels of Matthew, Mark, and Luke agree that when Jesus arrived in Jerusalem he went into the Temple and made a disturbance there. In our earliest account, Mark, we are told that he drove out those who were selling and buying in the Temple, overturned the tables of those who were exchanging money and the chairs of those selling doves, and did not "allow anyone to carry anything through the Temple." He then declared, from a passage of scripture, that the Temple was to be "a house of prayer for all the nations," but that they had made it "a cave of thieves." This irritated the Jewish chief priests and scribes, who began to look for a way to destroy him; but "the multitude" was astonished at his teaching (Mark 11:15–19).

To understand this passage it is necessary to know the context. Who is selling animals? Who is exchanging money? And why?

People coming to Jerusalem from long distances would not be able to bring their sacrificial animals with them, and so, to make it possible for Jews to sacrifice in accordance with the laws of Moses, it was necessary to have animals for sale on site, at the Temple. But it was not acceptable that Roman currency could be used to purchase these animals: Roman coins had an image of the emperor on them, and he was considered a divine being in parts of the world. Images themselves were not allowed in the holy city; coins dedicated to a foreign god were strictly verboten. So there needed to be a currency exchange, in which Roman currency could be exchanged for Temple coins, which had no human images on them.[29]

All of this sounds so sensible that it is difficult to see why Jesus would have found it objectionable. Surely he didn't object to sacrificing animals: this was commanded by the word of God in the law of Moses. And there had to be a way of acquiring animals. It made sense that one could not use Roman coinage to do it. So what was the problem?

The only hints come in the text itself. Jesus appears to have thought that the commerce in the Temple made it "a cave of thieves." Did he mean that it was completely unacceptable for people to be making money off the Temple sacrificial system? That somehow the system had grown corrupt and had to be replaced? We do know of other Jews from Jesus's day who thought the Temple was a corrupt place that was going to be destroyed by God, other apocalyptically minded Jews who opposed the priests and those who sided with them in their worship in the Temple. So possibly that is what Jesus had in mind.

Scholars often maintain that this attack on the Temple—if that's how it is to be understood—makes best sense within the context of Jesus's broader message, that destruction was soon to arrive with the coming of a cosmic judge from heaven, the Son of Man, and that those who would be destroyed would not only be the enemies of Israel (the Romans) but also many people within Israel itself (the priests and those who sided with them). If this view is correct, then possibly the disturbance in the Temple was meant as a kind of "enacted parable," where Jesus was acting out a kind of physical demonstration of his message, that a full-scale destruction was soon to come.[30]

If so, then, as I earlier indicated, it makes sense that there is a gist memory here that is historically right, that Jesus did make some kind of disturbance in the Temple that led to his opposition by the Jewish authorities, eventuating in his death. But could it have happened as narrated? Two points should be made here. The first is that the Gospel of John also has an account of this episode, with strikingly different details. For example, there we are told that Jesus made a whip and used it to drive out those selling animals and the moneychangers. That sounds even more violent, especially for those who think of Jesus as a pacifist. What is yet more striking is that even though the Synoptic Gospels place the episode in the last week of Jesus's life, the Gospel of John places it at the very beginning. There it happens in chapter 2, one of the very first things Jesus does in his public ministry of more than two years.

How could John be right if the Synoptics are right? Are we really supposed to think that Jesus did the same thing *twice*? Moreover, if he did it at the beginning of his ministry, why wasn't he arrested and brought up on charges then? In light of this question, how do we even explain the account in the Synoptics? In their version Jesus is not arrested on the spot. He spends another week in Jerusalem before he is tracked down. Why would that be? If Jesus made this big a disturbance in such a dangerous time, precisely in the place where most soldiers would have been located, surely he would have been seized and taken off immediately.

It should be stressed that for Mark, this was indeed a very big disturbance. In fact, it was impossibly big. Mark indicates that Jesus did not allow anyone to carry anything through the Temple (11:16). It is important to realize that the Temple sacrificial system simply could not function if priests and their assistants were prevented from carrying anything: sacrificial knives, bowls to catch the animals' blood, the carcasses themselves, and so on. Mark is saying that Jesus shut down the entire Temple cult, by himself. Is this plausible?

Probably from watching too many Hollywood versions, many of us think of the Temple facility as about the size of a large house. In fact, it was enormous. The space within the Temple walls was large enough to accommodate twenty-five American football fields. How are we to imagine that Jesus shut down the entire operation? It seems completely implausible. And implausible that if he did so he was not arrested and put away. Even though there may be a valid gist memory behind these accounts, the versions as narrated in the Gospels appear to represent distorted memories.

But that does not mean that we should simply discount these memories and throw them on a trash heap of historical inaccuracies.

They can again tell us a lot about the people who cherished such recollections and sought to share them with others. The Christian storytellers who passed along the traditions of Jesus's actions in the Temple were trying to emphasize something that was very important to them. True religion, for them, is not a matter of outward form and conformity to established ritual. It is a matter of the heart.

When Jesus engaged in his act at the Temple it was, on the one hand (for the Christians remembering the event), an attack on the old Jewish religion that he had surpassed. God no longer dwelled in the Temple of the Jews. Jesus came to indicate that God had established a new order, based on Jesus's own words and actions, not on the Jewish sacrificial cult.

On the other hand, this memory of Jesus's cleansing of the Temple served to emphasize that Jesus changed the worship of God in an even deeper and more profound sense. Worshipping God is not a matter of outward form, conforming to set rituals and established cultic practices. God can be found not in human buildings, institutions, and rites, but in the act of prayer—which is open to all people, Jew and gentile. God, in fact, can be found among all those who follow Jesus in cleansing their religion of outward show and ceremony and in seeking God with a pure heart.

Swords in the Garden

In all four Gospels, at least one of Jesus's followers is armed when he is arrested. In the Synoptics, this unnamed follower draws his sword and strikes the slave of the high priest, cutting off his ear (see Mark 14:47). In John's Gospel we learn that the sword-bearing disciple was Peter (John 18:10). Jesus puts a halt to his follower's violent inclination, however, and humbly submits to his arrest. In Luke's version he does so only after healing the ear (Luke 22:51).

From the eighteenth century until the present day (see my discussions of Reimarus in chapter 1 and Aslan in chapter 2), there have been scholars, and nonscholars, who have thought that this incident in the garden is both altogether plausible and indicative of the character of Jesus's message and mission. In this opinion, the incident must be historical for a rather simple reason. What later Christian would make up such a story? When Christians were telling and retelling their accounts of Jesus's life in the years after his death, of course they would want him to appear entirely palatable to their audiences. Nothing would make Jesus more palatable in Roman eyes than the view that he was a peace-loving promoter of nonviolence, not a violent insurrectionist against Rome. If Jesus allowed his followers to be armed, however, that would suggest he was in favor of them carrying out acts of violence. If later Christians would not make up the idea that Jesus promoted violence, then no one could make up the idea that his followers were armed. Following this logic, the story of the sword in the garden is not an invented tradition but a historical fact. Jesus's followers, therefore, were armed. Moreover, if they were armed, so this reasoning goes, then Jesus must have anticipated and even promoted an armed rebellion.

There's a good deal of sense to this view and it is easy to see why it is attractive. Still, at the end of the day I don't find it convincing. This is for two reasons, one that is obvious but ultimately unpersuasive, and the other that is less obvious but absolutely (to my mind) compelling. The obvious objection is that throughout all of our traditions, Jesus is regularly and consistently portrayed as a teacher of nonviolence. "Love your neighbor as yourself." "Love your enemies." "Love those who persecute you." "Blessed are the peacemakers." "Render unto Caesar the things that are Caesar's." "The one who lives by the sword will die by the sword." Throughout independent accounts of Jesus's life he is shown to promote loving and submissive nonviolence. Doesn't that squelch the possibility that Jesus favored armed rebellion and that his followers were armed?

The reason that argument is not totally persuasive is that Christians may have *wanted* to portray Jesus as nonviolent, and remembered him as nonviolent, for reasons for their own. Christians themselves were often opposed by the authorities and would have wanted to stress that they were no threat and no danger. In their own defense they argued that they were peace-loving people. But how could they really be peace-loving if they worshipped and strove to emulate a person crucified for insurrection against the state? The Christian response could have been to emphasize that Jesus's execution was a complete miscarriage of justice. In this view he was a peace-loving rabbi who urged a pacifist message of nonviolence. In theory the Christians could have put this message—extensively—on his lips.

Still, the abundant number of such pacifist statements on the lips of Jesus should give us pause and make us suspect that they might well represent accurate memories of his teachings, especially in light of the second reason for thinking that Jesus's followers did not put up an armed defense of him when the crowd came to arrest him. I think this reason is absolutely compelling. If Jesus's followers tried to defend him with a sword, or more than one sword, why weren't they arrested as well? If the problem with Jesus is that he was about to lead an armed rebellion, then surely his followers would have been as much of a threat as he, especially if they start whacking away at people's ears with their swords.

I don't think Jesus's followers were armed in the garden when Jesus was arrested. Why then do we have discussions of the followers' swords in the various Gospel accounts? My sense is that the sword attack is a story that was invented by an early Christian (either consciously created or simply generated as someone happened to tell the story and unconsciously elaborated it) who was trying to illustrate Jesus's teaching that "the one who lives by the sword will die by the sword."

This view will require a short explanation. Many of Jesus's best sayings in the Gospels may indeed go back to him: "Sabbath was made for humans, not humans for the Sabbath"; "Those who are well have no need of a physician but only those who are sick"; "A prophet is not without honor except in his own country." A large number of these great one-liners are delivered at the end of stories for which the sayings are particularly apt. It has long been recognized that, as happens even in modern contexts, sometimes a story will be told to set the stage for the delivery of a great, climactic statement.

I think that may have happened in the case of the story of the sword in the garden. Originally there was a saying, possibly something Jesus actually said, about swords and not wielding them: "the one who lives by the sword will die by the sword." As that saying was rehearsed over the years, there emerged a story that illustrated the point that Jesus's followers should not arm themselves with swords. This story was retold until it became the Gospel account that someone wrongly used the sword to attack Jesus's enemies. By way of contrast, Jesus himself passively submitted to being arrested. If I'm right, then the sword fight in the garden is a distorted memory. If it were an accurate memory it is very hard to see why the disciples were not arrested.

The reason why the event was later remembered in a way that was not historical is deeply significant. Later Christian storytellers wanted to emphasize that even though they worshipped one who had been crucified for crimes against Rome, he decidedly did not urge a political rebellion. Moreover, they themselves did not oppose the ruling authorities, they did not believe in violence against those in charge, they did not believe in taking up arms in opposition to the state. During Jesus's life, some of his followers may have thought that this is what it meant to be among his disciples. But Jesus was quite clear and explicit. That is not what it meant to follow him. Following him meant living in peace, both with one another and with the ruling authorities. Urging or wanting a violent uprising would only lead to death. Armed rebellion was not the way of either Jesus or his true disciples.

The Barabbas Episode

As I earlier indicated, Mark's Gospel indicates that it was Pilate's custom to release a prisoner guilty of a capital crime to the Jewish crowd in honor of the Passover festival. He asks if they would like him to release Jesus, but they urge him to release for them Barabbas instead, a man in prison for committing murder during an insurrection. Pilate appears to feel that his hand is forced, so he sets Barabbas free but orders Jesus to be crucified (Mark 15:6–15).

This Barabbas episode was firmly set in the early Christian memory of Jesus's trial—it is found, with variations, in all four of the Gospels (Matt. 27:15–23; Luke 23:17–23; John 18:39–40). I do not see how it can be historically right, however; it appears to be a distorted memory.

For starters, what evidence is there that Pilate ever released a prisoner to the Jewish crowd because they wanted him to do so, or because he wanted to behave kindly toward them during their festival? Apart from the Gospels, there is none at all. In part that is because we do not have a huge number of sources for the governorship of Pilate over Judea, just some highly negative remarks in the writings of a Jewish intellectual of his day, Philo of Alexandria, and a couple of stories in the writings of the Jewish historian Josephus. These are enough, though, to show us the basic character of Pilate, his attitude to the Jews he ruled, and his basic approach to Jewish sensitivities.[31]

The short story is that he was a brutal, ruthless ruler with no concern at all for what the people he governed thought about him or his policies. He was violent, mean-spirited, and hardheaded. He used his soldiers as thugs to beat the people into submission, and he ruled Judea with an iron fist.

Is Pilate the sort of person who would kindly accede to the requests of his Jewish subjects in light of their religious sensitivities? In fact he was just the opposite kind of person. We have no record of him releasing prisoners to them once a year, or ever. Knowing what we know about him, it seems completely implausible. I should point out that we don't have any evidence of *any* Roman governor, anywhere, in any of the provinces, having any such policy.

And thinking about the alleged facts of the case for a second, how could there be such a policy? Barabbas in this account is not just a murderer, he is also an insurrectionist. If he was involved with an insurrection, that means he engaged in an armed attempt to overthrow Roman rule. If he murdered during the insurrection, he almost certainly would have murdered a Roman soldier or someone who collaborated with the Romans. Are we supposed to believe that the ruthless, iron-fisted Pilate would release a dangerous enemy of the state because the Jewish crowd would have liked him to do so? What did Romans do with insurrectionists? Did they set them free so they could engage in more armed guerrilla warfare? Would any ruling authority do this? Of course not. Would the Romans? Actually we know what they did with insurrectionists. They crucified them.

I don't think the Barabbas episode can be a historical recollection of what really happened. It's a distorted memory. But where did such an incredible story come from?

We need to remember what I stressed earlier, that these accounts of Jesus's trial repeatedly emphasize that Pilate was the innocent party. It was those awful Jews who were responsible for Jesus's death. For the Christian storytellers, in killing Jesus, the Jews killed their own messiah. That's how wicked and foolish they were. They preferred to kill rather than revere the one God had sent to them. That is one key to understanding the Barabbas episode. The Jews preferred a violent, murdering insurrectionist to the Son of God.

There is even more to it than that. We have no evidence outside these Gospel accounts that any such person as Barabbas existed. It is interesting to think about the name of this apparently nonexistent person. In Aramaic, the language of Palestine, the name Bar-abbas literally means "son of the father." And so, in a very poignant way, the story of the release of Barabbas is a story about which kind of "son of the father" the Jewish people preferred. Do they prefer the one who is a political insurgent, who believed that the solution to Israel's problems was a violent overthrow of the ruling authorities? Or do they prefer the loving "Son of the Father" who was willing to give his life for others? In these Christian recollections, the Jewish people preferred the murdering insurrectionist to the self-sacrificing savior.

It is interesting to note that in some manuscripts of Matthew's account of the Barabbas episode there is an important addition. In these manuscripts—which may well represent what the Gospel writer originally wrote—Barabbas is actually named "Jesus Barabbas." Now the contrast is even more explicit: which kind of Jesus do the Jews want? Which Jesus, the son of the father, is to be preferred? In this account, of course, the Jews are remembered as preferring the wrong one. But for the Gospel writers that's because the Jews are always doing the wrong thing and always opposing the true ways of God.

The Ripping of the Curtain in the Temple

I will end this chapter by giving just one final example of what appears to be a distorted memory from the Passion narratives. Again, I have not intended to give an exhaustive account but simply to point out some of the striking instances.

In the Synoptic Gospels, though not in John, when Jesus dies, the curtain in the Temple is ripped in half, from top to bottom. There are some differences among the three recollections of this event. One of them appears to be irreconcilable. In our earliest account, Mark, the curtain rips the moment after Jesus dies (Mark 15:38); in Luke's version it rips while he is still living (Luke 23:45). They both obviously can't be right.

For a different reason, the event as remembered by Matthew is almost certainly not right. In his version, not only does the Temple curtain rip, but there was then an earthquake and "the rocks" split apart (all of them?) and, most remarkable of all, "the tombs were opened and many of the bodies of the saints who had fallen asleep [i.e., died] were raised; and coming forth from their tombs after his resurrection they came into the holy city and appeared to many" (Matt. 27:52–53). Really? Masses of dead people brought back to life, walking around Jerusalem? Apart from fundamentalists and other strict literalists, there are very few readers credulous enough to think that this can be an accurate memory.

What about the ripping of the curtain itself? This too can scarcely be a historical description of something that actually happened. How would there be no record of it? Josephus, for example, speaks of the curtain in the Temple—and he was intimately acquainted with the Temple and all its fixings in the years before the war with Rome, some thirty-five years after Jesus's death. Would he not know that the Temple curtain no longer existed? Or are we to think that the Jewish priests stitched it back together? If so, wouldn't Josephus mention that there had been a catastrophe with it?

If the story cannot be literally true, but represents a distorted memory, what is it all about? There is no real mystery about that. As we will see more fully in chapter 7, Mark's Gospel, in some senses, is all about the death of Jesus. One old scholarly view that continues to be held is that Mark is best seen as "a Passion narrative with a long introduction." As I already pointed out, an inordinate amount of space in Mark's Gospel is devoted to Jesus's last days and hours. Even before that period, throughout this Gospel Jesus regularly and repeatedly refers to what will happen at the climax of his life: he will be rejected, crucified, and raised from the dead. Earlier in his ministry he explicitly predicts on three occasions that this will happen, and there are yet other allusions to his death in his life and teachings (Mark 8:31; 9:31; 10:32–33).

Why does Jesus have to die, for Mark? It is because he needs to "give his life as a ransom for many" (Mark 10:45). Jesus's death will bring about a new relationship between God and his people; it is how people will be made right with God.

What does that have to do with the curtain in the Temple? Mark almost certainly is referring to the thick curtain that was believed to separate the "Holy of Holies" from the rest of the Temple. The Holy of Holies was the special room at the spiritual center of the Temple where God himself was supposed to dwell. Nothing else was in this room. No one could go into it, into God's presence, except once a year, on the Day of Atonement, Yom Kippur, when the high priest would enter to perform a sacrifice for his own sins and for the sins of the people. This is where atonement was made before God by the cultic leader of the Jews. No one else could enter into God's presence.

That is, for Mark, until Jesus died. When Jesus died the curtain was ripped in half. Now God has come forth from his holy place, and people—all people—have access to God, not through Jewish sacrifice, not through the Jewish priests, not through the Temple cult, but only through Jesus. It was Jesus's death that placed people directly in God's presence through his own atoning sacrifice.

The ripping of the curtain was not a historically accurate memory. It didn't happen. But it was "true" for the Christians of Mark's community who believed that through Jesus's death they had received a new relationship with God through the atonement that Christ achieved.

Memories of Jesus's Passion

I have given only a handful of examples of memories that appear not to be historically accurate. These "distorted" memories could have arisen in any number of ways in the years after Jesus's death up to the time when they were first written in our surviving Gospels. Of course it is possible that some Christian storytellers consciously invented stories that they passed along to others. It is possible in fact that some of these stories were invented by the Gospel writers themselves. If that was the case—it is impossible to know, really—then the stories may not have been embedded in the memories of the persons who invented them, at least if the person intentionally told the story while knowing it didn't really happen. But it is also possible that people who invented stories really believed they happened. As we saw earlier, if you imagine that something happened, even something implausible, it is very easy indeed for that imagination to become a memory and for that memory to be every bit as vivid as something that really did happen.

It is also possible that a number of these distorted memories were inadvertently created and circulated. In my personal opinion, this probably happened a lot. Why not? It happens a lot all the time, today, that stories just seem to emerge from nowhere. Why would it have been any different two thousand years ago?

Whether the persons who first told the stories did so intentionally, knowing full well that they didn't happen, or inadvertently, thinking they did, in either case once the stories were in circulation and people told and retold them, these other people almost certainly did remember Jesus in such ways.

Memory can be studied to see if it records something that really happened or not, and if so whether the memory is true only in its gist or accurate down to the details. But as I have also tried to emphasize, it is also possible to study a memory in itself, to see what it can tell us about the views of the person passing it along and the context within which he did so—whether it is an accurate memory or not. In chapters 7 and 8 I will be dealing with that latter approach to memory at even greater length, not by discussing individual incidents from the life of Jesus, but by considering large-scale memories of Jesus as embodied in our early Christian writings. Before doing so, I need to deal with one other matter, the question of oral cultures and whether they can be counted on as preserving their traditions with greater accuracy than literary cultures. That will be the subject of the next chapter as we consider, as well, distorted memories about the life and ministry of Jesus.

CHAPTER 5

Distorted Memories
and the Life of Jesus

In the previous chapter I talked about memory champions who train their minds to perform absolutely remarkable feats, using methods that have been around since Greek antiquity. Like serious bodybuilders, they have exercised their brains to bulk up their memories in ways almost unfathomable to the rest of us mere mortals. Those who have gone through this discipline insist that their memories are not necessarily better than others. They are simply trained.

There are other people whose memories are not trained to be remarkable. They were simply born that way. Some of these people are literally phenom of nature.

None is better known than the person called (to preserve his anonymity) "S" by one of the most famous neuropsychologists of the mid-twentieth century, Alexandre R. Luria (1902–77), a professor of psychology at the University of Moscow. Luria writes about his long-term involvement with S in his fascinating little book *The Mind of a Mnemonist.*[1]

He first came to know S in the 1920s, when S had been referred to him because of some unusual features of his mind. In his preliminary testing, Luria gave S long sequences of numbers and long lists of words, sometimes meaningful and sometimes nonsense, up to sixty or seventy items altogether. After hearing a list spoken once, S could repeat it back, in order, correctly, without mistake. In fact, when asked, he could repeat the list *backward.* Luria claims that he never could find a limit to S's memory. Make a list ever so long, and S could memorize it on the spot and flawlessly reproduce it, forward or backward.

For a neuropsychologist, this was the encounter of a lifetime. And in fact Luria studied S for decades. He eventually found him able to perform yet more remarkable mental feats, with no evident effort. Among the most astounding was one that took many years to discover. Some sixteen years after first meeting S, Luria asked him to recall some of the lists he had created for him at the beginning of their relationship (Luria had kept his notes). S would think for a second, recall the moment when the list was first given to him, how he was sitting, how Luria was sitting, what was in the room at the time—and then repeat the list without making a mistake.

These remarkable cognitive abilities were not necessarily beneficial for S's life. We might think that it would be great not to forget anything, but the reality is that it can create enormous problems, since we almost always tend to forget things that are less important for our daily lives. If we remembered absolutely everything, life and its struggles might be even more difficult than they are already. That proved to be the case with S, who never could hold down a job, even when he went on tour as a professional mnemonist, wowing the crowds by his ability to remember anything they would throw at him.

In any event, S was clearly not wired like the rest of us.

Are Memories Stronger in Oral Cultures?

I have been told many times—not by memory experts, but usually by undergraduates, who have heard this from someone else—that the reason most of our memories are not very good is because unlike ancient people we live in a literary culture. In oral cultures people's memories were stronger, because they *had* to be. They had no written texts to rely on.

This question is obviously of enormous significance for our study of the traditions of Jesus that were in circulation by word of mouth over the forty to sixty-five years between his death and our first surviving records of his life. If people living in oral cultures, by the very nature of things or because of the special efforts they made, preserved their memories accurately from one telling to the next, from one person to the next, from one generation to the next, then the fact that our Gospels were written decades after the events they narrate should have no real bearing on the question of whether some, or many, of these traditions had been altered, amplified, or even invented during those intervening years. According to this view, the memories of Jesus among nonliterate people would have been faithfully preserved, so that we can trust that what was later written about Jesus's life was what really happened.

In evaluating the case, it is important to concede that extensive literacy does make some kinds of memory less important. It is certainly true that if we can write down and look things up we no longer need to memorize as much. (These days, we do not even need to write most information down—we can just Google what we need.) As a result, our minds are freed to do much deeper and sophisticated work. Thus it is no accident that advances in science, technology, engineering, and math have always happened in highly literate cultures.

JESUS BEFORE THE GOSPELS

The question is whether that also means that people in nonliterary cultures have better memories, since, after all, they have to remember more simply to get by. Those who think so argue that in oral cultures people tend to memorize things almost automatically. For that reason, they can pass down traditions by word of mouth without changing a thing, from one person to the next, year after year, decade after decade, century after century. Jesus and his disciples, according to this argument, would have preserved their traditions accurately, because that's simply what happens in oral cultures.

Is this true?

The first thing to stress is that it is certainly not true for biological reasons. The neuronal structures in the brain of someone living two thousand years ago in Galilee were not much different from those of someone living in New Jersey today. As cultural anthropologist Jan Vansina puts the matter, "So far there exists no proof that there is any inborn difference in cerebral faculties between the various races of man."[2]

The consensus among both anthropologists and cultural historians, in fact, is quite the opposite of what we might assume about oral cultures. As orality expert David Henigie indicates, people in oral cultures "generally forget about as much as other people." And because that is the case, people in such settings are at an extreme disadvantage in comparison with those of us in literary cultures. If they forget something, they "lose it forever." For us it is usually not lost, since we can look it up.[3]

Moreover, in writing cultures, it is possible to see if something is remembered accurately. We can check an oral report, or a written account, against a written record. Subsequent written sources (e.g., multiple editions of a textbook) can, in theory, be compared with each other to see what has been changed over time. Not so in oral cultures, as Henigie points out: "Oral tradition destroys at least parts of earlier versions as it replaces them."[4]

The thesis of this chapter is that traditions in oral cultures do not remain the same over time, but change rapidly, repeatedly, and extensively. That is especially important when considering the traditions about Jesus in circulation in the early church, among people who were by and large illiterate, during the first forty to sixty-five years of Christianity, before our Gospels were written. To set the stage for a consideration of the oral habits of early Christians in particular, we need to consider what we know about oral cultures in general and the ways they tend to preserve their traditions. For that, we may turn to some fascinating scholarship of the early twentieth century that addressed issues of orality and literacy.

The Beginning of Studies of Orality:
Singers in Yugoslavia

The twentieth-century study of oral cultures can be traced back to the groundbreaking work of Milman Parry (1902–35), a scholar of classics and epic poetry at Harvard, and his student Albert Lord (1912–91). As a classicist, Parry was especially interested in the Homeric Question, which is actually a set of questions about Homer, the alleged author of the great classics the *Iliad* and the *Odyssey*. Was there a Homer? Were these books actually written by him? Were the two books even written by the same person? Even more, is each book itself a single literary composition? Is each of them instead a collection of earlier stories that have been patched together? Is it possible that any one person could compose such lengthy texts in an age when there was not massive literacy? How could anyone remember that much poetry?

These questions had long intrigued scholars, especially in Germany but also in the English-speaking world. Normally these scholars had addressed the issues by analyzing in detail the internal tensions and contradictions of the Greek epics themselves. Parry thought there was a better way. In particular, he wondered whether oral cultures in the modern world could shed light on how long epics could be orally constructed, performed, and preserved. He found what he was looking for in Yugoslavia.

There had been an age-old tradition in Yugoslavia of singers who produced and recited oral epic poetry, tales—sung in verse—that were as long as the *Iliad* and the *Odyssey*. In the early twentieth century this tradition was still alive and well. Parry wanted to find out more about it and decided to engage in extensive fieldwork among Yugoslavian singers. This, he thought, could shed any light on what may have been happening millennia earlier in nearby Greece, back in the time when it was commonly thought that "Homer's" works were finally written.

Parry made a brilliant start on this work, uncovering the techniques that singers used to compose and retell their tales, and showing how very similar techniques can be detected behind the now-written texts of the *Iliad* and the *Odyssey*. Unfortunately Parry died a tragic death before bringing his work to fruition—killed, as it turns out, while unpacking his suitcase and inadvertently discharging a firearm. He was only thirty-three at the time.

Parry's student Albert Lord picked up his mantle to pursue the work. Lord eventually became a professor of Slavic and comparative literature at Harvard, a post he held for many years. His great classic on oral epic poetry was published in 1960 as *The Singer of Tales*.[5] This is a great book, of real historical importance to those interested in Homer and to those intrigued with the question we are addressing here, involving the preservation of tradition in oral cultures.

Lord persuasively made a crucial point that has been confirmed and reconfirmed by studies since his day: oral cultures have a different conception of tradition from written cultures. In written cultures, such as ours, the idea of preserving a tradition means to keep it intact, verbatim, the same, from one telling to the next. An "accurate" preservation of a tale, a poem, a saying, for most of us, is one that does not vary from its earlier iteration. The reason we think that way is that we have ways of checking to see whether it is the same tradition.

Oral cultures have no way of checking. All someone can do is try to remember if a spoken version of a tradition is the "same" as an earlier version. But in fact, being exactly "the same"—in our sense of verbatim repetition—is not a concern in oral cultures. That concern came into existence in written cultures, where such things could be checked. Those passing along traditions in oral cultures are not interested in preserving exactly the same thing. They are interested in making the same thing relevant for the new context. That necessarily involves changing it. Every time. For that reason, when someone in an oral culture claims that the current version of the tradition—a story, a poem, a saying—is "the same" as an earlier one, they do not mean what we mean. They mean "the same basic thing." They do not mean "exactly" the same. At all. This is crystal clear from Lord's work and by significant amounts of work done since his day.

Parry and Lord listened to and recorded Yugoslavian oral epic poetry and extensively interviewed both Yugoslavian singers and those listening to them. Reading the results of their fieldwork leaves no doubt about their findings. In that oral context, every time a story is told it is changed. The "gist" remains pretty much the same (see the previous chapter), but the details get changed. Often they get changed massively.

Because a singer changes the story every time it is performed, he in effect composes it each time anew. That means, though, that in oral performance, there is actually no such thing as the "original" version of a story, or poem, or saying. Every performance is and always has been different. The idea that there is an "original" that comes to be later altered derives from written cultures, where later forms of a text can be compared to earlier forms and there *is* some kind of original. But as Lord shows, "In a very real sense every performance is a separate song; for every performance is unique, and every performance bears the signature of its poet singer."[6] That last point is very important. Whoever performs the tradition alters it in light of his own interests, his sense of what the audience wants to hear, the amount of time he has to tell or sing it, and numerous other factors. And so, as a result, the one who sings the tales is at one and the same time the performer of the tradition and the composer.

One striking fact to emerge from Parry and Lord's extensive interviews is that the singers of these folk tales consistently and frequently insisted that their performances were "the same" every time. But when they said so, they did not mean that it was literally the same. For a singer, the fixity of the song "does not include the wording, which to him has never been fixed, or the unessential parts of the story."[7]

How different could "the same" song be in different versions? Social anthropologist Jack Goody has noted that when Milman Parry first met a singer named Avdo, he took down by dictation a lengthy song that he performed called "The Wedding of Smailagiæ." It was 12,323 lines long. Some years later Albert Lord met up with Avdo again, and took down a performance of "the same" song. This time it was 8,488 lines.[8] Parry himself observed this phenomenon. He one time had Avdo sing a song performed by another singer, named Mumin. Avdo strongly insisted it was the same song. His version was nearly three times as long.[9]

There are obviously important differences between what Parry and Lord found among singers of epic poetry in Yugoslavia and what we find in the Gospel accounts of the life and teachings of Jesus. For one thing, the Gospels are not poetry to be sung but prose narratives and collections of sayings. Moreover, as Lord himself notes, the kinds of epic tradition that he recorded are quite different from "when A tells B what happened and B tells C and so on with all natural errors of lapse of memory and exaggeration and distortion."[10] It is obviously the latter sort of tradition that we are interested in when dealing with stories and sayings of Jesus. Thus, my point is not that with the epic poetry of Yugoslavia we have an exact analog with the Gospels. It is rather that if we want to know about how oral cultures pass along their traditions, we should not make assumptions about what seems natural from our vantage point as readers living in literary cultures ("surely they would have remembered things better than we do!"). We instead need to see what experts in oral tradition have told us and see how that might be relevant for understanding the oral traditions of early Christianity.

Further Confirmation

The findings of Parry and Lord have, in broad outline, been confirmed by other studies of other oral cultures. No one had done more in that realm than the previously mentioned Jack Goody, who spent a highly productive thirty years as a professor of social anthropology at Cambridge University. In his various publications, Goody stresses that without a written text, it is impossible to know for certain if two versions of a tradition are the same (in our sense). Outside of writing (or tape recorders, VCRs, or more modern forms of electronic recording), there is no way to check one version with the other. Your only choice is to listen to both and see if they seem the same.

In his classic study *The Domestication of the Savage Mind,* Goody reports on his anthropological work in northern Ghana in West Africa, among the people known as the LoDagaa, a tribal society that was completely oral until schools were introduced in the modern period. Goody reports that the LoDagaa had one major myth, known as the Bagre, which came in two forms. The White Bagre was connected with a set of rituals, and the Black Bagre was more strictly narrative, a cosmological myth that detailed how humans were created and came to be cultured with the development of farming, hunting, ironmaking, and the brewing of beer.

When asked, members of the LoDagaa would sometimes indicate that there was only one correct version of the myth. But as Goody discovered, that was not at all the case. In fact, even the poem itself encourages people to incorporate elements they had learned at other recitals. As a result, when the myth was recited, new passages were constantly being introduced; other passages were changed or deleted. As Goody summarizes, "We have here a process of composition that . . . gives rise to a number, indeed, an infinite number of variants."[11]

Goody was able to demonstrate this phenomenon by recording different versions of the Bagre; he found that some elements that were absolutely essential to the myth in 1951 were completely absent in 1970. These changes involved portions that one might expect would be transmitted intact. The Invocation to the myth is only about a dozen lines long and is, as Goody indicates, something that "everyone knows" (more or less as Christians all know the Lord's Prayer). And yet, "taping shows that the wording of the Invocation can vary significantly from one recitation to the other, even in the case of recitations by the same individual, and even in individuals who will correct you when your version does not correspond to their (current) version."[12]

At one point in 1970 Goody took two recordings of the Black Bagre by the same speaker, a few days apart. One of them was 1,646 lines long; the other was 2,781. Another time he recorded two versions of the White Bagre: one was 6,133 lines, the other, 1,204. And "yet," as he emphasizes, "the local population see it all as the same ritual and recitation," even though "the differences are enormous."[13] Goody's conclusion is that we ourselves, in our context, would not call these recitations "the same." The differences are extremely deep, even if in a very broad sense the gist of the myth survives in all the retellings.

Given these realities, as attested by numerous anthropological studies, why do people in literate cultures so often claim that people in past oral cultures had phenomenal memories and worked hard to recount the details of their past with great accuracy and consistency? As one expert in orality, the renowned cultural historian Walter Ong, answers, "Literates were happy simply to assume that the prodigious oral memory functioned somehow according to their own verbatim textual model."[14]

Here again one might object that Yugoslavian epic poetry and Ghana cosmological myths are not really the same as prose narrative traditions that attempt to recount what happened in the past—traditions such as those that were in circulation in the years after Jesus's life before being written in the Gospels. But there have also been field studies of traditions of this kind, and they too point in the same direction.

Narrative Traditions in Oral Cultures

The classic study in this area was produced by anthropologist Jan Vansina, based on field research he conducted in Africa, especially Rwanda and Burundi, in 1955–60.[15] In his work, Vansina uses the term "oral traditions" to refer to "all verbal testimonies which are reported statements concerning the past." In other words, a tradition needs to be a statement about something that happened, which is delivered orally from one person to another. A key point for Vansina is that tradition involves a chain of transmission that can be charted as follows: observer - prototestimony - chain of transmission - final informant - recorder - earliest written record.

To break down this graphic: you first have to have an observer of an event (or the hearer of a saying). That person delivers a first account of what has been observed (the "proto-testimony"). After that, the account is passed along by word of mouth from one person to the next (the chain of transmission) until it comes to a final person ("final informant"), who delivers it orally to one other person ("recorder"), who writes it down for the first time ("earliest written record").[16] The utility of this model and this way of understanding the transmission of tradition for our interests here should be obvious: this is exactly what happened with the traditions about Jesus as passed down from eyewitnesses to the authors of our earliest written accounts, either the Gospel writers or the authors of the now-lost written reports they utilized.

The problem with this chain of transmission is that something can go wrong at every point (if by "go wrong" we mean "changed from what actually happened"). Vansina's assessment, based on his years of experience in the field, sums it up nicely and is worth quoting at length:

A testimony [report about the past] is no more than a mirage of the reality it describes. The initial informant in an oral tradition gives, either consciously or unconsciously, a distorted account of what has really happened because he sees only some aspects of it, and places his own interpretation on what he has seen. His testimony is stamped by his personality, colored by his private interests, and set within the framework of reference provided by the cultural values of the society he belongs to. This initial testimony then undergoes alterations and distortions at the hands of all the other informants in the chain of transmission, down to and including the very last one, all of them being influenced by the same factors as the first.[17]

These views have been borne out by more recent research on oral tradition, even in written cultures, such as that reported by Duke psychologist David Rubin in his important study *Memory in Oral Traditions:*

When the recall of one person is the initial stimulus for that of another, the first person's recall is all that is transmitted of the original; there is no chance for a new context to recover information that was known by the first person, but was not told. The recall of the second person will be a product of the recall of the first person, the biases or style of the second person, and the conditions of the second person's recall.[18]

Vansina argues that when testimonies are recited frequently, because of the vagaries inherent in the oral mode of transmission, they change more often than when recited only on occasion. That is certainly worth bearing in mind when considering the early Christian traditions about Jesus's life and death, which certainly were recounted constantly within virtually all early Christian communities. As Vansina puts it, in words reminiscent of Albert Lord: "Every time a tradition is recited the testimony may be a variant version."[19]

Traditions experience massive changes not simply because people have bad memories. That may be true as well, but even more important, as Vansina discovered, when people pass along "testimonies" about the past, they are telling the stories for a particular reason to a particular audience, and "the amount of interest [the teller] can arouse in his audience largely depends on the way he tells the story and on the individual twist he gives it." As a result, "the tradition inevitably becomes distorted."[20] Moreover, since the story is told from one person

to the next and then to the next and then to the next, "each informant who forms a link in the chain of transmission creates new variants, and changes are made every time the tale is told. It is therefore
not surprising to find that very often the original testimony has disappeared altogether."[21]

Anyone interested in knowing about the historical Jesus based on
the chain of testimonies about him that eventually came to be written
down should certainly sit up and take note.

From his experience, Vansina found very much the same attitude
toward keeping a tradition "the same" as Parry, Lord, and Goody: "It
happens that the same persons with regard to the same series of events
will tell two different, even contradictory stories."[22] Even so, as with
these other researchers, Vansina found that despite enormous differences and even discrepant accounts, the "gist" of a report is often
retained in the various retellings. He did note, however, that this was
not always the case.

In summing up this assessment of what we now know from such
anthropological studies, I think it is fair to say that people in oral cultures do not preserve their traditions intact with verbatim accuracy
from one telling to the next. They not only do not do so, they also
do not care to do so. Storytellers in oral cultures tell their tales to
communicate with their audiences in very specific contexts. Both the
audience and the context will affect how the story is told or the
teaching is recounted—whether it is told expansively or briefly;
which entire episodes will be added or deleted; which details will be
changed, expanded, or passed over completely. Someone who then
hears that version of the story or teaching will later tell her own version. Whoever hears that version will tell his own version. And on it
goes, until someone writes it down. The gist of these stories is more
likely to survive relatively intact over the course of time, but not always. Elements are constantly added to the stories and other elements

are deleted or altered. For that reason it is extremely difficult to separate out the elements that have been added or altered to an "original testimony" (to use Vansina's term) from the gist that represents an "accurate memory" of the past.

Still, as we saw in the previous chapter, there are ways to do so. If there are several written versions of the same event—say, in the life of Jesus—and they evidence differences large or small, especially if those differences create irreconcilable differences, then we know that something has been changed, probably as the stories were circulating by word of mouth among storytellers in the years after Jesus's death (although possibly some of the changes were made by the people writing the stories). In addition, if there are reports that are completely implausible for other reasons, those too indicate where storytellers have been applying their craft in recounting the tradition while passing them along year after year prior to the appearance of the Gospels. On the other hand, there are certain memories of Jesus extensively and thoroughly documented throughout our sources that are completely plausible and do not appear to represent the biased perspectives of later Christian storytellers. These would be gist memories that provide a basic outline of what we can say about the historical Jesus. We have seen all this with respect to the accounts of Jesus's last days and hours. We now turn to the written records of his life and teachings, to find altered and even invented traditions.

Gist Memories of the Life of Jesus

In all our Gospels, the majority of the narrative is devoted to recounting what Jesus did, said, and experienced prior to his last week in Jerusalem. If we are looking for gist memories that appear to be true to historical reality among these materials, most scholars would agree with at least the following:

- Jesus was born and raised a Jew.

- He came from Nazareth in rural Galilee.

- As an adult he was baptized by an apocalyptic prophet named John the Baptist, who was preaching the imminent judgment of God and baptizing people for the forgiveness of sins in preparation for this climactic moment in history.

- Afterward Jesus engaged in his own itinerate teaching and preaching ministry.

- Like John, he proclaimed an apocalyptic message of the coming Kingdom of God.

- Much of his teaching was delivered in parables and in thoughtful and memorable aphorisms that explained the Kingdom of God and what people should do in preparation for it.

- As a distinctively Jewish teacher, much of Jesus's ethical teaching was rooted in an interpretation of the Torah, the law of Moses, as found in the Hebrew Bible.

- Jesus's teachings about the Torah led to controversies with other Jewish teachers, especially Pharisees.

- Jesus had a number of followers, from whom he chose twelve to accompany him on his preaching ministry.

- Jesus was occasionally opposed by members of his own family and by people from his hometown of Nazareth.

- His followers, however, maintained that he spoke the truth; they may also have claimed that his words were vindicated by the miraculous deeds he performed.

If these gist memories are accurate, we have a fair outline of information about the man Jesus himself during his public life, beginning with his baptism by John. We also have numerous questions, too numerous to handle in a short treatment such as this. Here are some of them. More exactly, what did Jesus teach? Do his famous parables actually go back to him, or were some of them invented, or at least altered, by later storytellers? Did he really deliver the famous Sermon on the Mount, or is that an invention of the evangelist Matthew (it is found only in Matt. 5–7)?[23] Did Jesus really deliver his famous discourses found in the Gospel of John, such as the one given to Nicodemus where he indicates that one has to be "born again" (or did he mean "born from above"?)? Did he teach extensively about his own identity? Did he actually claim to be equal with God? And what about his activities? Can we know what actually happened at his baptism by John? Or how he called his disciples? Can we know if he did miracles—walk on the water, calm the storm, feed the multitudes, heal the sick, cast out the demons, and raise the dead? Such deeds are recorded in the Gospels. Are they accurate memories?

We will begin by addressing some of the questions about Jesus's teachings, since among the gist memories of Jesus's life, none is more thoroughly attested to or reliable than that during his ministry he was a Jewish teacher.

An Illustration of the Method: The Sermon on the Mount

As we saw in chapter 4, when evaluating the accounts of Jesus's trial before Pilate, in one and the same episode there may be some elements that are completely plausible and well attested (Jesus was executed on order of the governor of Judea, Pontius Pilate), other elements that represent discrepancies among the Gospels and thus show that memories of the event were changed over time as the stories were being recounted (the role of the Jews in the trial), and yet other elements that are implausible and almost certainly not historical (no one was there to hear what Jesus said to Pilate in private in the Gospel of John). The same is true of accounts of Jesus's teaching, as we can see by considering the Sermon on the Mount, found in Matthew 5–7.

This long sermon is one of the best-remembered selections of Jesus's teaching even now, nearly two thousand years later. It is here that Jesus delivers his famous Beatitudes, beginning with one of his most memorable lines: "Bless are the poor in spirit, for theirs is the kingdom of heaven." It is in this sermon that Jesus speaks some of his most memorable metaphors: "You are the salt of the earth. . . . You are the light of the world." Here he also gives his well-known "antitheses": "You have heard it said that you shall not commit adultery. . . . But I say to you that everyone who looks at a woman in order to lust after her has already committed adultery with her in his heart." And the Lord's Prayer, "Our Father, who art in heaven . . ." Here as well one finds some of Jesus's famous ethical injunctions: "Do not lay up for yourselves treasures on earth where moth and rust consume and where robbers break in and steal." This is the teaching of Jesus in a glorious three-chapter nutshell, arguably the most famous religious discourse of all time.

Surely Jesus did deliver a number of these teachings at one time or another. But it is also important to note that there are certain features of this sermon that seem implausible. At the beginning of this account Jesus is said to have seen the "great crowds" that had come to him from Galilee and Jerusalem and Judea, and from the other side of the Jordan River. Massive crowds. Then, going up on a mountain, he sat down and began to teach his disciples. Was he teaching only the disciples? That would make sense, since who else would be able to hear him? But if he was teaching only his disciples, why would Matthew bother to mention that he began teaching only after noticing the large crowds that came to him? Are we to imagine he didn't want anyone else to hear? But if, as is commonly understood, he was also teaching the crowds, how is that even imaginable? How could a massive crowd possibly hear anything he had to say if he was in an outdoor setting sitting on a mountain?

Moreover, how would Matthew, writing fifty or sixty years later, know exactly what Jesus taught on the occasion? Was someone taking notes? Certainly not the disciples—they were all illiterate peasants from rural Galilee. Is it possible that the words of Jesus could be preserved intact for more than fifty years as storytellers recounted what happened that afternoon? Think about it for a second. Suppose you were asked to recall a conversation, word for word, that you had this time last year. Could you get it exactly right? Suppose you tried it with a speech that you heard once, say, twenty years ago. Or suppose you tried it with a sermon you heard fifty years ago. Would you remember the exact words? Matthew himself wasn't there to hear these words. He was a Greek-speaking Christian who lived outside of Palestine, five decades after the events he narrates. What are the chances that he got the words of the sermon down accurately?

But was there even a sermon given that afternoon? It is important to note that the Sermon on the Mount cannot be found in Mark, Luke, or John—or in any other Gospel from the ancient world.[24] Yet it is such a powerful and moving account of Jesus's words. Why would the others not include it in their Gospels if it was otherwise known?

Could it, then, be a creation of the author of Matthew, or of someone living in his community before him? It is striking in this connection that many of the sayings in the Sermon on the Mount are indeed found in the Gospel of Luke, though not in Mark. That means that they come from the Q source I discussed in chapter 4. For example, Luke also has an account of the "Beatitudes," the Lord's Prayer, and many of the sermon's aphorisms, metaphors, and ethical injunctions. But in Luke these sayings are scattered throughout the Gospel in various places and various contexts. Of course, Jesus may well have said the same thing, or similar things, in different times and places. He almost certainly did. But why are the Q sayings found in Matthew's Sermon on the Mount located in relatively random places in Luke? Many scholars think it is because Luke is following the sequence of the sayings presented in Q, but Matthew has gathered many of these sayings together to create the Sermon on the Mount.[25]

For all these reasons it has long appeared to scholars that the Sermon on the Mount represents a collection of sayings of Jesus that Matthew himself has shaped by arranging a large number of Jesus's teachings into one long and memorable sermon. The sermon poses several other difficulties as well, the most interesting of which is that some of Jesus's sayings here are recorded in different forms elsewhere in the Gospels. Sometimes the differences are really different, to the point that they appear to be discrepancies.

This creates an enormous problem for trying to establish what Jesus really taught—not just in this sermon, but generally. A large part of the problem involves a factor you may have already inferred. As I stressed earlier in the chapter, in oral cultures especially, every time someone passes along a tradition of something she has heard—for example, about someone else's teachings or actions—she changes the story in light of her audience and context. That would obviously have been true of Jesus as well. He certainly delivered numerous teachings numerous times on numerous occasions in numerous contexts to numerous audiences. And those who talked about his teachings would have changed them regularly as they recounted them as well. As New Testament scholar Werner Kelber has expressed the matter, "All too often when we think of transmission of traditions, we think of it primarily as the passing on of fixed forms. In other words, we think of it in literary terms. In orality, *tradition is almost always composition in transmission.*"[26]

Let me give two illustrations of the problem from sayings in the Sermon on the Mount. Some of the Beatitudes come from Q material, but the differences between Matthew and Luke (the only Gospels that record them) are significant, not only because they give different nuances but actually represent very different ideas. In Matthew Jesus says, "Blessed are the poor in spirit, for theirs is the kingdom of heaven" (Matt. 5:3); but in Luke he says, "Blessed are you poor, for yours is the Kingdom of God" (Luke 6:20). At first that might seem like an unimportant difference, but in fact it's highly significant. There is a huge difference between being humble or lowly (poor in spirit) and being impoverished (poor). Of course the same person could be both, but many people are one or the other. Which one is blessed? Did Jesus say one of these things, or the other, or both?

So too the later Beatitude in Matthew: "Blessed are those who hunger and thirst for righteousness, for they shall be satisfied" (Matt. 5:6). But in Luke it is, "Blessed are you who hunger now, for you shall be satisfied" (Luke 6:20). It is very different to crave for righteousness in your life and to crave for food in your belly, as anyone who has not eaten for days will tell you. Which was Jesus concerned for and whom was Jesus blessing?

As I've indicated, it is possible that the answer is "both." It is also possible that since Matthew and Luke both got their sayings from Q, one of them changed them in light of his own interests. Did Matthew change them to emphasize humility and righteousness, or did Luke change them to emphasize Jesus's concerns for the poor and hungry? Or did they both change the sayings? Moreover, where did the author of Q get the sayings? Did he also change them? Did the author of the source that he got the sayings from change them? And have the sayings changed so much in the process of retelling that it's almost impossible to know what Jesus said, other than that he blessed someone experiencing something now for what was going to happen later?

The same issue emerges when considering Jesus's teaching on divorce in the Sermon on the Mount. The problem here is that there are actually four, or possibly five, different versions of what Jesus said about breaking up a marriage, with striking differences among them. In Matthew 5:32 Jesus says that if a man divorces his wife except on the grounds of sexual immorality (presumably on her part) he makes her commit adultery; and if a man marries a divorced woman he commits adultery. It is not obvious why a man would make his wife commit adultery by divorcing her. Possibly the logic is that if they are "united" as "one" in marriage, and he divorces her, but then she remarries, she is considered to have committed adultery against him, even though he was the one who pushed for the divorce. Still, it is hard to see how the man "makes" her commit adultery: did he force her to remarry? In any event, that rule does not appear to apply if she first committed a sexual impropriety, presumably with someone else. Moreover, if he marries any divorced woman (even if she was divorced for the reason of sexual impropriety of her husband?) he commits adultery.

That one saying is hard enough to understand, but matters get harder when the other versions of the saying are considered. Later in Matthew, Jesus indicates that if a man divorces his wife for any reason other than sexual impropriety and marries someone else, then *he* commits adultery—evidently because he is already united with his first wife. But here there is nothing said about the original wife: does she too commit adultery? In Mark 10:11–12 Jesus teaches that if a man divorces his wife and remarries another he commits adultery, just as does a woman who divorces and remarries. But here there is no "exception" clause: adultery committed if the divorce happens for *any* reason, including for sexual impropriety. That is a very big difference from the sayings in Matthew.

In Luke's version the man who divorces, again apparently for any reason, and remarries, commits adultery. And he also commits adultery if he marries a divorced woman, whether or not she was divorced because of sexual impropriety (Luke 19:18). But why has he, rather than his new wife, committed adultery?

The matter gets more complicated by what we find in one of Paul's letters, where he indicates that he has a teaching of Jesus that a woman should not divorce her husband, but if she does, she should either remain single or be reconciled with her husband (1 Cor. 7:10–11). A husband, however, should not divorce his wife. What are we to make of the first injunction? It appears to allow divorce grudgingly, and only if the woman does not remarry but remains single. So has she committed adultery? Apparently not—as long as she doesn't marry someone else. A few verses later Paul gives one of his own teachings that he appears to think does not go back to something Jesus said but stands within the general framework of Jesus's teaching, that a believer can grant a divorce to a nonbelieving spouse if the spouse wants it. But nothing is said about whether adultery is then committed if a person is remarried. And here divorce is allowed in a case other than sexual impropriety.

This is a real tangle. Did Jesus think divorce was ever allowed? For Mark, the answer is no. But for Matthew there is an exception: it is allowed in cases of sexual impropriety. In Paul's understanding it is allowed with a nonbeliever. Further, is the problem the divorce or the remarriage? Is remarriage allowed in the case of divorce for sexual impropriety? Or not? For marriage to a nonbeliever? Or never?

To repeat: it is possible that Jesus taught each and every one of these various things. But if so, one has to ask: what did Jesus actually think about divorce? Did he think different things at different times? Can we say nothing more than that he generally thought it was a bad thing? In some cases?

One thing we can almost certainly say is that Jesus was *remembered* as teaching different things about divorce (either slightly different or significantly different). And it is not difficult to see that the storytellers who were remembering those precise teachings could well have been influenced by the views of divorce in their own communities, or that they were influenced by the views they *wanted* to have in their communities. Some Christian communities had stricter rules than others (no divorce could be allowed, ever, under any circumstance; or, sometimes it was allowed depending on the circumstance); some of the communities were concerned principally with what constitutes adultery in the case of a separation; some were more concerned about the moral propriety of the man, and others about the woman. For each of the surviving recollections of Jesus's teachings on the matter, the "present" of the community has appeared to influence the memory of the "past" sayings of Jesus.

Distorted Memories of Jesus's Teaching

To this point I have been examining teachings of Jesus that he probably delivered in some form or other, even if the substance of what he said got changed as the sayings were transmitted from one person to another. There are a number of other teachings of Jesus found in the Gospels of the New Testament that on close inspection appear to be things he did not actually say. On the contrary, there are reasons for thinking that they may have been placed on his lips by later followers. In each case it is important not only to consider whether Jesus actually delivered the teaching, but also what it might mean that later Christians "remembered" him delivering the teaching. Here I will give just a few examples.

In Matthew 22:1–14, Jesus gives his famous Parable of the Marriage Feast. There was a king who was throwing a wedding feast for his son, but when he sent his slaves out to call in those who were invited, they didn't come. So he sent out other slaves urging the invitees to come. Again, none of them heeded the call. Instead they seized the slaves, abused them, and killed them. As a result, in Jesus's words, "The king became angry and sent out his soldiers and destroyed those murderers and set fire to their city" (Matt. 22:7). He then sent out his slaves to others, and invited them in from far and wide, both good and bad, until the wedding hall was filled with guests.

The parable continues with one of the most confusing episodes in the Gospels: the king arrived in the wedding hall and saw a guest without a wedding garment. He ordered his servants to bind the man hand and foot and cast him into the outer darkness, where "people will weep and gnash their teeth." And why? Because "many are called but few are chosen" (22:14). Thus, even those called to the feast can come only if they are chosen to be there and have the appropriate apparel. It's a very strange ending.[27]

My primary interest, though, is the core of the parable itself. It is not particularly difficult to interpret. The king is actually the King of Kings, God himself. His son is Jesus. The invitees are the Jewish people. The slaves who invite them to the feast are the prophets, who are seized, abused, and killed. God is wrathful at this shameful treatment of his own messengers. He sends forth the troops to destroy the city of the Jews, Jerusalem. Then others are invited to God's feast. These are non-Jews, the gentiles, who heed God's call.

This parable makes perfect sense as a lesson in the later Christian context, after the death of Jesus. Some decades later the mission to convert the Jewish people failed, leading to the beginning of the gentile mission, when the church came to be filled with those from outside Israel. Most important, however, is that the passage especially makes sense after 70 CE, the year in which Jerusalem was destroyed by the Romans, as the parable states: "the king sent out his soldiers and destroyed those murderers and set fire to their city." Later Christians said that this catastrophe occurred because God was avenging the rejection of his son by the Jews. For these followers of Jesus, the destruction of Jerusalem was not simply a political and military nightmare. It was a divine act against those who refused to flock to celebrate in honor of God's son. This is why the parable is widely seen as a story that was generated both after an influx of gentiles into the church and, in particular, after the Jewish War of 66–70 CE. At least in its present form, it is probably not a recollection of a saying of Jesus himself.

For a different reason, the same thing can be said of another familiar passage. In Matthew 25:1–13 we find the parable of the Wise and Foolish Virgins. There were ten virgins who brought their lamps to welcome a bridegroom who was bringing his bride home after the wedding. But the bridegroom was delayed, and the virgins fell asleep. At midnight the cry was heard that he had now come, and the virgins went out to meet him. Five of them had brought plenty of oil for their lamps, but five others—the foolish virgins—had not. Their lamps were going out so they needed to go off to buy more oil. In their absence, the bridegroom arrived, and when they showed up he would not allow them in the house, saying that he did not know who they were. The parable ends with the injunction "And so watch, because you do not know the day or the hour."

This has long been recognized as a parable that makes sense in the context of the early church long after the death of Jesus. The bridegroom (as in the previous parable) is Jesus. He is soon coming home. That is, he is returning back to the earth at his Second Coming. The "virgins" are his attendees: the Christians. Some of them are doing what they need to do to greet him when he returns. Others are not prepared and are caught by surprise.

The key to interpreting the parable is to realize that the bride-groom has been delayed in coming. This is a parable that was told in a context in which Jesus had been expected to return right away but it hadn't happened. He had been delayed. The parable urges Christians to continue to be ready, since Jesus could return from heaven at any "day or hour," and they do not want to be caught unawares. Since that appears to be the clear context, it does not seem to be a parable actually delivered in Jesus's day, at least in this form, but to have been generated by early Christian storytellers who were re-counting his teachings.

For a third example of a distorted memory of Jesus's teaching I turn to a famous passage in the Gospel of John, Jesus's dialogue with Nicodemus (John 3:1–15). Nicodemus is said to be a Jewish leader who comes up to Jesus and affirms that Jesus must come from God because of the great things he has done. Jesus then tells him, "Unless a person is born *anothen,* he cannot see the kingdom of heaven" (John 3:3).

I have left the Greek word anothen untranslated because it is the key to the conversation as it proceeds. It is a Greek word that actually has two different meanings, depending on the context in which it is used. On one hand it can mean "a second time." If that's what it means here, then Jesus is telling Nicodemus that he must be "born again." But it can also mean "from above." If that's what it means, then Jesus is telling Nicodemus that he must have a birth from God above if he is to see the kingdom of heaven.

The reason this double meaning matters is because Nicodemus takes Jesus to mean that he has to be born a second time, and he is incredulous. He responds by asking how a person can crawl back into his mother's womb to be born again. Jesus tells him that he does not mean a second, physical birth. He is talking about a birth from heaven, a birth made possible by the spirit of God, who comes from above.

Anyone who has had such a heavenly birth, to accompany his earthly birth, can then ascend to heaven and have eternal life.

This is arguably the most famous passage of the New Testament Gospels that just about no one "gets" because they don't read it in Greek. It is only in Greek that it actually makes sense, since the double meaning of the word anothen cannot be replicated in English. And so English translators of John 3:3 have to decide whether they translate the word as "again" or "from above." Either way creates problems for the translation, since the word has to mean both things for the conversation to make sense, with Nicodemus understanding the word in one way and Jesus meaning it in another.

It is precisely this key point—that the pivotal word means both things—that shows the conversation almost certainly didn't happen, at least as described in the third chapter of John. The double meaning that cannot be replicated in English also cannot be replicated in Aramaic. Recall: Jesus, an Aramaic-speaking Jew, is allegedly talking with a Jewish teacher in Jerusalem, where, again, Aramaic was the native tongue. They would have been speaking Aramaic. But the double meaning of the key Greek word in the passage doesn't work in Aramaic. In other words, the Aramaic word for "from above" does not mean "a second time" (and vice versa). And so, since the entire conversation between Jesus and Nicodemus is predicated precisely on a double meaning of a word that in Aramaic doesn't have a double meaning, it could not have taken place as described.

The conversation is not described in any other ancient Christian source. It appears not to have been a conversation that Jesus really had, with Nicodemus or anyone else. It is a conversation that was either created by the author of the Gospel of John or by a Greek-speaking storyteller before him who passed it along, until it came to be written in the Gospel. It is not a memory of something that Jesus actually said, it is a memory of a teaching of Jesus that is meant to deliver a message to the community of the people (or person) recalling his teaching in a new context.

We could spend days talking about teachings of Jesus that do not appear actually to go back to him. I am not trying to provide an exhaustive account, or even a reasonably complete one. I am simply picking a few examples to make my point. People today "remember" Jesus as having taught lots of different things that the man himself almost certainly did not teach. Each saying of Jesus—there are literally hundreds of them from our early Gospels—would need to be examined in a similar way, to see if it is implausible or if it appears in various forms that are not reconcilable with one another, to determine if it represents a distorted memory or if, possibly, it represents something that Jesus really did teach.

The very fact that he did teach is beyond real question. That he taught about the coming Kingdom of God also seems relatively certain. That he told his followers that they needed to prepare for that kingdom by repenting and doing God's will as expressed in the Torah—as Jesus himself interpreted it—seems highly probable as well. But individual teachings of Jesus, as now found in the Gospels, need to be examined one at a time to see if they represent accurate or altered memories of Jesus. Moreover, if they are altered memories, we should always be eager to consider them for what they can tell us about the contexts in which they were "recalled." That is, we should always consider how later circumstances may have affected storytellers and led them to remember Jesus as teaching something relevant to their own situation.

The Teachings of Jesus: Changing the Gist

It can be argued that even the "gist" memories of Jesus's teachings came to be changed, significantly, with the passing of time. I earlier noted that Jesus almost certainly proclaimed the imminent arrival of the Kingdom of God. This is the core element of Jesus's teaching in our earliest Gospels. It is at the heart of what he proclaims throughout the Gospel of Mark, starting with the very first words off his lips in 1:15: "The time has been fulfilled and the kingdom of God is at hand. Repent and believe the good news." These words convey an apocalyptic image: the current age we live in now is controlled by evil forces, but its allotted time is nearly finished. God's own kingdom is just about here. People need to prepare for its appearance by repenting and believing the good news. This message continues throughout Mark until the climactic chapter of Jesus's teaching, his famous apocalyptic discourse of chapter 13, where he spells out in graphic detail what will happen very soon when a massive cataclysmic end to history arrives and the Son of Man appears from heaven to reward the elect.

Apocalyptic proclamations of the coming kingdom can be found in the sayings of Q, as well as in sayings found just in Matthew and just in Luke. The earliest sources we have for the teachings of Jesus thus have him proclaiming that the end of this age will occur soon, within the lifetime of his apostles (see Mark 9:1; 13:30).[28]

The earliest Christians, after Jesus's day, also expected the imminent end of the world as they knew it. Paul thought Jesus would return in his own lifetime (e.g., see 1 Thess. 4:14–18 and 1 Cor. 15:5–53). So too, almost certainly, did the other apostles, including Jesus's own disciples. But with the passing of time, that apocalyptic expectation began to fade. Jesus did not return; the Son of Man did not arrive; the end did not come. Some Christians then came up with other sayings they placed on Jesus's lips, telling people to continue to look for him to come, even though there had been a delay—such as the parable of the Wise and Foolish Virgins mentioned already. Other Christians began to think that Jesus must never have said the end was coming soon, since, in fact, it had not come. As such Christians told traditions about Jesus's teachings, they changed them accordingly.

It is striking that in the last of the New Testament Gospels to be written, the Gospel of John, Jesus no longer preaches about the imminent end of the world, the coming of the Son of Man, and the arrival of the Kingdom of God. He no longer preaches about what will happen to the future of earth. He instead preaches about what will happen to people when they die. For John's Gospel, Jesus's message is no longer that the Kingdom of God is soon to arrive here on earth. It is that people can have eternal life above, up in heaven with God (John 14:2). Jesus now does not warn of the coming apocalypse. He teaches about having eternal life. It is a life that has come from heaven, in the person of Jesus himself, a divine man who has come down from above so that he can lead others back to the realm whence he came (John 3:13–16). Those who believe in him will have eternal life (John 3:16, 36). No longer is the point about an apocalyptic break in the history of earth; it is instead about living with God forever in the world above. And that comes only by "believing in" Jesus (John 3:15–16; 14:6).

That is why, in the Gospel of John, Jesus takes a completely different tack toward speaking about himself from the earlier Gospels. In Matthew, Mark, and Luke (as well as in their sources, such as Q), Jesus says almost nothing about who he is. He does call himself the Son of Man, he does say that he must be rejected and killed and raised, and he does by implication say a few other things about his identity (see, e.g., Mark 8:31; 9:31; 10:32–33; Matt. 11:27). But his identity is by no stretch of the imagination the focal point of his teaching. Quite the contrary; in the Synoptics the focal point is God, his coming kingdom, and the need to live in ways that will prepare one to enter it. Not so in John, where the imminent arrival of the Kingdom of God is absent. In John, Jesus principally preaches about himself. He is the one who has come down from heaven to bring eternal life.

And so it is in John, and only in John, that Jesus makes bold and astounding claims about himself as a divine being. "I am the light of the world." "I am the bread of life." "I am the way, the truth, and the life, no one comes to the Father but by me." "I am the resurrection and the life. Anyone who believes in me, even if he dies, he will live, and anyone who lives and believes in me will never die." "I and the Father are one." "Truly I tell you, before Abraham was, I am" (John 9:5; 6:35; 14:6; 11:25; 10:30; 8:58). And on and on. Jesus spends almost his entire preaching ministry in John talking about who he is, where he has come from, and what he can provide. There is nothing like this in the Synoptic Gospels. The very gist of Jesus's teaching has come to be transformed.

It comes to be transformed yet again in the later Gospel of Thomas from outside the New Testament, a Gospel that I mentioned in chapter 1 and will talk about at greater length in chapter 6. This Gospel was written some years after John; often it is dated to about 120 CE. If the gist of Jesus's teaching changed in the Gospel of John, in the Gospel of Thomas it has changed yet again. Now Jesus's preaching of the coming kingdom—the core of his message in our earliest Gospels and their sources, and probably the teaching of Jesus himself—is no longer simply transformed (as in John). Now it is actually preached against, by Jesus himself. Jesus now proclaims that salvation does not come *to* this world. It comes *from* this world: a person can be saved from the material trappings of this world by understanding and correctly interpreting the secret teachings of Jesus. Since eternal life will not be lived here on this planet, but in the realm of heaven above, anyone who thinks that Jesus proclaimed a coming Kingdom of God has completely misunderstood both what the Kingdom of God is and what Jesus preached. Moreover, for Thomas, unlike the earlier Gospels, salvation does not involve belief in Jesus and his death and resurrection; it comes by correctly interpreting his teachings.

Thus while it is fair to say that in oral traditions the gist of a message often remains the same, that is not always the case. Sometimes, demonstrably, even the gist of a memory can change. In this case, the gist memory changed for a very specific reason: the earliest recollections of Jesus's teaching of the coming apocalypse were not borne out by the realities of history. And so these memories faded and then disappeared, to be replaced by the teachings of a nonapocalyptic, or even an antiapocalyptic Jesus. As we have repeatedly seen, memory is not just about what happened in the past; it is also about the present of those who are remembering the past.

Distorted Memories of Jesus's Deeds and Activities

We now can move to some of the gist memories about Jesus's deeds and activities, to see how details came to be changed in their retelling, and to ask whether there could be instances in which the gist itself does not actually go back to an accurate memory of Jesus but was invented by later Christian storytellers. Even though, again, I will be highly selective, I have chosen to discuss three of the most significant recollections of Jesus's activities, involving his baptism, his connections with his followers, and his reputation as a miracle worker.

THE BAPTISM OF JESUS AND HIS RELATION TO JOHN—The earliest account of Jesus's baptism is in Mark. It is the first episode that the Gospel narrates. John is said to be preaching "a baptism of repentance for the forgiveness of sins."

Along with "all the country of Judea" (surely an exaggeration) Jesus comes to be baptized. When he comes up out of the water, the heavens split open, the Spirit descends upon him like a dove, and a voice comes from heaven, "You are my beloved son; I am well pleased with you" (Mark 1:9–11).

It appears that this simple narrative created problems for early Christians, for a fairly obvious reason: in early Christian ritual it was widely thought that the person doing the baptizing was spiritually superior to the one being baptized. So how could Jesus be baptized by someone else? Wouldn't that suggest his spiritual inferiority? Mark's Gospel already works to counter the idea that John could have been Jesus's spiritual leader and teacher by having John proclaim that he was merely a forerunner: someone else was coming soon who would be greater than he.

But there was an even bigger problem that Mark doesn't try to resolve. If John's baptism was for "repentance," to show, or to bring about, "the forgiveness of sins," why was Jesus baptized? Did he need to repent and be forgiven of his sins? The early Christians obviously did not think so. What sins?

But if he had no sins, why was he baptized? Matthew's Gospel provides an answer, which appears to have come about later in the tradition as the story was told and retold. Here, when Jesus arrives at the Jordan to be baptized, John tries to prevent him, by indicating that it is Jesus who should baptize *him*. But Jesus urges him to go ahead and do his duty, "to fulfill all righteousness" (Matt. 3:13–17). Here the earlier problem Christians would have had with the baptism is dealt with efficiently. Jesus now does not actually need to be baptized; he does so because it is the right thing to do. It is interesting to note that the voice from heaven that comes at the baptism in Matthew's account says something slightly different from Mark's. Here the voice speaks not to Jesus ("You are my son") but to either John or the crowd ("This is my son"). Did the voice say both things?

What is striking is that the voice says something completely different in some of the manuscripts of the Gospel of Luke, manuscripts that appear to give the story as originally found in the Gospel.[29] Here the voice says "You are my son, today I have begotten you." Now God from heaven seems to be declaring that Jesus has become the Son of God at his baptism, so that it is a ritual act of adoption, rather than a baptism for forgiveness.

But did the voice say all *three* things? In one other early Christian Gospel, known as the Gospel of the Ebionites, the voice does indeed say three things at the baptism. First it says the words of Mark to Jesus and then the words of Luke. Then John the Baptist asks who Jesus is, and the voice comes a third time saying the words of Matthew.[30] This is a clever solution to the problem, one that many literalistic readers today might still find plausible!

But the problem remains: why was Jesus baptized at all? We have seen that Matthew has one solution. Luke and John appear to have another. Luke's account (read it closely) does not explicitly say that John baptized Jesus: it only says that "after Jesus had been baptized" (Luke 3:21–12). Is Luke trying to distance Jesus from the baptizing hands of John? That appears more clearly to be the case in the Gospel of John, where there is no account of Jesus being baptized at all, only a reference to John the Baptist's preaching and his declaration that he had (earlier) seen the Spirit descend as a dove and remain on Jesus (John 1:29–34).

These later Gospels also go to greater lengths to show that John was Jesus's inferior, merely the forerunner of one who would be "greater." In John's Gospel (unlike the others) the Baptist admits that he himself is not the messiah, or the prophet Elijah, or the prophet who is to come (John 1:24–27). He is instead simply preparing the way for another—that is, for the one who will be all these things, the

Son of God on whom the Spirit of God will rest. According to this account, John is the one who informs his own followers that Jesus is the "Lamb of God who takes away the sins of the world" (1:29, 36).

Luke's Gospel goes even farther. In this account, John recognizes Jesus as superior even before either one of them is born. It is only in this account that we are told that John and Jesus are blood relatives: in the other versions there is no mention of them having any association or connection prior to John's baptizing activities. But here we are told that Jesus's mother, Mary, is a relative of John's mother, Elizabeth. When Mary hears from the angel Gabriel that she will conceive by the Holy Spirit, she also learns that Elizabeth has already become pregnant. She goes to visit her, and as soon as she gives her greeting, John the Baptist, in utero, leaps for joy, because the mother of the Lord has come to visit (Luke 1:39–45). Here there is no doubt about the matter: John may have preceded Jesus, but he was fully inferior and subordinate to him.

One can see how stories change over time. Scholars widely acknowledge that the gist of this memory is true: Jesus of Nazareth was baptized by John the Baptist, an apocalyptic preacher performing a baptism of repentance for the forgiveness of sins. Later followers of Jesus continued to want to tell the story, of course. The fact that Jesus was himself baptized showed Christians that anyone who wanted to join his church also had to be baptized. But as later storytellers recounted the episode, they were forced by their understandings of Jesus to alter it so as to emphasize, in a number of different ways, both that Jesus did not need to repent or be forgiven of sins, and that, even though baptized by John, he was spiritually superior to him.

JESUS AND HIS FOLLOWERS—There can be almost no doubt that Jesus had followers during his public ministry, and more specifically that he chose twelve men to be a specially close group of disciples.

There was also a group of women with whom he was in contact during his ministry. In evaluating the memories of these followers, I have selected two stories, one involving the men and the other a woman. My basic view is that the gist memory is right: Jesus did have these followers. But the details about their relationships no doubt were changed in the process of storytellers telling and retelling their traditions. Again, these changes can tell us something about what these storytellers wanted to emphasize as they recounted their tales of the past to help guide them in their lives in the present.

One of the frequently noted discrepancies between the Synoptic Gospels and John involves how it is that the disciples closest to Jesus (e.g., Simon Peter and his brother Andrew) came to follow him. In Mark's account it happens at the outset. After Jesus is baptized he goes off to the wilderness to be tempted by Satan for forty days. Then, after John the Baptist is arrested, Jesus comes into Galilee preaching his apocalyptic message. The very next thing he does is call his disciples.

He is passing by the Sea of Galilee and he sees two brothers, Simon and Andrew, fishing. Jesus tells them to follow him. They drop their nets and do just that. He walks a bit farther on and sees James and John, the sons of Zebedee, mending their nets. He calls them to follow him, and they leave their father behind—much to his chagrin—to do so (Mark 1:16–20). This is a story that is typical of Mark: terse, to the point, and powerful. These are people who have never laid eyes on Jesus. But he is a charismatic presence with an authoritative voice. He speaks and people not only listen, they also jump to obey. On the spot. No questions asked.

The account of Jesus's first followers in John is completely different. Again it happens at the very beginning. John the Baptist—who, in this account, is not yet arrested (a discrepancy with Mark)—sees Jesus and announces that he is the Lamb of God (1:29). The next day,

John is with two of his own followers, and again he declares that Jesus is the Lamb of God. The two go after Jesus to speak with him. One of the two is Andrew. He then leaves to find his brother Simon, and announces to him that he has "found the messiah." Simon comes and Jesus tells him that even though his name is Simon, he will call him Cephas (the Aramaic equivalent of the Greek name Peter; both names mean "Rock"; John 1:42).

There are, then, striking differences between the two traditions. In John's version, Jesus acquires his followers while John is still actively baptizing, not after his arrest. Andrew and Peter come to him separately, not at the same time, and they both seek Jesus out: he does not first find them. Here there is no sense that Jesus can simply speak and people will follow him with no hesitancy. Moreover, it should be noted that here in John, even before Jesus has done anything publicly, Andrew and Peter come to him precisely because they think he is the messiah. Anyone familiar with Mark's Gospel realizes that this is not at all what happens there. In Mark Jesus spends weeks, and months, with the disciples, who simply can't figure out who he is (see Mark 6:51–52; 8:21). It is only until halfway through the Gospel—the end of chapter 8 (out of sixteen chapters)—that Peter finally realizes that Jesus is the messiah. And then he completely misunderstands even what that means, as we will see in chapter 6. When Peter shows he is still clueless about Jesus's identity and mission, Jesus calls him "Satan" (Mark 8:27–33). There is no such passage in John's Gospel. Here Peter understands who Jesus is, even before Jesus has done anything, already in chapter 1.

These, then, are very different accounts of how Jesus acquired his first followers. If anyone tries to reconcile the two by playing interpretive gymnastics—for example, by saying that the account in John 1 happened first, which prepared the way for what happened in Mark 1—they have completely misunderstood the point of both accounts.

Mark's call narrative loses its force if the disciples already knew Jesus from before. As we will see in chapter 7, Mark's emphasis—that is, the reason he is apparently remembering the event as he does—is that he wants to emphasize something very important about Jesus. Jesus was a man of authority. When Jesus spoke, people jumped to obey. Even if they had never laid eyes on him before.

On the other hand, John's account cannot "work" if Mark's account is right. In Mark, Jesus meets with the disciples only after John was arrested. But in the Gospel of John, Jesus meets with the disciples and immediately begins his ministry (chapter 2: the wedding at Cana and the cleansing of the Temple). There is no hiatus that would allow the disciples to return to their boats to be fishing for Jesus to call them, as in Mark 1. John's Gospel is trying to emphasize something different from Mark's. In John's Gospel the first followers of Jesus seek him out and become convinced by his words that he is the one sent from God. They represent the faithful Jews (in the midst of an unfaithful world), those who are looking for a messiah, who, once they find Jesus, realize, on the spot, that he is the One. Indeed, that is what everyone who finds Jesus will discover: he is the savior from God who takes away the sins of the world.

The historical Jesus had not only the twelve men disciples but also an unknown number of women followers. One of the most impressive stories about a woman and Jesus shows just how important women were to his life and ministry. In all four Gospels a woman anoints Jesus's body with oil, and one or more of the men who see her do it object. Jesus, however, justifies what she has done and rebukes the men for not understanding.

The earliest account again is in Mark (14:3–9). On the day before his arrest, Jesus goes to Bethany, just outside of Jerusalem, and comes to the home of Simon the leper. An unnamed woman arrives with an alabaster flask of very expensive ointment and pours it over his head.

Those standing by (presumably the disciples) become upset and angry: this ointment could have been sold for a substantial amount of money and given to the poor. Jesus rebukes them and says she has done a beautiful thing to him, having anointed his body ahead of time for burial. Here is another prediction in Mark's Gospel that Jesus is about to die. And this woman has prepared him for it. It is unclear in the account whether she *knew* he had to die, or if she was simply honoring him and he took it to be symbolically significant. In either case, that part of the story—where Jesus commends her for preparing him for burial—seems to make best sense as an elaboration by a later storyteller, precisely after Jesus had died. But the way the story ends certainly speaks a real truth: Jesus announces that wherever the Gospel is preached, this unnamed woman's kind and prophetic action will be told "in memory of her." So it has.

John's Gospel contains significant and probably irreconcilable differences from Mark (John 12:1–8). Again the action takes place in Bethany. Nevertheless, it is not in the house of Simon the leper but in the home of his friends Mary, Martha, and Lazarus. Moreover, it is not an unnamed woman who anoints Jesus, but his hostess Mary herself. In addition, it is not the other disciples who complain about what she has done, but specifically Judas Iscariot, who wishes he could have pilfered the profits had the ointment been sold. As stories get told, sometimes details change and names are added and other human-interest touches accrue. That seems to be the case here, as the story now is used to tie together other figures well known from John's Gospel.

Luke, as it turns out, does not have this version of the story, but a different one that has long been recognized as a radical transformation of the account in Mark. Here the episode does not happen the day before Jesus was arrested, but relatively early in his ministry (Luke 7:36–50). Jesus is invited to the house of a Pharisee named Simon (not Simon the leper, and obviously not the house of Mary and Martha). An unnamed woman comes with an "alabaster flask" of ointment, weeps at his feet, and anoints them with the ointment. Now it is Simon (not one or more of the disciples) who objects, and not because of the expense but because she is a sinful woman and no prophet would allow himself to be touched by such a one. Jesus tells Simon a parable about a man who had two debtors, one who owed him a little and the other who owed him a lot. If both were forgiven, Jesus asks, which would feel more grateful? Obviously the one who had the huge debt. This woman has innumerable debts to God—since she is a sinner—unlike this outwardly righteous Pharisee; and so she to whom much has been forgiven loves much, much more than the Pharisee secure in his righteousness.

Luke, or a storyteller before him, has altered a story of Jesus's "anointing for burial" into a story of Jesus's forgiveness of a social outcast. In some ways it is the same gist memory: Jesus was anointed with expensive oil by a woman in someone's private home. But the details are so radically different that one wonders if it can fairly be called the same story.

The authors of three of our Gospels (Mark, Matthew, and John) "remember" the event because they want to proclaim that Jesus knew full well that he was about to be crucified. This was the plan of God. The woman who anointed Jesus performed this service, in these recollections, because she had a divine intuition that his death was imminent. She was one who understood—in contrast to Jesus's male disciples, who failed to recognize his ultimate purpose.

Luke remembers the event completely differently, in no small measure because he wants to use it for a different end. The point here is not that Jesus is soon to die. The point is that Jesus and the forgiveness he embodies are available to all people—not just to the highly religious, very rich, and inordinately successful who seem to be blessed by God. He and his salvation are for all people, even the lowest of the low, the social outcasts, who will be far more devoted and grateful to him, and to God through him, precisely because they have so much for which they need to be forgiven.

THE MIRACLES OF JESUS—When one discusses the activities and deeds of Jesus, it is very hard indeed to avoid talking about his miracles. Miracles are everywhere in the Gospel accounts of Jesus's life. He is miraculously born to a woman who has never had sexual relations. From the beginning of his public ministry to the end he does one miracle after the other, conquering nature, healing the sick, casting out demons, and raising the dead. So abundantly attested are Jesus's miracle-working abilities that even scholars who are otherwise skeptical of the supernatural biases of our sources sometimes claim that whatever else one can say about him, Jesus was almost certainly a healer and an exorcist.[31]

It has long been interesting to me that such moderate skeptics choose to believe that Jesus could heal people and cast out demons, but do not conclude, as well, that he could perform miracles with nature: walk on the water, calm the storm with a word, multiply loaves, turn water into wine. Is it because the healing and exorcism miracles are even more abundantly attested than the nature miracles? Probably. But could it also be because these nature miracles are so much harder to believe? Possibly that as well.

I am not going to discuss the problem that historians have with the category of miracle. I have already delved into that question at length in earlier books, and feel no need to repeat myself here.[32] My strong conviction is that whether one is a believer or not, if one wants to discuss what probably happened in the past, it is never appropriate or even possible to say that miracles have happened. That is absolutely not because of a secular, antisupernaturalist bias (as some apologists gleefully love to claim). I had the same view even when I was a committed Christian. Instead, it has entirely to do with what it means to establish historical probabilities. Supernatural miracles can never be established as probable occurrences. By definition they are utterly *im*probable. But again, I will not go into that in this context.

Instead I want to consider whether it is absolutely certain that Jesus was already understood to be a miracle worker even in his own day, prior to his death. My view of that question is a minority position, but one that I want to explain. I think the answer is no. I am not saying that I know for certain that Jesus was not considered a miracle worker during his life. But I do think there are grounds for doubt.

Let me begin by making two points that I think everyone can agree on: (a) With the passing of time, Jesus's miracle-working abilities became increasingly pronounced in the tradition, to an exorbitant extent; and (b) the stories of his miracles were always told to make a theological point (or more than one point) about him.

That Jesus's miracle-working abilities increased the more Christians told stories about him should be pretty obvious to anyone familiar with the noncanonical Gospels. In chapter 1 I referred to some of the striking accounts: as a newborn Jesus was a walking, healing Son of God; as an infant he ordered palm trees to bend down to provide his mother with some fruit; as a five-year-old he could make mud sparrows come to life, wither playmates who got on his nerves, and kill with a word teachers he found irritating; after his miraculous life, at his resurrection he emerged from the tomb as tall as a mountain; and on and on. These, of course, are simply the narratives I've already mentioned—not the sum total of what one can find in the accounts.

Not only does Jesus become increasingly miraculous with the passing of time, these miracles are all told to make a point. The stories about Jesus as the miraculous wunderkind reveal that he really was the Son of God endowed with supernatural power straight from the womb; as a five-year old he was already the Lord of life and death; as the resurrected savior he was manifestly a superhuman being of giant proportions. In more general terms, the miracles in our later accounts repeatedly show that Jesus was the spectacular Son of God. He was far superior to all his enemies (even if these were only the aggravating kids down the street). He was more powerful than nature itself.

I should stress, though, that these same theological lessons can also be drawn from the canonical accounts. The authors of these accounts, as well as the storytellers who gave them their material, were all, to a person, believing Christians who understood Jesus to be the powerful Son of God who was superior to all things on earth, superior to his earthly opponents, superior to pain and suffering, superior to all bodily ailments, superior to the devil and his demons, superior to nature, and superior to death itself. The stories of Jesus's miracles in the Gospels are not disinterested accounts of what happened in Galilee, told for antiquarian interests by those who wanted to provide an objective overview of events in an outpost of imperial Rome. The stories were being told—always were being told—to convince people that Jesus was the Son of God.

It is important to note that miracles in our surviving Gospels consistently serve to validate Jesus's message. This is true not only of later noncanonical Gospels, but also of the canonical ones, as can be seen by considering their views of miracles in reverse chronological order. In the Gospel of John the point is made repeatedly by the author himself. The miracles are "signs" of Jesus's identity, as the author himself says repeatedly (Jesus's miracles are not called signs in the Synoptic Gospels). Without such signs, no one will believe (4:48). In this Gospel, and only in this Gospel, Jesus identifies himself by his numerous "I am" sayings, and his miraculous deeds prove that what he says about himself is true.

And so Jesus says that he is "the bread of life," that is, the one who can provide what is needed for eternal life; he proves it by multiplying the loaves for the multitudes (John 6). He says that he is the "light of the world" (John 8); he proves it by healing a man born blind (John 9). He says that he is "the resurrection and the life"; he proves it by raising a man from the dead (John 11). Jesus's words and deeds interconnect and entwine with one another in this Gospel. Storytellers—or the author of the Gospel himself—took accounts of Jesus's words and of his deeds and made them coalesce into a seamless whole.

That is happening long before John's account, however. Luke's understanding of Jesus, among other things, is that in the life and ministry of Jesus the Kingdom of God can already be seen. This is an important nuanced difference from the earlier Gospel of Mark, one of Luke's sources. In Mark, Jesus predicts that the end of the age will come in his disciples' lifetime. People living in Jesus's day will see the Son of Man coming in power to establish God's kingdom (Mark 8:38–9:1; 14:62). For Luke—living after these people were all dead—Jesus's teaching is different. True, the end is still to come. But for Luke, in another sense, the kingdom was already present in Jesus's ministry. And so in Luke, unlike his predecessors Mark or Q, Jesus can say that the Kingdom of God "will not come with signs to be observed" but instead it is already "in your midst" (17:20–21).

This does not mean, as it is commonly misinterpreted, that the Kingdom of God is inside each of us. When Jesus says these words in Luke, he is talking to his enemies the Pharisees. He certainly does not mean that they, of all people, have the kingdom in their hearts. They—precisely they—do not. What Jesus means is that the kingdom of God is among them in his own ministry. The signs of the kingdom are not just about an apocalyptic moment soon to come; they are indicative of the presence of the kingdom already in Jesus's life and work.

In the other two Synoptics there is a different understanding, one that can be seen most clearly in the saying preserved in Matthew 11:2–6. Here we are told that John the Baptist, who is now in prison, has heard about "the deeds of Christ," and sends some of his disciples to him to ask if he is the one to come at the end of time, or if there is someone else. Jesus replies, "Go and report to John the things you hear and see: the blind come to see and the lame walk; lepers are cleansed and the deaf hear, and the dead are raised . . . and blessed is the one who takes no offense at me." Is the end upon us? John wants to know. Yes indeed. Jesus's miracles demonstrate it. Or as he says later in Matthew, "If it is by the Spirit of God that I cast out demons, then the Kingdom of God has come upon you" (Matt. 12:28).

This appears to be the earliest interpretation of Jesus's miracles. They are signs that the Kingdom of God will soon arrive. In other words, they coalesce with Jesus's apocalyptic message. There is a deeply seated logic to seeing and portraying the miracles in this way. At the earliest known layer of our traditions, Jesus's spectacular deeds are, in effect, proclamations of the kingdom: real, tangible declarations about the realm of God that is very soon to arrive. In the Kingdom of God there will be no natural disasters; Jesus controls nature even now. In the kingdom there will be no more demons; Jesus casts out demons now. In the kingdom there will be no more disease or bodily ailments or physical impairments; Jesus heals the sick now. In the kingdom there will be no more death; Jesus raises the dead now.

When storytellers recounted the life of Jesus in the days, years, and decades after his death, they not only delivered his teachings (in their own words, of course). They showed that his teachings were true. They proved it. They proved it by showing that his words were verified by his deeds. He not only proclaimed that the kingdom was imminent. He demonstrated that it was, by all the powerful things he did. For them, this was evidence, cited to convince others they were trying to convert and to assure those who were already converted.

How soon did the Christian storytellers begin to tell such accounts? Was it as early as the life of Jesus himself? Were such stories told by eyewitnesses? Or were they later generated after Jesus's death during the course of the Christian mission to convince the world that Jesus really was the powerful miracle-working Son of God who not only conquered the forces of evil at his resurrection but that he had been conquering them all along, throughout his entire ministry, a ministry that proved the truth that the apocalypse was soon to appear and that the Kingdom of God was about to arrive?

In the end there is no way to know. Possibly people were saying such things about Jesus during his life. But the fact that these deeds are so thoroughly ascribed to Jesus by later authors, living decades after the fact, is not in itself proof that they must be historical or even that they must have originated as stories during Jesus's lifetime. The gist of a message can change. Storytellers not only came up with their own ways of expressing the traditions they passed on, they not only made up and altered details, and they not only embellished their accounts and added entire episodes. Sometimes their inventiveness went to the very heart of the matter so that what later became the gist of the tradition was not in fact an accurate memory, but one that had been generated as the stories were told and retold, hundreds of times, by hundreds of people, in hundreds of situations. Jesus became increasingly powerful with the passing of time. Was he really the miracle-working Son of God during his lifetime? That is not a question that historians can deal with directly.[33] But it is not at all implausible that the miracle-working deeds of Jesus were later memories told by those who had come to believe that he had been raised from the dead and exalted to heaven. His current powers as Lord of all, according to these memories, were present already during his life as demonstrations that the end was near.

Memories That Change in the Retelling

To sum up what we have seen in this chapter, oral traditions change as they are told and retold from one person to another. They change every time they are told. If what we have in the Gospels are not eyewitness reports (on which, see chapter 3), but accounts in circulation, not just for weeks or months, but for years and decades, then almost certainly they were changed. We know in fact that they were changed, because we can compare different accounts of the same words or activities of Jesus and find discrepancies. Yet other accounts are historically implausible, and so appear to have been created in the years of transmission as people recounted what they had heard about the life of their Savior.

But the study of memory does not have to be concerned only with such negative findings, with memories that appear to have been "distorted" over time. It can also be very positive, not simply to determine which memories are true to history, but also to see what they can tell us about the groups of people who were passing them along to others. Different people, and groups of people, remember things differently, as the present they inhabit affects their memories of the past they recall. We have already seen this in our various discussions of memories of Jesus that have been altered, or even invented, in the years and decades after his death. But we will now see it in an even more sustained way, over the course of the next two chapters, as we consider the work of modern sociologists who have explored how and why social groups remember the way they do. This is often considered one of the most interesting phenomena that memory studies can address, and is certainly one of particular relevance for understanding the early Christian memories of Jesus.

CHAPTER 6

Collective Memory: Our Earliest Gospel of Mark

I FIRST BEGAN TO REALIZE THAT MEMORY is radically affected by a person's social context when I moved to the South in 1988. I had spent my entire adult life in other climes, five years in Chicago and ten in various places in New Jersey. Over the course of those fifteen years, I had little reason to think about the American Civil War. It was simply part of the background knowledge of the past that all of us had, the war against slavery that had been won by the side that subscribed to all that was good, fair, and true. Those poor Confederate soldiers may have fought valiantly for their cause, but their cause was misguided and it was a good thing they lost. Everyone thought that. Right? I had no idea that there was another side to the story, one that was still held with some fervor more than 120 years after the war had ended.

It was in the South that I first "learned" that the Civil War was not about slavery but about states' rights. Down here it was sometimes referred to with a term I had never heard before: "the war of northern aggression."

At first I thought this was some kind of southern humor, a witticism made up by some clever local. But I kept hearing the term—it was how many people simply remembered the war—and I soon realized that in fact that's how a lot of southerners were raised to think about it. Just as surprising to me was the fact that they did think about it. With great regularity. For parts of the South, the Civil War continues to be a present reality. They're still fighting it.

Remembering the past is not simply a mental exercise each of us engages in when we recall what happened to us personally. To use the technical term I introduced in chapter 1, memory is not simply "episodic." There are other kinds of memory, and one of them involves remembering the past of our society. For that reason, memory is studied not only by psychologists but also by social scientists—both the anthropologists interested in oral cultures, as we saw in the previous chapter, and sociologists who explore how memories of the past come to be constructed and discussed by various social groups.

That different social groups "remember" the past (not their personal past, but the past of their society) in different ways will make sense to anyone with a wide range of experience. If we stick with the theme of war, it is quite clear that the important events of World War II are remembered very differently indeed by persons from Germany, Russia, Japan, or America. As are the American Indian wars by a person of European descent living in Philadelphia and a Native American living in New Mexico.

The families we have been raised in; the social, ethnic, and religious groups we belong to; the people in our environment that we associate with; the news media that we access—all these factors affect how we remember the past. That is why there are such different memories of the New Deal, or the civil rights movement, or the events leading up to the second war in Iraq. Some of these memories can be personal—most of us had very strong opinions about the wars that came in the wake of September 11. Others of them are of things we did not ourselves experience. Sociologists call these "group" recollections of a past that was not necessarily experienced personally "collective memories."

Just as is true of individual memories, these collective memories can be feeble, frail, or even false, and they can be studied to see if that is the case. Doing so often requires some rather serious subjective evaluations: how would one establish that the memory of the Civil War as a war of northern aggression is distorted? For this reason, it may be more fruitful to assess collective memories in another way. That is by seeing what such memories tell us about the group of people who remember the past in the ways we do.

Using our sources of information to see what actually happened in the past is a matter of history. But studying how groups of people *remember* the past is, in the words of cultural historian Jan Assmann, a matter of "mnemo-history," or, to use a simpler term, "memory-history." The difference between history and memory-history is fairly straightforward. It is possible to study the American war in Vietnam as history. In doing so one might examine the precedents to the war, the political situation that led up to it, the gradual involvement of American troops, the escalation, the strategies, the miscalculations, and so on and on. But it is also possible to study the war as memory-history, by isolating one or more groups of Americans—say, draft dodgers from the '60s on one hand and military veterans on the other—to see how they remember the war. That may not tell you much about what really happened, but it would tell you how people today remember the past, and that can reveal a lot about those people and their histories, beliefs, convictions, attitudes, struggles, and allegiances.

The preceding two chapters have taken into account how the memories of Jesus, over the years and decades prior to the writing of our Gospels, came to be altered or even invented by Christians who were telling their stories about him. In those chapters we were interested not only in trying to isolate and assess such distorted memories, but also in seeing what such memories could tell us about the lives, the concerns, the interests, and the contexts of those who recalled Jesus in these ways. In the current chapter and the next, this latter interest will now come directly to the fore, as we focus on the task of "memory-history," the overwhelmingly positive attempt to see how the past—in this case, the life and death of Jesus—was remembered by particular ancient Christian communities in their "collective memories."

On Collective Memory: Maurice Halbwachs

The term "collective memory" was coined by French philosopher and sociologist Maurice Halbwachs (1877–1945). His most important and influential book appeared (in French) in 1925 and was published in English (along with another of his writings) under the title *On Collective Memory*.[1] Halbwachs acknowledges the rather obvious point that it is individuals, not social groups, who remember the past (society does not have some kind of enormous hippocampus!). But in his view, individual memories are always reconstructed based on our relation to society around us, especially our various social groups, such as our families, friends, local communities, and nations. For Halbwachs, it is impossible for us to remember without having a social framework within which to place a memory. That is to say, in his rather radical claim, there is no such thing as a memory outside of a social context. If you remember something that happened to you, it is always in relation to the people you know, or the things you have

learned and experienced from other people. It can never be in complete isolation from your social surroundings.

Halbwachs was notoriously suspicious of psychological research
that tried to investigate memory as an individual phenomenon. In his
view, "There are no recollections which can be said to be purely
interior, that is, which can be preserved only within individual memory."[2] That is because what we remember has been deeply and inex-
tricably influenced by our social surroundings. We cannot exist,
either physically or mentally, apart from these surroundings. If you
try to escape from your social setting, you necessarily move into a
different social setting. But you are still in a social setting. Even if you
become a hermit, you know about what it means to be a hermit because you learned about it in a social environment. For Halbwachs
"one can escape from society only by opposing it to another society."[3]

The society you live in provides not just the background but also
the very framework for what you recall about the past. In one of
Halbwachs's most famous lines, "There exists a collective memory
and social frameworks for memory; it is to the degree that our individual thought places itself in these frameworks and participates in
this memory that it is capable of the act of recollection."[4] In other
words, without a social framework, you would not be able to organize your thoughts or recall a coherent past.

Halbwachs would agree with those psychologists who say that
memory is a matter of "constructing" the past and that the construction of memory happens by recalling traces of what happened and
filling in the gaps with similar sorts of information drawn from memory.[5] For example, if you remember a gathering one evening long ago
in your family home, you will reconstruct that memory not only by
calling back to mind precisely what happened on that occasion, but
also by filling in the many gaps of your memory by recalling—

inadvertently—the things that typically happened on such social occasions. In that act of reconstruction, you will often confuse one set of events for another. When it comes to a memory of this sort, "We compose it anew and introduce elements borrowed from several periods which preceded or followed the scene in question."[6]

Moreover, Halbwachs would agree that the reason you remember anything at all about the past is because it has some relevance for the present. As one of his later followers expressed the matter, "For Halbwachs, the past is a social construction mainly, if not wholly, shaped by the concerns of the present. . . . He argues that the beliefs, interests, and aspirations of the present shape the various views of the past as they are manifested respectively in every historical epoch." The key here is that the past is a "social" construction—not simply a matter of the individual psyche.[7]

This is true also of the past that we have not ourselves experienced. Among other things Halbwachs was interested in the collective memory found in religion. He maintained that religious memory works in the same way as collective memory generally: "It does not preserve the past but reconstructs it with the aid of the material traces, rites, texts, and traditions left behind by that past, and with the aid moreover of recent psychological and social data, that is to say, with the present."[8] Moreover, as is the case of collective memory more generally, when people remember the past of their religion—that is, when they recall the great figures, movements, and events of their religious heritage—they reconstruct it by adapting "the image of ancient facts to the beliefs and spiritual needs of the present." As a result, "the reality of the past is no longer in the past."[9]

The work of Halbwachs was absolutely groundbreaking and continues to assert its influence even today, some ninety years after his book first appeared. Many of his views have been contested, of course, and some recent sociologists have expressed an uneasiness about his more radical positions. Sociologist Barry Schwartz, one of the leaders in the study of collective memory today, maintains, for example, that Halbwachs's emphasis on the present as the key to the past may be going too far. For Schwartz, it is not only the case that people remember the past because of the present, and that what is happening in the present affects how the past is remembered; it is also the case that what really happened in the past affects how we think and understand the present. In his view, Halbwachs drew too hard a line between the concept of "memory" and that of "history." It is not simply that history is concerned only with what actually took place before now and memory is concerned only with how we recall what took place. Memory does affect how we construct the past in our minds, but the past also affects how we remember in the present. And in some ways, one of the most interesting questions we can pursue is how and why we remember the past in the ways that we do, especially when we compare the past as it appears really to have happened with how it is remembered by various social groups.

Schwartz showed how this can be done in his brilliant analysis of collective memories of Abraham Lincoln, an analysis that I referred to in chapter 1. Something similar can be done, obviously, for any figure from the past, even the historical Jesus. How one studies the memory of such figures is a matter much discussed among both sociologists and cultural historians, none more influential than a German Egyptologist named Jan Assmann.

Jan Assmann and the Study of "Memory-History"

Assmann agrees with Halbwachs about the social character of memory: our memories of the past are created collectively, not individually, and our reconstructions of the past are always built on the frameworks that have been provided by society. We organize our thoughts about what happened before now based on what we are experiencing in the present in the society of other people. And so when we consciously or even inadvertently remember the Civil War, or World War II, or the war in Vietnam it is because something in our present situation has called it to mind; moreover, it is our present situation that shapes how we remember these catastrophic events. One downside to this reality is that if there is no contemporary framework for a recollection of the past—if there is nothing in the present that leads us to recall what happened before—that part of the past will simply be forgotten, erased from memory.

The upside is that it is possible to study the collective memory of past events to see what it can tell us about the social groups who are constructing and preserving this memory. As we have seen, this is Assmann's "mnemo-history," or what I am calling "memory-history."

In one of his most important books, *Moses the Egyptian: The Memory of Egypt in Western Monotheism,* Assmann engages in memory-history by seeing how Moses was remembered at key moments in Western civilization. As Assmann explains, "Unlike history proper, mnemo-history is concerned not with the past as such but only with the past as it is remembered.[10] In other words, "Mnemo-history analyzes the importance which a present ascribes to the past."[11] When it comes to a figure such as Moses, this kind of approach does not try to determine what we can know about the man himself, what historical facts about him we can establish as relatively certain. It instead looks at how Moses was remembered at different times and places.

Assmann's book engages in a memory-history of Moses, as he was remembered in discussions from antiquity all the way up to Sigmund Freud. Moses is arguably the most important figure in the entire Hebrew Bible, the great prophet, savior, and lawgiver of the people of

Israel. Four of the first five books of the Bible (Exodus through Deuteronomy) are almost entirely directly or indirectly about him.

As he is portrayed in Exodus (see Exod. 1–2), Moses was born of a Hebrew mother during a time when the nation of Israel was enslaved in the land of Egypt. We are told that the ruler of Egypt, the pharaoh, had ordered that all male Hebrew children be killed at birth, to prevent Israel from becoming too numerous in the land. Moses's mother hid her child in a basket by the shore of the Nile. He was serendipitously discovered there by the very daughter of the pharaoh, who took him into her home and raised him as her own son. As an adult, Moses rebelled against his Egyptian upbringing and became the great leader of the Israelites who brought his people out of their slavery at the Exodus event (Exod. 2–15).

Many centuries later, in the New Testament book of Acts, we are told that as a youth Moses had been "instructed in all the wisdom of the Egyptians" (Acts 4:22). This is something that is never indicated in the extensive accounts of his life in the Hebrew Bible itself, and it is one of the things that strikes Assmann. He uses this as an example as he explains how memory-history works: "Mnemo-history does not ask 'Was Moses really trained in all the wisdom of the Egyptians?' Instead it asks . . . why the Moses discourse in the seventeenth and eighteenth centuries almost exclusively based its image of Moses not on Moses's elaborate biography in the Pentateuch, but on the single verse in the New Testament."[12]

The task of memory-history, then, is to explore how an important figure or historical event is later portrayed, understood, or "remembered." Before applying this approach to Jesus by examining the written documents that appeared after his life, it is important to see more clearly how it works. This I would like to show by citing a particularly enlightening modern example, the memory of "Masada," especially among Israeli Jews.

The Collective Memory of Masada

Many Americans of my generation first came to know about Masada from a blockbuster miniseries of that title in 1981, starring Peter O'Toole. Israelis don't know the story of Masada from television, but from personal experience as part of the fabric of the "founding myth" of the modern State of Israel.

The term Masada refers to both a place and an event. Masada the place was a mountain fortress built in the first century BCE. It was on an impressive thousand-foot plateau just over a mile from the western shore of the Dead Sea, about sixty miles southeast of Jerusalem. Some years before Jesus was born, King Herod the Great built and fortified a large complex on this site. The remains of the complex still exist; it has become one of the main tourist sites in all of Israel, even though it is never mentioned in either the Hebrew Bible or the New Testament.

Masada the event refers to what happened at this location during the Jewish war against Rome in 66–73 CE. Our principal source of information of the event is Josephus, the first-century Jewish historian who was personally involved in the prosecution of the war, first as a general of Jewish troops fighting the Romans, and then, after his surrender, as an interpreter used by the Romans during their siege of Jerusalem, a siege that ended in 70 CE with the storming of the city, the destruction of its walls, the burning of the Temple, and the massacre of thousands of Jews.

But the fall of Jerusalem was not the end of the Jewish rebellion. There were some holdouts who had fled Jerusalem. The most famous of these were on Masada.

Immediately before the war began in 66 CE, a group of Jewish rebels attacked the Roman garrison on Masada and took it over. With the weapons they acquired there, they came to Jerusalem and initiated a kind of civil war within its walls, among other things killing a number of Roman soldiers. This led to the Great Revolt as the nation as a whole was spurred to oppose the Roman authorities who had earlier conquered the land. The Roman legions marched in from Syria, the war began, and it lasted for three and a half years until the destruction of Jerusalem.

The rebels who had started the revolt, though, had returned to Masada, where they holed up for the duration of the war. Counting the women and children, more than 950 people were there. Three years after the fall of Jerusalem, when the Romans were still engaged in mopping-up exercises after the destruction of the resistance, the army came to Masada and laid siege to it. There was no real way for them to engage in a frontal attack, given the geography of the place. There was just one narrow road up to the top, which could easily be defended.

The Romans decided to assault the fortress by building an enormous earthenwork siege ramp up to it from the western side, from which they could launch their attack with military equipment. The Jews on top could do nothing but watch it happen. According to Josephus, as the ramp was nearing completion, the Jews at the top made a decision. Flight was impossible, but so was self-defense. Surrender was not plausible: it would mean execution for the fighters and almost certain slavery for the women and children. And so the leader of the group, a man named Eleazar, delivered two impassioned speeches, urging a course of action that he saw as the only noble solution: mass suicide. This is what they did. Soldiers killed the women, children, and one another; the last ones standing committed suicide. When the Romans finally breached the walls, there was no one there—just two women and five children who had escaped the massive self-destruction, and from whom Josephus later learned the tale.[13]

It is the event of Masada that lives on in Israeli memory today. As is always the case, the past is remembered because of the present. In this instance, for much of the past century, the "last stance" of Jews against the Romans has been remembered as a time that—like now—Israel was surrounded on all sides by enemies, when Jews chose to "fight to the finish" until "the last drop of blood." This is how the story is told and retold in Israel—and outside of it—today. Anyone who goes to Masada on a tourist visit—there is now a cable car that goes to the top—hears the story, sees the remains of the fortress, and contemplates the act of bold defiance in the face of hostile opposition. For Israeli Jews, especially in the decades immediately before and after they achieved statehood in 1948, this was a story not only about what happened once two thousand years ago, but also about something that had to continue to happen as the nation fought to the bitter end for its independence in a sea of worldwide animosity.[14]

But Masada was not always remembered that way, as modern scholars of collective memory have shown so well. A seminal article written by the aforementioned Barry Schwartz, along with fellow memory experts Zael Zerubavel and Bernice Barnett, has shown that Masada in fact played no role in Jewish collective consciousness from antiquity to modern times.[15] It is not mentioned in the Jewish Talmud or in any other sacred text. There is no holiday associated with it. Jews throughout history never said anything about it in writing. It was forgotten for nearly two millennia.

It became part of the Jewish consciousness, in a big way, in the early part of the twentieth century with the poem "Masada" published in 1927 by a Ukrainian immigrant to Israel, Yitzhak Lamdan. In the 1920s, of course, the State of Israel did not exist, so it was not under military siege. Lamdan's poem then did not liken the military situation of the rebels on Masada to the Israelis of the modern day. Instead it argued that the *social* situation was comparable. This was a period when Jews in Eastern Europe were being denied access to the West. As one observer explained, at this time "there were only two places for the Jew: places where he could not go, and places where he could not live." Palestine was the only option, the only place on earth where a last-ditch stand could be made.[16]

Lamdan's poem concedes that Jews who came to Israel to make this stand may indeed be making a futile effort. As was the case with Masada historically, this could well be a situation where there was "no exit." But it was the one option available.

Remembering Masada in 1927, then, meant recalling the past in light of the present. After Israel was established as a sovereign state in 1948, the meaning and message of Masada changed—in light of the then present circumstances. Since then, for much of the following few decades, "like the besieged and outnumbered defenders of Masada, contemporary Israelis find themselves surrounded by hostile and numerically superior forces."[17] And so Masada became "a symbol of military valor and national commitment." Most Israelis interpreted the mass suicide "as a heroic affirmation of national dignity and will."[18]

One of the authors of this study, Jewish studies scholar Yael Zerubavel, has since written an impressive full-length study of the collective memory of Masada: *Recovered Roots: Collective Memory and the Making of Israeli National Tradition*.[19] In this work Zerubavel shows how the leaders of modern-day Israel used the Masada story to advance their national agenda, making the events of Masada "one of the most prominent national myths of Israeli society."[20] Three features of Masada helped contribute to its modern collective memory: it is a powerful and fascinating story; the fortress site itself is breathtaking; and the archaeological remains—including the remains of the earthenwork ramp and the outlines of the ancient Roman army camps— are both fascinating and impressive. Anyone who goes to Masada and hears the story cannot fail to be moved. For Israeli Jews, Masada became an emblem of what it meant to be Israeli.

Israeli leaders realized this virtually from the beginning. The archaeologist principally responsible for excavating the site was none other than Yigael Yadin, who before his digs in 1963–65 had been the chief of staff for the Israeli Army. As he himself indicated in a radio broadcast on April 27, 1966, "Through visits to Masada we can teach [our brethren from the Diaspora] what we today call 'Zionism' better than thousands of pompous speeches."[21] This lesson was long conveyed to Israelis through the stories they told of the place, through obligatory field trips by youth groups to the site, through tourism, and even through school textbooks. As Shmaryahu Gutman says in the introduction to a children's book on Masada (in Hebrew):

Masada is a symbol of Jewish and human heroism in all its greatness. A generation of youth was raised by Masada. This is the generation that created the state, the generation of defense in its various manifestations. Masada has been the source of power and courage to liberate the country, to strike roots in it, and defend its whole territory.[22]

What is most striking to scholars of collective memory, however, is how this widespread collective memory came at the expense of actual historical events, as narrated in our ancient sources themselves. Zerubavel points out that the typical narrative of Masada, as widely proclaimed throughout Israeli culture of the twentieth century, was produced through a "highly selective representation of Josephus's historical record. By emphasizing certain aspects of his account and ignoring others, the commemorative narrative reshaped the story and transformed its meaning."[23]

No one has exposed this problem more thoroughly than Nachman Ben-Yehuda, an Israeli who himself was raised on the Masada myth, who later became completely disconcerted when he learned its precarious historical basis. In his book *The Masada Myth: Collective Memory and Mythmaking in Israel,* Ben-Yehuda points out that in the modern myth, the Jewish rebels on Masada are considered "freedom fighters." But Josephus indicates that they were a group known as the "Sicarii." As Josephus himself explains, the Sicarii (called this because of their use of a dagger, in Latin *sicarius*) were Jewish assassins, involved in the killing of fellow Jews who were seen as collaborators with the Romans. These Sicarii did not simply wait out their end on top of Masada during the Jewish war. They in fact committed horrible acts of violence, precisely against other Jews, most notoriously by raiding the village of Ein Gedi, where they slaughtered numerous fellow Jews to take their supplies back to Masada. These rebels are portrayed in the modern myth as withstanding a Roman siege for three years of constant fighting; in fact the siege probably took only a few months. The modern myth claims that the rebels fought valiantly "until the bitter end," "until the last breath," "until the last drop of blood." But in fact, there is no indication in Josephus that the rebels fought at all. There were no battles, no armed engagements—a reality borne out by the archaeological explorations of the site. Rather than fighting to the end, the Sicarii leaders convinced (through force?) hundreds of people to submit to a suicide pact. Instead of engaging with the Romans, they opted to kill themselves.[24] In the words of Yael Zerubavel, to create the modern myth of Masada, the modern storyteller "elaborates where Josephus is silent and silences some of his more elaborate descriptions."[25]

In some ways, then, the study of collective memory can tell us more about who is doing the remembering in the present than about the actual persons and events they are recalling from the past. There is, of course, a relationship of the past event to the present memory. The modern tale of Masada has not been made up whole cloth. There really was a Roman siege that led to hundreds of Jewish deaths, in precisely the site that is celebrated today. But the tale about the event still in wide circulation today is not giving—and is not particularly interested in giving—the historical past as it really happened. It is interpreting the event in light of the present situation.[26]

Sociologists who explore collective memory would say that this is what always happens when we remember the past. Our present circumstances affect how we remember whatever it is we choose to recall. It is possible, then, not only for historians to establish (to some degree) what did happen in the past, but also for memory-historians to show how that past is being remembered, and for what reasons.

For the rest of this chapter and the next I will apply these insights to the memories of Jesus in the early church. I cannot delve into every memory in every Christian community—that would take an entire book, or even series of books. I have instead chosen, first, to discuss, at relative length, the distinctive recollections of Jesus found in three of our early Christian texts, the Gospels of Mark, John, and Thomas. I will then undertake a much shorter assessment of collective memories in a range of other early Christian writings, to give a fuller sense of the kaleidoscopic images of Jesus in early Christian memory. All of these books were produced at different times and in different communities, each of which had its own history and circumstances. As a result, each of these writings remembers Jesus in distinctive ways.

Jesus as Remembered in the Gospel of Mark

The Gospel of Mark is the shortest of our canonical Gospels and the earliest, written in about 70 CE. It is, therefore, our oldest surviving account of the life, death, and resurrection of Jesus.[27] For years—centuries, actually—Mark was somewhat discounted by readers and scholars of the Bible as a kind of condensed version of Matthew. Today scholars widely realize that this characterization is both wrong and unfair. It is wrong because Mark's Gospel *preceded* Matthew and was the basis for much of its own narrative. It is unfair because Mark is far more than simply a shorter version of a more complete Gospel. It is a real literary gem with a powerful message and a subtle way of expressing it. Approaching Mark from the perspective of memory-history can uncover a rich and textured recollection of the life and death of the Christian Savior. In this Gospel we find a gripping memory of Jesus as the messiah that no one understood.

The Beginning of the Gospel

The theme of the Gospel is expressed already in its first verse, which is sometimes thought to serve as a kind of title for the book: *The Beginning of the Gospel of Jesus Christ*. As with much of Mark, this statement is short and to the point. It is also intriguing and puzzling. It may not appear all that odd to a modern reader, for whom it may seem somewhat banal. But for any reader in the ancient world who knew the meaning of its key words, their significance could not be missed. For my purposes here, I should say something about two of the terms, "Gospel" and "Christ," since these are what create the powerful tension.

The word "gospel" comes from the Greek word *euanggelion,* which means "good news." It was a word used to describe some great and glorious event, such as a triumph in a military conquest, or the great benefactions that an emperor had provided or was about to provide for his people.[28] So what is the great news that Mark has to proclaim? Its hero comes to be misunderstood, rejected, betrayed, denied, mocked, tortured, and crucified. If that's the good news, what's the bad news?

The other word, "Christ," simply compounds the puzzle. The term *christ* is a Greek translation of the Hebrew word *messiah*. Christians today are, of course, accustomed to thinking that the Jewish messiah was predicted to be one who would suffer and die for the sake of others. In the Jewish world of Jesus's day, however, that's a view that precisely no one had. Or had ever had. The messiah was not supposed to be crushed by his enemies. Just the reverse.

There were various expectations among ancient Jews about what a future messiah would be like.[29] The word "messiah" itself simply meant "anointed one." It was originally used of the kings of Israel, such as King David or King Solomon, who, at their coronation ceremony, were anointed with oil as an outward sign of God's favor being showered upon them. When a king was anointed, he was thought to stand in a special relationship with God, as his own son (see 2 Sam. 7:11–14). In the days of Jesus, when there was no king sitting on the throne of Israel, no ruling anointed one, some Jews anticipated that there would be a *future* king, a descendant of David, who would overthrow Israel's enemies and set up a good kingdom in Israel like back in the golden days. That was the messiah.

Other Jews expected a more cosmic kind of messiah, a heavenly judge who would come to destroy the oppressors of Israel and set up a mighty Kingdom of God with Jerusalem as its capital. Yet other Jews expected a great priest to appear as the messiah, one who would powerfully rule the people of God through his authoritative interpretations of the Law of Moses.

There were, in short, a variety of expectations of what a future messiah might be. All these expectations had one thing in common: the messiah would be a figure of grandeur and power who would overthrow God's enemies and rule God's people in great majesty.

And who was Jesus? Everyone reading the first line of Mark's Gospel knew full well who Jesus was. He was an itinerant preacher from an impoverished rural part of Galilee who was denounced by the Jewish leaders and executed by the Romans for crimes against the state. That's the messiah? A crucified criminal? Jesus was not simply different from what anyone expected a messiah to be. He was the opposite.

Yet Mark begins his narrative by announcing that this Jesus was the messiah. And somehow his public humiliation and destruction was a good thing (the "good news"). Mark clearly has his work cut out for him. In a sense, that is what his title announces he is about to do: he is about to explain how it is that a crucified criminal was in fact the anointed one of God. In doing so Mark is most likely not simply recording his own personal memory of Jesus. He was not a disciple or an eyewitness to Jesus's life. Instead he was narrating a memory of the Christian community in which he lived and possibly had been raised—wherever it was located—some forty years after Jesus's death.

Jesus the Authoritative Son of God

Mark's account of Jesus begins with a series of episodes designed to show that Jesus did in fact have the credentials of the messiah, appearances notwithstanding. The narrative opens with John the Baptist, a fiery apocalyptic preacher urging people to prepare for the coming of the Lord (Mark 1:2–9). For Mark, John is not the leader Jesus followed or the teacher he learned from. He is the forerunner of one who was greater. Jesus receives John's baptism and is immediately declared to be God's chosen one. In fact, God himself makes the declaration. As Jesus comes up out of the waters the heavens split open, the Spirit of God descends upon him like a dove, and a voice comes from heaven, "You are my beloved Son; I am well pleased with you" (1:9–11).

After a forty-day temptation by Satan in the wilderness, apparently a kind of preparation for what lies ahead, Jesus returns to Galilee and begins to preach a message very similar to that of his predecessor: the time allotted to this current age has been fulfilled and a new order is about to arrive. The Kingdom of God is almost here. People need to repent and accept this good news (1:14–15). The imminent arrival of God's mighty kingdom is a key theme in Mark. The world will be turned upside down and all that is wrong with this world will be made right. But there is something that has to happen first. The future king has to be rejected and killed before he can return to wreak vengeance on his enemies.

Why should anyone see Jesus as that future king? Mark shows why in his opening stories. Not only does he himself declare that Jesus is the anointed one in the title of his book, and not only does God declare it at his baptism, but also Jesus himself begins his public ministry by showing all who can see that he is the authoritative leader God has chosen for his people.

As we have seen, at the outset of his public ministry, Jesus is passing by the Sea of Galilee and sees two fishermen, Simon and Andrew. He calls out to them to become his followers. They drop everything and come. Farther on he sees two more fishermen, James and John, the sons of Zebedee, mending their nets. He calls them as well, and they too leave everything—including their perturbed father—to follow him. Jesus here is remembered as an authoritative leader. When he calls, people immediately respond with no hesitation or doubt (1:16–20).

Jesus goes into the town of Capernaum, enters the synagogue on a Sabbath, and teaches. The Jewish congregation is amazed "for he taught them as one who had authority, and not as the scribes." Jesus is remembered as an authoritative teacher. When he teaches, the people all marvel (1:21–22).

Into the synagogue comes a man who is possessed by a demon. The demon recognizes Jesus and cries out that he, Jesus of Nazareth, is the "Holy one of God" who has come to destroy the evil spirits of the world. Jesus orders him to be silent and casts him out of the man. Again the crowds are amazed: "With authority he commands . . . the unclean spirits, and they obey him" (1:21–27). Jesus is remembered as an authoritative healer and exorcist. When he speaks, even the forces of evil do his bidding.

Jesus's fame spreads everywhere throughout Galilee. He engages in a ministry that is truly awe-inspiring: healing the sick, casting out demons, and raising the dead. He gathers massive crowds around him. And he preaches about the Kingdom of God that is soon to arrive.

Jesus the Misunderstood Son of God

It is clear throughout the first half of Mark's Gospel that the masses are drawn to Jesus because of his spectacular teachings and even more spectacular miracles. One might think that with this huge uprising, the Jewish nation would turn to Jesus, recognize that he is the coming messiah, and crown him king. But that is not how Mark portrays Jesus's life. In fact, quite the contrary. One of Mark's most striking memories of Jesus is that despite his astounding words and deeds, no one really understood who he was.

The misunderstanding of Jesus is demonstrated time and again throughout Mark's narrative. In chapter 3, members of Jesus's family come to take him out of the public eye because they think that he has gone out of his mind (3:20–21).[30] The people from his hometown cannot believe that he is saying and doing these things: isn't he a local fellow, the carpenter whose family is well known? They reject him and his message (6:1–6). The Jewish leaders think they do know how Jesus could do such amazing deeds: he is a blasphemer against God and is empowered by the devil (2:7; 3:22).

Most shocking of all—and surprising to those who are accustomed to the memories of Jesus recorded in our other Gospels—even Jesus's own disciples don't understand who he is. Early in the account Jesus chooses twelve men to be his close disciples (3:13–19), and he gives them special, private instruction (4:10–20). But they simply don't get it. When he calms a violent storm with a word, they ask who he could possibly be (4:41). When he walks on water "they did not understand . . . for their hearts were hardened" (6:51–52). After he feeds the multitudes with simply a few loaves and fishes—on two separate occasions—he is himself amazed at the fact that they still don't realize who he is (8:21).

It is striking to see who actually does recognize Jesus's identity in the first half of Mark's Gospel. God obviously knows, since he declares Jesus his son at the baptism (1:9–11). Jesus knows because God tells him at that moment. The demons know, but Jesus urges them to be silent about it (3:11). Apart from that, there are only two people who know: Mark, who is writing these things, and you, the one who is reading them. No one else knows.

What is yet more striking, Jesus himself seems to want to keep it all a secret. Not only does he command demons not to reveal who he is (3:11; see also 1:34), when he heals someone he orders him not to tell anyone (1:44); when he performs miracles he sometimes does not let the crowds observe (5:40); when his disciples see his revealed glory he orders them not to divulge it (9:9); when anyone starts to have a sense of his identity he commands their silence (8:30).

Eventually the disciples begin to get an inkling of who Jesus really is, but once they start to understand, they in fact misunderstand. This growing but vague sense of Jesus's identity is portrayed symbolically in Mark's Gospel in one of its key stories, which happens almost precisely halfway through the account near the end of chapter 8. A blind man is brought to be healed by Jesus. Jesus spits on his eyes, lays his hands on him, and asks if he can see anything. The man responds that he can now see people, but they are fuzzy, like walking trees. Jesus again lays his hands on the man's eyes, looks intently at him, and asks if now he can see. His vision then becomes perfectly clear (8:22–26).

That this story is meant to be a symbolic account of people who do not see well, but eventually come to see, is clear from its narrative context. In the very next story Jesus asks his disciples who people say he is. They tell him that some say he is John the Baptist come back to life; others the great prophet Elijah; and yet others one of the prophets. He then asks who they themselves think he is. Peter responds: "You are the messiah" (8:27–30).

You would think this would be the right answer. In a sense it is. But not in the sense that Peter thinks. He is seeing Jesus, but only vaguely, like a person who sees people as walking trees. Mark shows that Peter still does not understand by what happens next. In response to Peter's confession, Jesus indicates that he must suffer, be rejected, killed, and then rise from the dead. Peter rebukes him: that can't possibly happen to him (after all, he is the messiah!). Jesus rebukes Peter in turn, calling him "Satan" and saying that he does not understand the things of God (8:31–33). Jesus then begins to preach to the crowd that following him does not mean a path to glory but a path to suffering: anyone who does not take up a cross and come after him cannot be his disciple (8:34–37).

From that point on, the narrative of Mark moves inexorably toward the climax: Jesus's trip to Jerusalem to be rejected by the Jewish leaders and the Jewish people, leading to his arrest, trial, and crucifixion. On two more occasions Jesus predicts it will happen (9:31; 10:33–34). Each time the disciples show that they just don't understand. They assume that coming to Jerusalem will lead to Jesus's kingship over Israel, where they too will rule (9:32 and especially 10:35–36). But for Mark, that is not what it means for Jesus to be the messiah. As the messiah, Jesus must suffer and die. He came "not to be served but to serve, and to give his life as a ransom for many" (10:45).

For Mark, Jesus is not to be the messiah that anyone ever expected. He is the messiah who must die for the sake of others. It is no wonder that the disciples never get it. This is a completely new and different understanding of what it means to be God's anointed one. But for Mark, the way of the messiah is a way of pain, suffering, and death—not only for Jesus himself, but also for his followers. They too must give their lives for others, both in how they live and in how they die.

That will not be the end of the story, however, as Jesus himself indicates. He will rise from the dead. Then a catastrophe of worldwide proportions will come. Horrible suffering such as the world has never seen will appear. There will be massive wars, famines, and natural disasters. The followers of Jesus will be hated and persecuted. Tribulations will be intense and false hopes will be dashed. The world itself will collapse upon itself. Only then will Christ come in his glory and bring the Kingdom of God to those who are his chosen (Mark 13:1–36).

Mark's message, then, is one of suffering and ultimate vindication. Jesus must experience an excruciating execution, but he will then be raised from the dead. His followers too must endure horrific tribulation; but then they will be brought into God's glorious kingdom.

The final chapters of Mark's Gospel—all of chapters 11–16—are about Jesus's final fate. He goes to Jerusalem with his disciples; he cleanses the Temple and proclaims its coming destruction; he rouses the ire of the Jewish leaders by his words and deeds; he proclaims his apocalyptic message of coming doom upon the earth but the ultimate triumph of God; he has his last supper; he is betrayed by Judas Iscariot; he is arrested, tried, and condemned to death; he is flogged and crucified.

How can this be the fate of the messiah? Doesn't the death of Jesus as a crucified criminal precisely demonstrate that he *cannot* be the messiah? Not for Mark. For Mark, Jesus is the suffering messiah who was then vindicated by God. But why must he suffer? As Mark says, it was "as a ransom for many." Jesus's death was the sacrifice that restored people to a right relationship with God.

That is made clear in the crucifixion scene itself. Jesus is condemned to death. He is taken off and crucified. People who are passing by observe the spectacle and mock him. The Jewish priests mock him. Both robbers being crucified with him mock him. At the end he seems to feel abandoned even by God: "My God, my God, why have you forsaken me?" (Mark 15:34). Then he dies. But immediately two things happen that show that this awful outcome was in fact according to the will of God. As soon as Jesus breathes his last, the curtain in the Temple is torn in half, and the centurion overseeing the execution announces, "Truly this man was the Son of God" (Mark 15:38–39).

As we saw earlier, the ripping of the curtain is meant to show that now God—the one who dwelled in the Holy of Holies in the Temple—is accessible to all people, not simply the high priest of the Jews once a year. Jesus's death has brought people directly into the presence of God.

And someone finally realizes it. It is not one of Jesus's family, or townsfolk; it is not one of the Jewish religious leaders or even one of Jesus's own disciples. It is the pagan centurion who has crucified him. Here—finally, for the first time in this Gospel—is someone who realizes that Jesus is not the Son of God *despite* his death but precisely *because of* his death. Jesus is the dying messiah who brings salvation to the world.

Mark ends his Gospel by showing that God himself put his stamp of approval on Jesus's life and death. Three days after the crucifixion, some of his women followers go to the tomb and find that Jesus is no longer there. A young man tells them that he has been raised; they are to go and tell the disciples that Jesus will meet with them in Galilee. But the women do not tell the disciples. They flee the tomb in terror and don't tell anyone (16:1–8). In this Gospel, the disciples never do come to understand.

Mark's Memory of Jesus

This is how Mark—or, more probably, the Christian community in which Mark lived—remembered Jesus. He was the suffering messiah, the Son of God whose horrible suffering and execution at the hands of his enemies did not invalidate his claim to be the messiah. They made him the messiah. His death and resurrection brought salvation to others. Jesus did not bring the Kingdom of God to earth during his lifetime, and for Mark, he never meant to do so. He set the example that his disciples were to follow by suffering for the sake of others, in anticipation of ultimate vindication. Jesus himself was vindicated by God, who raised him from the dead. His later followers would also suffer. That might be difficult to understand, just as it was difficult to understand how Jesus could be the messiah if he suffered. But the community's persecution would earn it a great reward when Jesus returned as the mighty cosmic judge in glory at the end of days, to establish the Kingdom of God in power.

Why would a group of Christians remember Jesus in this way? As I have stressed throughout this study, we remember the past because it is relevant to our present, and what we are experiencing in the present radically affects how we remember the past. It is unfortunate that we do not have any other information about Mark's community and its experiences that would lead it to recall the life and death of Jesus in the way it did. All we have is the Gospel itself. Still, it is possible to read this Gospel and come up with some plausible suggestions about this community and its experiences.

This appears to be a community that is suffering hardship. In large part Mark is explaining why that is. Those who follow Jesus will naturally experience tribulations—of all sorts—just as Jesus did and just as he expected them to do. This community may be experiencing hunger, war, disaster, and above all persecution (13:7–13). Jesus predicted these things would come. They are almost certainly having to confront Jews and Jewish communities that flat-out reject their claims that Jesus is the messiah. How could Jesus be the messiah? He was a crucified criminal! Mark's community has an answer to that. Yes, Jesus was crucified, ostensibly for crimes against the state. But that's not the real reason for Jesus's death. Jesus died for the sake of others. It is proved by the fact that he was raised from the dead. Those who follow him will experience a fate similar to his. All this is according to the plan of God.

But the plan of God is even bigger than this. Yes, of course, the messiah was all along expected to be the ruler of the great Kingdom of God. And yes, it is also true that Jesus did not establish this kingdom during his lifetime. But he never meant to do so. God had a different design. First Jesus had to be rejected and killed. Even so, God showed that he was the messiah—not only in the spectacular works that he did while alive, in healing the sick, casting out demons, raising the dead, and exercising authority over nature itself, but most especially in what happened after his death, when in fulfillment of the scriptures God raised him from the dead.

That too is not the end of the story, however. Jesus is to be the ruler of the Kingdom of God. He is coming back very soon. When he does, he will judge the earth. His kingdom will be established here, and he will rule. His disciples will rule along with him. Jesus's followers may be suffering now, but they will be vindicated. Like the disciples, who even after Jesus's death still did not grasp his identity, Jesus's present-day followers may have trouble understanding this. But they need to hold on for just a little while longer, and the end will come. Then the Jesus who is remembered as the great, powerful, but misunderstood Son of God, who himself suffered but was vindicated, will himself vindicate those who trust in him and believe in his death and resurrection. They, then, will inherit the great Kingdom of God. This is Mark's memory of Jesus's past and his hope for his community's future.

CHAPTER 7

The Kaleidoscopic Memories of Jesus:
John, Thomas, and a Range of Others

I N THE PREVIOUS CHAPTER WE MOVED beyond the question of how the memories of Jesus were molded, influenced, altered, or even invented in oral traditions circulating during the forty to sixty-five years after his death, to consider one example of a "collective memory." There we considered our earliest surviving Gospel, the one attributed to Mark.

In this chapter we move on to other collective memories. Arguably the most interesting feature of our earliest Gospels—both those inside the New Testament and those outside of it—is just how differently they record their memories of Jesus. This rich variety becomes clear when we stop thinking of these books purely in historical terms, as data sets that can help us establish a historically accurate portrayal of Jesus, and begin thinking about them as records of how Jesus was being remembered by later Christian communities. This is a shift of focus from history to memory-history.

There were, of course, a number of commonalities in the memories of Jesus cherished by various Christian churches in one place or another. They did, after all, comprise followers of the man Jesus, a real historical person who lived and taught in Galilee and was crucified under Pontius Pilate in Judea. And so, many of their memories of Jesus will overlap. What is startling to many readers, though, is just how widely these memories vary. How does this rich variety help us understand the communities who preserved and recorded their recollections of the one who stood at the foundation of the church, the man Jesus?

We begin our exploration by considering two writings at some length—the canonical Gospel of John and the noncanonical Gospel of Thomas. As we will see, the memories of Jesus recorded in these two books differ radically from those found in Mark, as well as from one another. We will then move, in much shorter order, to look at collective memories embodied in six other writings, three of which are found in the New Testament and three from outside of it. The end result, I hope, will be to show that there was not one remembered image of Jesus among his early followers, but a kaleidoscopically varied set of images.

Jesus as Remembered in the Gospel of John

John is widely believed to be the last of our canonical Gospels to be written; it is usually dated toward the end of the first century, say, 90–95 CE. From the earliest of times it has been recognized as significantly different from the other three, Synoptic, Gospels. Already in the second century it was thought that the Synoptics gave a kind of nuts-and-bolts historical view of the things Jesus said and did, whereas John was a more "spiritual" Gospel, concerned with conveying the mystical truth of Jesus's teachings and true identity. Here Jesus is not portrayed merely as a human chosen by God to be his messiah, the one who needed to die for others and then be raised from the dead. He certainly is that, but he is also remembered as being much more. In this book Christ is a divine being who came down from heaven, a being equal with God, through whom the entire universe was created, who shared with God all his glory in eternity past but who has become a human to reveal the truth so that anyone who believes in him can have everlasting life.

Christ the Incarnate Word of God

Just as was the case with Mark, the Gospel of John begins by laying out in clear terms who it understands Jesus to be. But the beginning could not stand in sharper contrast to Mark. Rather than starting with a title and an account of Jesus's apocalyptic forerunner, John begins with a poem that celebrates the identity of Christ as the preexistent divine being who created the world and then came into it as God made flesh.

This is the famous "prologue" that comes to us in John 1:1–18. In powerful and poetic language the prologue starts not by naming Jesus or even indicating that it is talking about him. Instead, it begins with an elegant celebration of the "Word" of God:

> In the beginning was the Word, and the Word was with God, and the Word was God. This one was in the beginning with God. All things came into being through him and apart from him not one thing came into being that came into being. In him was life and the life was the light of humans. And the light shines in the darkness, and the darkness has not overcome it. (John 1:1–5)

Scholars have wrangled for centuries over how best to understand these famous opening lines, but some things about them can be said with relative certainty. It becomes clear only much later—in vv. 14–17—

that this "Word" in fact is Christ before he became human. In trying to explain who Christ is, the author appears to be alluding to the creation account found in the opening of Genesis, the first book of Bible, which also starts with the words "In the beginning." In that well-known account we are told that God "created the heavens and the earth" (Gen. 1:1). Here in John we are told that it was through "the Word" that all things –that is, the heavens and the earth—came into existence. That of course makes sense. For how does God create all things in the book of Genesis? "And God said, 'Let there be light.'" In the Bible's version of creation, God makes light, and eventually all things by speaking a word. That is what John's Gospel is referring to: God's Word.

Here, however, the Word of God is not simply something that God speaks. It is its own distinct entity, which exists as God, yet also exists apart from God. It is not identical with God himself, but yet, at the same time, is itself God. How are we to understand this?

When the Gospel of John was written, philosophical traditions of Judaism had developed a concept that scholars call "divine hypostases."[1] A "hypostasis" is a kind of personalized attribute of God. That is to say, God has certain attributes—for example, he is wise. But if he "is" wise, that must mean that he "has" wisdom. If he "has" wisdom, then wisdom must also be something separate from him that he possesses. Since it is his own wisdom, that thing that he possesses in some sense is identical to him. Yet it is also distinct from him, since he has it. So some Jewish philosophers began to consider "Wisdom" as both a divine attribute and as something distinct from God. You can see that already in the Hebrew Bible, for example, in the description of creation in Proverbs 8, where God's "Wisdom" is one who accompanies God and is the one through whom God creates all things (Prov. 8:22–36).

The "Word" of God was like that as well: a distinct entity from God and yet at the same time God. God would have always existed with his Word. And so John states, "In the beginning was the Word, and the Word was with God, and the Word was God."

What makes John quite distinct from Proverbs or other books that talk about divine hypostases is that here the Word becomes a human being. We are told in the prologue that the Word through whom all things were created and who brought both light and life to this world "came to his own, but his own people did not receive him" (1:11). More clearly still, "The Word became flesh and dwelled among us, full of grace and truth; and we have observed his glory, glory as of the unique Son from the Father" (v. 14). Who is this Word become flesh who brings grace and truth? It is Jesus Christ (v. 17). Even though no one has ever seen God, Christ as the unique Son has made him known to others (v. 18).

This understanding of Jesus as the incarnation—the coming in flesh—of the preexistent Word of God who created all things and brought life and enlightenment to the world is far more exalted than anything one can find in Mark and the other Synoptics. Here we have a poem of praise glorifying Christ as God. He is not God the Father, obviously, but God the Son, who made the world and then came into it to bring truth from above and reveal who God the Father is. In many ways, the Gospel of John intends to show how that happened through the life and death of Jesus.

Those Who Attest to Jesus

In broad outline, the narrative of Jesus's life that begins in John 1:19 is comparable to what we find in Mark: here too we learn about John the Baptist and Jesus's earliest followers. But as we have already seen in chapter 5, these stories are told in very different ways. Unlike Mark, in this case John the Baptist explicitly identifies Jesus as the one who is to come; more than that, he publicly indicates that Jesus is the Son of God and "the Lamb of God who takes away the sins of the world"

(1:29). As a result, it is no secret, for this Gospel (unlike Mark) that Jesus is the Son of God who must die for the sake of others as a sacrifice for sin. This understanding is proclaimed from its very opening narrative.

Moreover, in this Gospel Jesus does not pass through more than half of his ministry before someone recognizes that he is (in some sense) the messiah, as in Mark. When John the Baptist's own followers come up to Jesus, they immediately—already in chapter 1—realize who he is, and they set off to tell others about him (1:35–51). One of Jesus's first followers is Andrew, who goes and finds his brother Simon and tells him, "We have found the messiah." Another follower is Philip, who announces that Jesus is the one who was predicted in the Law of Moses and the prophets (1:43–45). His friend Nathaniel immediately comes to realize that Jesus is the Son of God and the "king of Israel" (1:49). All this is before Jesus has even begun his ministry.

Even so, as already seen in the prologue, for this Gospel Jesus is much, much more than the messiah, the king, and the Son of God who has to die for others. He is God incarnate. He is clearly not the Father himself, but he is a divine being who shared the glory of God the Father from the beginning, who has now become a human. Moreover, here, in contrast to Mark, Jesus does not keep his identity a secret, for example, by ordering others to be silent about it. Instead he broadcasts it loud and clear, in public and in private, in virtually everything he says and does.

Jesus's Self-Revelation

It is interesting that in the other canonical Gospels Jesus resolutely refuses to perform miraculous deeds to prove who he is. Instead, his miracles reveal his compassion for others and serve to show that the Kingdom of God is soon to come, as we saw in chapter 5. In one key passage in Matthew, Jesus's opponents ask him to perform a "sign" to prove himself, that is, a miraculous deed that will offer a vivid demonstration of his identity. Jesus flat-out refuses to do so and says that he will perform "no sign" for that generation (Matt. 12:38–42). This makes for a remarkable contrast with the Gospel of John. Here, of course, as in the Synoptics, Jesus does miraculous deeds. But they are not to show that the kingdom is soon to arrive.[2] They are to reveal who Jesus is. In fact, whereas he won't do signs to establish his identity in the Synoptics, that is precisely what he does in John. Here his mighty deeds are not called "miracles"; they are "signs." They are meant to prove who he is, a divine being who has come from his heavenly glory to reveal the Father.

The first sign Jesus does is not found in the other Gospels, but has long been the favorite miracle of Jesus on college campuses everywhere. Jesus is at a party where the supplies are running low, and so he turns the water into fine wine (2:1–11). Oh, for power like that. For his next sign Jesus heals the son of an official in Capernaum (4:46–53). In this context Jesus explicitly indicates that no one will be able to believe unless they see the signs (4:45). We are told that Jesus did many such public signs (2:23). Altogether, seven are explicitly narrated during his public ministry (chs. 1–11), before his fateful trip to Jerusalem the last week of his life, which occupies roughly the final half of the Gospel. The author tells us, though, that Jesus did many other signs that are not recorded in his book. The ones that are recorded are specifically designed to show that "Jesus is the Christ, the Son of God," so that anyone who believes in him will be rewarded with eternal life (20:30–31).

One of the striking features of John's portrayal of Jesus is that in addition to doing signs to prove who he is, Jesus proclaims his divine identity publicly and repeatedly. This again is in sharp contrast with Mark and the other Synoptics, where he scarcely ever teaches anything about himself except that he must be rejected, executed, and raised from the dead. In these earlier Gospels, Jesus constantly proclaims the Kingdom of God and urges people to live in ways that are appropriate to it. Not in John. Jesus does not talk about the coming kingdom here. He talks about himself, who he is.

As we have seen, in many instances he uses his signs precisely to prove that what he says about himself is true. Thus he indicates he is the "Bread of Life." That is, he is the one who can provide the sustenance that will bring eternal life. He feeds the multitudes, not out of compassion, as in Mark, but to show that what he has said about himself is true. He is the one who provides everlasting sustenance. He has come down from heaven so that no one need ever hunger again; anyone who believes in him will live forever (John 6:1–59).

He says he is the "Light of the World," and he heals a man who was born blind to prove it. Jesus is the one who brings enlightenment, and not simply for sight in this world, but the kind of enlightenment that will bring eternal life (8:5; 9:1–41). He says he is the "resurrection and the life"; anyone who believes in him will never die but will live forever. Then he raises a man who has been dead for four days, to prove it. Jesus not only can bring the dead back to life, he also can assure that people will never die. Those who believe in him will have everlasting life (11:1–44).

In John's Gospel, Jesus not only proclaims who he is through his signs, he also spends his entire preaching ministry telling others that he is the one who has come from heaven to bring eternal life to all who will believe in him. He proclaims this message not just to his followers and not just to the crowds, but also to his enemies, who in this Gospel are simply called "the Jews."[3] Jesus is in constant trouble with the Jewish authorities, who regularly consider his claims about himself to be blasphemous and try to kill him for it.

In chapter 8, Jesus tells "the Jews" that their ancestor Abraham looked forward to his own day. They are incredulous: how would he know about Abraham? Jesus is not even fifty years old! He responds with the famous line "Truly I tell you, before Abraham was, I am." Not only is Jesus claiming to have existed before Abraham (eighteen hundred years earlier); he also is calling himself "I am," the very name of God revealed to Moses in the Hebrew Bible (Exod. 3:14). Jesus's opponents know full well what he is saying about himself. They take up stones to stone him (8:48–59).

Two chapters later the Jews in Jerusalem question Jesus and he again declares his identity: "I and the Father are one." Once more they break out the stones (8:22–31).

Throughout this Gospel, then, Jesus spends his public ministry declaring who he is and doing miraculous signs to prove it. He is the one who has come from God, who himself is equal with God, who was with God in the beginning, who has shared God's glory, who has come into the world to reveal who God is, that anyone who believes in him can have everlasting life. Yes, he is also the one who died for the sake of others and was raised from the dead (John 18–21). But this one who did such things is God on earth, a preexistent being who is equal with God the Father himself and who created the universe before becoming a human, to redeem it.

John's Alternative Memory of Jesus

In some very basic respects John's recollection of the life and death of Jesus is similar to what you find in Mark and the other canonical Gospels. Here too Jesus begins by associating with John the Baptist and calling followers; here too he does great miracles and delivers astounding teachings; here too he is rejected by the Jewish religious authorities, betrayed by one of his own disciples, handed over to the Roman governor, Pontius Pilate, for judgment, condemned for sedition against the state, crucified, and raised from the dead. The broad outlines are very much alike.

But the specific memories are very different indeed. Jesus's entire proclamation is different. No longer does he deliver an apocalyptic proclamation about the massive suffering in store for the earth in the last days before the cataclysmic end of all things and the appearance of a cosmic judge of the earth who will bring in the Kingdom of God to be ruled over by Jesus and his followers. This proclamation is completely absent from John's Gospel. Instead, Jesus preaches about himself.

In addition, unlike the other Gospels, Jesus is portrayed as a divine being who has become human. He existed before the world in the glory of the Father and has now become a human to reveal the truth that can bring eternal life. Anyone who believes in him will live forever with God in heaven; anyone who rejects him will be subject to God's eternal wrath (3:36).

It is striking to realize who, in this Gospel, rejects Jesus's message, incurring wrath upon themselves. It is "the Jews." Obviously by this John is referring, in part, to the Jewish leaders. But it is actually more than that. In fact, it is all the Jews, at least the Jews who refuse to acknowledge that Jesus is the messiah, the Son of God, the one who has come from heaven to reveal the truth that can set all people free.

What is the situation of John's Christian community that has led them to remember Jesus in this way, as opposed to some other way—for example, the way he was remembered by Mark? Once again, scholars have had to take their cues from the Gospel itself to see if it provides any hints about the present situation of John's church that has influenced how they have remembered the past. Some scholars have found such hints, most strikingly in the intriguing story in chapter 9 where Jesus heals a man who was born blind, much to the consternation of his Jewish opponents, who object that doing such things on the Sabbath is forbidden by God.[4]

As I have already pointed out, in part this story is meant to show that Jesus is who he says he is. He is the light of the world (John 8:5), and he shows it by restoring sight to one who has always been blind. Also, even more obviously, the story is meant to highlight the contrast between the helpful, compassionate, healing Savior and his mean-spirited, legalistic, Jewish opponents. They not only object to Jesus doing such things on the Sabbath, they even doubt that he is able to do so. Anyone who breaks the Sabbath can't be from God, and so such miracles are not possible (John 9:16–18).

But the man who has been healed insists that it really was Jesus who did the miracle. So the Jewish leaders bring in the man's parents to ask them what they can say about their son's blindness and healing. John explicitly indicates that the parents will not come out and say that Jesus healed their son, "because they were afraid of the Jews; for the Jews had already agreed that anyone who confessed Jesus to be the messiah would be cast out of the synagogue" (9:22).

It is almost universally agreed among critical scholars that this cannot be describing the state of affairs in Jesus's own day. There were no synagogues in the 20s CE that had passed rulings on whether anyone could think of Jesus as the messiah. This verse is clearly referring to something that must have happened after Jesus's day, when some Jews came to follow Jesus and insisted that, despite his death, he really was the future ruler of the earth.[5]

We don't know the precise details of how the events unfolded, but based on the most influential studies of the matter by modern scholars, the rough outline appears to be this.[6] There were Jews in some locality or other (we don't know where) who came to believe that Jesus was the messiah. They tried to convert other Jews. Most of the other Jews thought this was an absurd claim and rejected it. But the Christian Jews wouldn't give it up or be quiet about it. Every Sabbath they argued their case. They finally began to make a nuisance of themselves. What was the Jewish community to do with such nuisances? They finally told the believers in Jesus that they had to leave.

They were no longer welcome. They were kicked out of the synagogue.

What were the excluded Jews to do? They had no option. They started their own worshipping community apart from the synagogue. That is the situation presupposed by the Gospel of John. It is written by an author who is in a community of people who have been (or are descended from people who had been) excluded from a synagogue.

How would this tragic event in the life of this community have affected its memories of the past? Recall: we remember the past in light of the present so that our present influences how we remember. Scholars in the social sciences have long known that splinter groups that break off from a larger community often develop a kind of fortress mentality of "us" versus "them." That appears to be what happened in John's community, and it led to its distinctive recollections of Jesus. One pressing question these people must have asked was why their friends, families, and fellow Jews had rejected the messiah, Jesus, sent from God. They came to think that these others must not have understood him because they were not chosen to believe; they were incapable of seeing the truth because they were alienated from the truth. The truth came from God above, but they were from this world. Christ himself must have come from above, from God. But the unbelievers were earthly and could only understand earthly things (see John 3:5–21).

As John's Christian community thought more and more about the matter, and discussed it among themselves, telling their stories about Jesus in light of their situation, this understanding of divine truth coming from above in the person of Jesus began to take more definite shape. Jesus was no longer simply a man chosen by God to be his messiah who would die for others, as in Mark. He was a divine figure who revealed God; he was God's way of communicating to people; he was God's word to this world; he in fact was "the Word of God" who had come from above. Having eternal life with God above meant recognizing this revelation that had come from above when God's Word became a human. Those who did not accept this Word of God would be forever punished by God, because they had rejected God's own Word (see John 3:16, 36).

For this community, ultimate salvation no longer was a future event that was about to happen in this world when the cataclysmic apocalypse hit and the Kingdom of God arrived. That may have been the view of earlier communities, such as Mark's. It may even have been the view that Jesus himself preached. But it wasn't the view of John or his community. That older view understood the divine plan in temporal terms; you could draw it on a timeline so that it would, in a sense, be laid out horizontally along an axis that divided this present evil age controlled by the forces opposed to God from the future good age in which God would rule this world in the Kingdom of God. This was a kind of temporal dualism, in which history was split into two radically distinct ages.

The fortress mentality of John's community retained a dualistic understanding of the divine plan, but in a sense the temporal, horizontal dualism seen in Mark came to be flipped on its axis. Now the dualism was not horizontal but vertical, not temporal but spatial. The new dualism was between this world down below at one extreme and the world above at the other. It wasn't about now and then; it was about down and up. Salvation would not come in the future after the apocalypse hit. It would come in the world above. Believing in Christ would not allow you to enter into a future kingdom that was coming to earth. The kingdom was not coming in the future. The kingdom was now. In heaven. Above. To enter that kingdom you "must be born from above." Those who believe in Christ as the one sent from God to reveal his true identity will have eternal life with the Father and Son in heaven (see John 3:3, 16, 31–36; 14:1).

Those are the people in John's community. The people on the outside, including above all, "the Jews," who have rejected this message, have lost out on the possibility of everlasting life. Jesus is remembered as the one who delivered the message. Moreover, he himself is that message. He is the one who has come from above to take his followers back with him to their eternal home. This will happen to anyone who sees Jesus's great signs and realizes that he is the God who has become human to save people out of this world (John 20:30–31).

Jesus as Remembered in the Gospel of Thomas

Of all the noncanonical Gospels discovered in the modern period, none has proved more significant than the Gospel of Thomas. I have already said a few words about this Gospel and cited some of its sayings in chapter 1. Here I need simply remind you that it was discovered in 1945 in a cache of writings that were, for the most part, originally Gnostic compositions of one sort or another, even though the majority of scholars today would not call Thomas itself a Gnostic Gospel.[7] There is no real debate, however, over the most distinctive feature of this Gospel. Unlike the canonical Gospels it is not a narrative of Jesus's life, ministry, death, and resurrection. There are no narratives in the Gospel of Thomas at all. It consists entirely of sayings of Jesus. Altogether there are 114 sayings by the modern reckoning (the sayings are not numbered in the manuscript itself).

These sayings are simply given one after the other. There is no obvious organizing pattern for them, apart from the fact that similar sayings will sometimes be arranged together. But on the whole, the Gospel simply gives a sequence of Jesus's teachings, most of them introduced with the words "And Jesus said." Apart from that there are no stories: no accounts of Jesus's birth, life, activities, miracles, death, or resurrection. It is nonetheless titled, in the manuscript, a

"Gospel." For this author it is a Gospel because it too is proclaiming the "good news" of Jesus. Here the good news is not about the salvation Jesus brought by dying for the sins of the world. It is instead the good news he brought through his secret teachings. Anyone who understands these teachings will have eternal life. Jesus's death appears to have nothing to do with it. This is a very different way indeed to remember Jesus and his significance.

The Opening Recollection of Jesus

As was the case with both Mark and John, the opening of the Gospel of Thomas provides a key to understanding its message and its portrayal of the significance of Jesus. Before the author launches into the first saying of the collection he gives a brief and telling introduction: "These are the hidden sayings that the living Jesus spoke and Didymus Judas Thomas wrote down."[8] There are several key words here. First, it is not simply the sayings of Jesus that are being recorded, but the "hidden" sayings. This Gospel is concerned with secret knowledge. These teachings cannot be understood by anyone with just a modicum of attention and intelligence. They are teachings for insiders. Is this book meant to be read only by members of Thomas's inner group, an elite few? It is hard to tell.

The introduction speaks of Jesus not as the messiah, or the Son of God, or the Word of God made flesh. He is instead simply called the "living Jesus." Does that mean that Jesus has come back to life after being dead, so that it is the resurrected Jesus who is speaking? Or does it (also?) mean that he is the Jesus who always lives and is the one who is able to provide life to his followers? Relatedly, the author does not indicate when he spoke these words. Was it during his ministry? After his resurrection?

It is also significant that Didymus Judas Thomas is the one who wrote these words. Unlike the authors of our canonical Gospels, this one actually tells us his name. Or rather he tells us what he wants his readers to *think* is his name. No one believes this was actually written by Didymus Judas Thomas. That's because Didymus Judas Thomas, in some circles of the early Christian church, was thought to be Jesus's twin brother.

The word *didymus* means "twin" in Greek; the word *thomas* means the same thing in Aramaic. So this is a twin. His name is Judas or, as sometimes translated, Jude (it's the same name). So whose twin is he? In the Gospel of Mark we are told that Jesus had four brothers, one of whom was named Jude (Mark 6:1–6). This Jude was later thought to have become a leader of the church after Jesus's death and to have written the letter of Jude in the New Testament. In Christian circles in ancient Syria, it was thought that he was actually Jesus's twin. This can be found, for example, in the famous Acts of Thomas, where they are identical twins. They looked just alike. How Jesus could have an identical twin and yet have been born of a virgin is something these traditions never even try to explain.[9]

For our purposes here, the simple identification of the alleged author is enough. These words are being written down by Jesus's twin brother. Who better to know his secret teachings?

Knowing them intimately is everything for this author. That becomes clear in the very first saying: "And he said, 'Whoever finds the interpretation of these sayings will not taste death.'" Throughout history many millions—billions—of people have thought it is important to understand what Jesus taught. But no one ever placed a greater emphasis on it than the author of the Gospel of Thomas. For him, understanding what Jesus really meant by his secret teachings is the way, probably the only way, to have eternal life. Salvation does not come by believing in Jesus's death and resurrection, or by accepting his virgin birth, or by acknowledging that he is God become a man. It comes by correctly interpreting what he had to say.

Some of Jesus's earthly followers—according to the Synoptic Gospels, at least—believed they would be rulers in the future Kingdom of God. For the Gospel of Thomas, future rule is not reserved for the twelve disciples. Nor will it involve simply ruling over the future kingdom. It is a rulership open to anyone who seeks the meaning of Jesus's words, finds it, realizes how disturbing it really is, and then marvels at the truth. Such people will rule over all things. And so the second saying of the collection: "Jesus said, 'The one who seeks should not stop seeking until he finds. And when he finds he will be disturbed; and when he is disturbed, he will marvel. And he will rule over the all.'"

Interpreting the Secret Teachings

As we have seen, a number of the sayings in the Gospel of Thomas—maybe half of them—are very similar to what you find in the Synoptic Gospels.[10] Numerous other sayings are very different from what you can find in the canonical Gospels, and in some ways these other sayings seem to provide the conceptual framework for Thomas, indicating the author's overarching understanding of Jesus's teaching about the world, the people who are in it, and how they can find salvation.

One recurring motif is that the material world is not a good place. In fact, it is dead and lifeless. The one who realizes what the world is will be able to escape it and have life. As Jesus says tersely in one place, "The one who has come to know the world has found a corpse; and the one who has found the corpse, the world is not worthy of that person" (saying 56).

This world is not portrayed as the good creation of the good God, as presented, for example, in the book of Genesis. Instead, it is a deeply impoverished place that is a realm of entrapment for human spirits who have the misfortune of residing here: "Jesus said, 'If the flesh came into being because of the spirit, it is a marvel. But if the spirit (came into existence) because of the body, it is a marvel of marvels. Yet I marvel at this, how this great wealth has come to dwell in this poverty'" (saying 29). This saying should not be interpreted as exulting in how marvelous it is that the spirit came into existence because of a body. Just the opposite. For Thomas, it would be amazing if the flesh came into existence because of the spirit; but if it were the other way around—it would be beyond marvelous. It would be literally unbelievable. Instead, the great wealth of the spirit has somehow come to be trapped in the poverty of this material world.[11]

Why has that happened? For this author it is because the human spirit has come down into this material world from a higher realm of enlightenment: "If they say to you, 'Where have you come from?' tell them, 'We have come from the light, from the place where the light came to be on its own, established itself, and was revealed in their image.' If they say to you, 'Is it you?' say, 'We are its children and we are the chosen of the living Father'" (saying 50). Thus we are children of God from the realm of light. We have come to be trapped in this impoverished realm, this corpse of a world. We were originally unitary creatures, pure spirit. Then we came into these wretched bodies and became both spirit and flesh, two things, not one: "On the day when you were one, you became two; but when you become two, what will you do?" (saying 11). It's a good question. What you might hope to do, at least, is to return to being one again, an enlightened spirit who is no longer dwelling in this impoverished material world.

In this world the human spirit is disoriented and confused, without clear insight, blind. It is like a person who is completely drunk and can't see straight. When Jesus came into this world to bring salvation, that is how he found people: "Jesus said, 'I stood in the midst of the world and appeared to them in flesh. I found them all drunk, and I did not find any of them thirsty. And my soul was anguished for the children of humankind, for they are blind in their hearts and do not see. For they came into the world empty, and empty again they seek to depart from the world. Yet now they are drunk; when they shake off their wine, then they will repent'" (saying 28). Only by coming to a clear understanding of the truth can a person escape the torpor that comes from living in this material realm.

That can come only through the secret knowledge that Jesus provides. This knowledge is principally self-knowledge, of who you really are as one who has come from the enlightened realm of God into this world. Those who do not come to realize this about themselves will never escape this miserable realm: "When you come to know yourselves, then you will be known, and you will understand that you are the children of the living Father. But if you will not know yourselves, then you are in poverty, and it is you who are the poverty" (saying 3b).

Those who realize the true state of things, as spirits imprisoned in the material trappings of the body, will be able to escape their bodies, discard their flesh, and find salvation. This emergence from the hateful material shell of the body is likened to children stripping off their clothes and tramping on them: "His disciples said to him, 'When will you appear to us and when shall we see you?' Jesus said, 'When you strip naked without being ashamed and take your clothes and place them under your feet like little children and stamp on them, then you will see the Son of the Living One, and you will not be afraid'" (saying 37).

If the material world is to be escaped by the spirits that are trapped within our bodies, how should we interact with the world? Like many other antimaterialist texts from antiquity, the Gospel of Thomas insists on a highly renunciatory approach to life. If the problem is the body, and if pleasure is what makes you appreciate the body, then you should engage in acts of self-denial to keep yourself from being tied to the body and thus to this material realm. Thomas, therefore, is often read as a highly ascetic text, one that urges its readers to avoid the pitfalls of bodily pleasure in light of the need to liberate the spirit from its material entrapments.

This then may be the ultimate teaching of the text. Knowledge of one's true situation, and of how to escape it, are absolutely key. It is no surprise, then, to find that so many of the sayings of the Gospel of Thomas focus on correct knowing and understanding (e.g., sayings 1, 3, 5, 16, 18, 39, 46, 56, 67, and so on). You must know who you are and what the world is. All this is revealed in the hidden teachings of Jesus. Those who understand these teachings "will not taste death."

The Community Behind Thomas

Many scholars have tried to establish what can be known about the history of Thomas's community, but again the reality is that we have very little to go on apart from the written text that survives. There are, however, several points to make.

For one thing, this author—like the authors of Mark and John—is deeply opposed to Judaism and the Jewish people. There is little to suggest his community is experiencing any active persecution. The engagement seems to be more distant. But the antagonism is nonetheless clear: this author mocks Jewish practices and insists they are not to be followed. In saying 6, for example, Jesus's disciples ask him if they should engage in acts of Jewish piety: fasting, prayer, giving alms, and dietary observances. Jesus does not answer their question until saying 14, so that some scholars think that originally these two sayings belonged together as a unity. Whether or not that is the case, Jesus's answer is clear: fasting is a sin, prayer will be condemned; giving alms damages the spirit; and Jesus's followers should eat anything that is given them.

Saying 27 is sometimes taken to be an attack on observing the Sabbath, if in a rather convoluted way, by saying that one needs to "make the Sabbath a Sabbath" (does that mean to give the Sabbath a rest—that is, not to keep it?).[12] So too saying 53 attacks the practice of circumcision: if cutting off a baby's foreskin were profitable, God would have had boys born without it in the first place.

Other sayings attack Jewish leaders, such as saying 39, where the scribes and Pharisees are said to have the keys to the kingdom but they fail to enter themselves and do not allow anyone else to do so. The Jews as a whole are similarly condemned: "For they love the tree but hate its fruit; and they love the fruit but hate the tree" (saying 43). Jews, that is, don't know what to think: they can't decide what to love and what to hate. They clearly don't have knowledge. If true knowledge is the only way to have eternal life, they have lost out.

Thomas is thus coming from a community that is opposed to Judaism and Jews, and this opposition is affecting how it remembers Jesus's teachings. It is also opposed to other Christians and Christian communities. In particular, it is opposed to those who think that the Kingdom of God will be an actual place to be found in this world (a view we found in the Gospel of Mark). Right off the bat in this Gospel, in saying 3, Jesus mocks this understanding of the kingdom as literalistic, crass, and wrongheaded. If Christian teachers think the kingdom of God is to come in a physical sense, where will it be exactly? In the sky? Then the birds will get there before you. In the sea? Then the fish will beat you there. No; for this Gospel the kingdom is an internal reality, within those who realize they are "sons of the living father." Thus it is already spread out over the earth.

A similar teaching occurs as well near the very end of the Gospel, in saying 113.[13] In this nearly final saying the disciples of Jesus ask when the kingdom is coming, and again Jesus stresses that it will not be a physical entity here on earth. Instead it is here and now, even if it is hidden from those who lack knowledge. Those who teach otherwise are false teachers. Who would those false teachers be? They would be teachers of other Christian communities.

What can we say then about Thomas's own community? It appears to be a group of Christians who have nothing to do with real-life Jews. Those people are outside the fold, ignorant, wrong, and beyond the pale. There is nothing to indicate that they are physical threats. The community may, however, be in conflict with other Christians. That would explain its repeated insistence on knowing the particular truths that come from the lips of Jesus. Those who hold to older views do not have or understand Jesus's "hidden" teachings about the need to escape from the material trappings of this world. For the members of this community, salvation is not coming to this world, as it is in the Gospel of Mark. Even more than in the Gospel of John, there is instead to be an escape *from* this world.

Now, however, that comes not by believing Jesus is the one who has come down from heaven to reveal the truth of the Father. It comes by understanding the secret teachings of Jesus, who has revealed the truth about this world and how we came to be here. We are from another realm and have become entrapped in this material existence, this "corpse," which has no possibility of coming to life. The material world will not be redeemed. It was never meant to be redeemed. It needs to be transcended and ultimately escaped by knowing the truth and by denying oneself the pleasures of this life through catering to the whims of the body. Only by sacrifice can one find the kingdom. Not sacrifice for the sake of others, but sacrifice of one's own pleasures. Those who live in this way will fully know the truth of Jesus's secret teachings and return to the spiritual realm from which they have come.

Yet Other Memories of Jesus

To this point we have seen three sets of memories of Jesus, from three different communities, in three different situations. All these communities were remembering the past because of and in light of their present. There can be no doubt that in many instances their memories were frail or faulty—at least in the historical sense that what they remembered about Jesus was not true to the Jesus who really lived, taught, and died in Roman Palestine. To be sure, it can probably be assumed, though it can never be proven, that people in these communities *thought* their memories of Jesus were historically true. For them, these really were the things Jesus said and did. But obviously all three communities could not be right about that. Their memories are very different, even contradictory.

The historical question of what could be shown to have actually happened in the life of Jesus was not the ultimate concern for people living in these churches. Their communities were not made up of historians interested in applying rigorous historical criteria to establish what Jesus really said and did. They were for the most part simple Christians who had heard stories about Jesus that had long been in circulation, stories about who he was, what he taught, what mission he came to fulfill. These stories about the past had always been told in light of how the storytellers perceived the relevance and significance of Jesus for the present. Those who held, preserved, and shared memories of Jesus did so because he meant something to them and their struggles. It was precisely those memories—stored, recalled, and shared by Christians encountering these struggles—that made it possible for them to make sense of the world and their lives.

I do not want to leave the impression that there are basically three kinds of memories of Jesus that have come down to us from the early church as laid out in the preceding chapter, those represented by the

Gospels of Mark, John, and Thomas. On the contrary, each author we know about from the early centuries of Christianity has a different memory of Jesus—either a greatly or a slightly different memory from everyone else. Our ancient Christian texts provide us with an entire kaleidoscope of images of Jesus.

This obviously is not the place to provide a detailed sketch of all the ancient memories of Jesus. But I would like to say just a few words about several of them, just to give a sense of this rich variety. To that end I have chosen six important Christian texts and/or figures, three from within the New Testament and three from outside. Each of these recollections deserves a full chapter—indeed, a full book. Some of them, in fact, have had many, many books devoted to them. Here I will merely summarize, as briefly as possible, the distinctive features of their memories.

Paul's Memory of Jesus

When speaking about Paul's memory of Jesus we are severely handicapped by the fact that the only writings we have from Paul's hand are seven letters sent to Christians who were experiencing problems he was trying to address. We don't have anything like a complete account of what he remembered or thought about Jesus. Nonetheless, it comes as a complete surprise to many readers of Paul that, as we saw in chapter 5, he says very little at all about Jesus's life on earth. Whereas Jesus's words and deeds are the very center of focus for the Gospels of the New Testament, they play a minuscule role in Paul's writings.

Paul's letters are for the most part interested in only two things when it comes to the earthly Jesus: his death and his resurrection. As he himself reminds his converts among the Corinthians: "I knew nothing among you except Christ, and him crucified" (1 Cor. 2:2). Later in the same letter he summarizes what he has always held to be "of first importance." This is the teaching that "Christ died for our sins in accordance with the scriptures . . . and that he was raised on the third day in accordance with the scriptures" (1 Cor. 15:3–5).

Paul, therefore, at least in his surviving writings, does not remember Jesus as a healer, an exorcist, a teacher of parables, or a preacher of the coming kingdom. It is Jesus the dying and rising messiah whom Paul speaks about, theologizes about, revels in, and proclaims. Those who trust Christ's death and resurrection will be right with God. What else could matter?

One corollary of this belief was that Paul's converts did not need to adhere to the Jewish law and in fact were not to do so (Rom. 3:19–26; Gal. 2:15–21). Whether Paul thought that was the case for those who were born Jewish is very difficult to say (he never indicates one way or the other); but it was certainly the case for gentiles. Any gentile who thought it was important to follow the law was in danger of losing salvation. What mattered was not the Jewish law (Gal. 2:11–21; 3:1–4; 10–14; 5:1) but Christ alone (Phil. 3:2–11), the messiah who died and rose again to bring salvation to the world.

Q's Memory of Jesus

We are even more handicapped when it comes to knowing the views of Jesus held by the unknown author of the now-lost document scholars have called Q.[14] If you recall, Q provided Matthew and Luke with many of their sayings of Jesus, including such memorable passages as the Beatitudes, the Lord's Prayer, some of the parables, and many of his ethical teachings. Back in the nineteenth century, when Q was first proposed as a hypothetical source behind these canonical accounts, it was presented as a collection of Jesus's teachings with no narrative of his death and resurrection.[15] You might imagine a possible objection to thinking that there once was some such writing: how could any early Christian author have written a Gospel without an account of Jesus's passion? Isn't that *everything*? Gospels by their very nature focus on Jesus's fate and vindication, right?

Well, wrong. When the Gospel of Thomas was discovered in 1945 it was immediately seen to be very similar to the hypothetical Q, a collection of sayings with no passion narrative. That does not mean that Thomas is Q. Far from it. There are lots of sayings in Q not in Thomas and vice versa. But possibly they were the same kind of document.

Any author who thought that it was Jesus's teachings, rather than his death and resurrection, that ultimately mattered stood at odds with Paul. But for Q, Jesus was indeed principally remembered as a teacher of great wisdom and high moral demands, as an apocalyptic prophet anticipating the imminent end of the age, and one whose miraculous activities showed that the day of judgment was soon to come. For the author of Q, Jesus's teachings provided the goal of the Christian life. Followers of Jesus are those who adhere to his directives for how to live, in anticipation of the coming kingdom of God.

Matthew's Memory of Jesus

In a sense, the anonymous author of the Gospel of Matthew agreed with both Paul and Q. In fact, he more or less combined their views into an amalgam that was, as a result, different from either one. The ultimate importance of Jesus for Matthew was that Jesus died for the sake of others and was raised from the dead. That is like Paul. But unlike Paul, Jesus's life prior to his death was absolutely crucial. In fact, in many ways it is the point of the Gospel: it is essential to know what Jesus actually did and, especially, what he said. Jesus teaches at length in this Gospel, nowhere more memorably than in the three-chapter Sermon on the Mount (see pp. 195–202). Much of that sermon comes from Q.

Matthew's memories of Jesus are fundamentally different from Paul's in yet another way. Whereas Paul was opposed to the followers of Jesus (at least gentiles) keeping the Jewish law, in Matthew Jesus is remembered as a Jew who himself perfectly kept that law and insisted that his followers do likewise. For Matthew, Jesus was the Jewish messiah sent from the Jewish God to the Jewish people in fulfillment of the Jewish law. Following Jesus meant patterning one's life on that of (the Jewish) Jesus and, therefore, adhering to the law—adhering to it, in fact, even better than the most religious Jewish leaders (see Matt. 5:17–20). This means not simply keeping to its explicit demands (e.g., "an eye for an eye and a tooth for a tooth") but also digging even deeper and fulfilling its ultimate intent ("turn the other cheek"; see Matt. 5:21–48), so as to be "perfect" before God (Matt. 5:48).

Thus, whereas for Paul Christ brought an "end to the law" (Rom. 10:4), for Matthew he is remembered as urging the continued observance of the law. Doing so is mandatory.

In Sum: Memories of Jesus in the New Testament

We have now seen a number of very different recollections of the life and significance of Jesus in the New Testament (Mark, John, Paul, Q, and Matthew). In fact, all the authors of the New Testament seem to have a different recollection. For some readers of the New Testament, the different memories of Jesus found throughout its pages are more striking than the similarities. For others, it is the similarities that are both more profound and significant. That is a debate we will never resolve. People simply see things differently. Those who are more analytical tend to see difference; those who are more synthetic tend to see similarity. My view is that there are both similarities and differences.

Reasons for these similarities are not hard to find. For one thing, the church fathers who decided which books to include in the New Testament made their choices for clear and firm reasons. They would never have included a writing that presented a view of Jesus that was completely at odds with what they themselves believed or with what other "acceptable" books had to say. And so their books of scriptural authority—those we have inherited today—are ones they believed all shared the same theological perspective.

Moreover, it cannot be emphasized enough that all the books of the Christian scripture are all found in one book, the New Testament. It does not come to us as twenty-seven books, or collections of books by a number of different authors. It comes to us as a single volume, in hard or soft covers. Since we obtain it as a single book, we tend to read it as a single book.

Any time you read a book by an author—even, say, a collection of essays—you simply assume that he will not contradict himself. If you see two passages that look different, you reconcile them in your mind, thinking they must present a single perspective, not different views at odds with one another. So too the Bible. People read it as a single book—especially people who think that rather than having a number of different authors, it has one author, God. Such people see unity everywhere and very little diversity.

On the other hand, people who focus on the fact that the New Testament has a number of different authors tend to read the book—or rather, the books—differently. Just as you would not expect fifteen or sixteen leading American politicians to agree on everything, you won't expect a comparable number of early Christians to agree on everything. To be sure, the politicians will all have many very basic similarities: they will all be firmly committed to the Constitution, for example, and to democracy, and to free enterprise, and to the four freedoms, and so on. But beyond those basic agreements, think about the differences between Barack Obama and Ted Cruz.

If someone were collecting a group of political authors for inspirational reading of the kind she herself enjoys, she probably would not include essays by both Obama and Cruz. More likely she would collect essays by Democrats, or by Republicans, and so the similarities would be manifest. But differences would emerge even there.

The New Testament is the official collection of twenty-seven books made by later church fathers. It naturally will have similarities. But as we have seen, those similarities sometimes mask very deep and deeply rooted differences.

Once we move outside the New Testament the differences are far greater and much easier for everyone to see. Here we will look briefly at three recollections of Jesus that are far less familiar to your average reader: the Gospels of Judas, Marcion, and Theodotus.

The Gospel of Judas's Memory of Jesus

One of the most recent Gospels to be discovered is the Gospel of Judas, unearthed in Egypt in the 1970s but published for the first time in 2006.[16] This was without a doubt the most significant Christian manuscript discovery since the famous Nag Hammadi Library in 1945.[17] Like most of the documents in the Nag Hammadi collection, the Gospel of Judas was instantly recognized as a Gnostic Gospel. Also like many of them, it was produced by an unknown author sometime in the middle of the second century.

As we have seen, Gnosticism was a widely diverse collection of various religions that shared certain features.[18] In particular, adherents of these religions maintained that true "knowledge" (Greek: *gnosis*) is what brought salvation from this fallen material world. Jesus was the one who provided that knowledge. He came from a divine realm inhabited by an entire range of divinities who had all come into existence in eternity past. By learning the secret knowledge he could convey, those "in the know" could escape the material trappings of this world and return to their rightful home in the heavenly realm.

The Gospel of Judas shares this view of Jesus and remembers him as one who revealed his secrets, not so much to his other disciples but principally to Judas Iscariot. In this Gospel Jesus is remembered as one who mocked the other disciples and their lack of knowledge. They seemed to think that the creator of this world was the true God. Nothing could be farther from the truth. Judas alone understood that Jesus did not come from the creator but from a higher divine realm. Evidently for that reason, it is to Judas that Jesus reveals the mysteries of this greater realm. This revelation forms the core of the Gospel, an account of how the divine realm came into existence, and then this material world.

But not even Judas is able to enter this realm. It is reserved for others, those who fully grasp the truth of Jesus's mystical and even mind-boggling teachings. In this Gospel it is not Jesus's death and resurrection that matter, in the least. The Gospel does not even narrate the passion, but ends at the point at which Judas betrays Jesus. That is not a bad thing in this Gospel, however; once Jesus dies he will return to the heavenly realm, and those who understand the secret knowledge he conveys will themselves go there for a blessed eternity apart from this material world and the God who created it.

Marcion's Memory of Jesus

We do not have any writings from the hand of the theologian, teacher, and evangelist Marcion even though he was, arguably, one of the most important Christian authors of the second century. Because he was widely condemned for propounding heresy, his works were not preserved, except as they are quoted by church fathers who found their views offensive and damnable. Unfortunately, as a result, we need to rely on what these fathers—Marcion's enemies—tell us about his views.[19]

From these quotations it is clear that Marcion would have agreed with the Gospel of Judas that Jesus did not belong to the creator of this world. He was not the son of the Jewish God. But Marcion would have fiercely disagreed with Gnostics who maintained that Jesus came from a divine realm inhabited by numerous other divinities, and that it was the understanding of the secret knowledge of the world, and of oneself, that led to salvation.

For Marcion there were two and only two Gods. These two, however, were vastly distinct. The God who created this miserable world was the God of the Old Testament, who chose the Jews to be his people and gave them his law. Since everyone had broken that law, he had condemned everyone—fairly, but harshly—to damnation. Jesus came from a different God, one who was above the creator, who sent Jesus to deliver people from the wrath of the God of the Jews. Since Jesus was not a part of the created order, he did not really have a human body. Otherwise, like us, he would be a creature made of matter. Thus Jesus only *seemed* to have flesh and blood. It was all an appearance.

When Jesus died he did not really shed blood and suffer and die. Evidently it was a deceit, meant to trick the creator God to give up his claims on people. It worked. Salvation comes then by faith in what Jesus did.

This memory of Jesus was ruled out of court by prominent church fathers. It was widely attractive to other people, but in the orthodox view that emerged, if Jesus wasn't really a human being, he couldn't save those of us who are. Marcion's recollection of a nonhuman Jesus was eventually thrown onto the trash heap of heretical views.

Theodotus's Memory of Jesus

In the city of Rome at the end of the second century and the beginning of the third there was a group of Christians who had a strikingly different understanding of Jesus, based on memories quite contrary to those preserved in the churches of Marcion. These Christians claimed allegiance to the teachings of a man named Theodotus, who by trade was a cobbler but by passion was an amateur theologian.[20] Theodotus insisted vehemently on a monotheistic view. There is only one God. There were not many, as the Gnostics claimed, and not even two, as Marcionites urged. There was one and only one God, as he himself declares in scripture, "There is no other God besides me . . . I am God, and there is no other" (Isa. 45:21–22).

The Christological corollary was clear to Theodotus and his followers. If the Creator God is the only God, then Christ himself could not be God. If Christ were also God, then there would be two Gods. But there is only one. And so Christ was not a divine being. He was a human, from beginning to end.

When the Theodotians recalled the events of Jesus's life, they remembered his birth as the result of the sexual union of Mary and Joseph. He was fully human and only human. At his baptism God sent his Spirit upon him in the form of a dove, to empower him for his ministry. At this point God "adopted" Jesus to be his son. Since Jesus was adopted as God's son, he was not actually divine—any more than the kings of Israel such as David or Solomon were. Jesus, like them, was a human being to whom God showed special favor.

It was the Spirit working through Jesus that allowed him to do his great miracles and deliver his spectacular teachings. In particular, being God's anointed meant that Jesus had to fulfill a mission of dying for the sake of others. He did so in obedience to the divine command, and so God raised him from the dead. But he was, and always had been, fully and only human.

Orthodox church fathers strenuously objected to this view. They thought of Jesus as human, yes, but also as divine. If he were not God, how could he fully mediate God's will to earth? If he were merely human, he could not have died as the Son of God for the sins of the world. He must then have been both human and divine.

Later Memories of Jesus

About a century after both Marcion and the Theodotians had their short time in the sun, it came to be thought throughout most of Christendom that each of their views of Jesus was completely right about one thing and completely wrong about another. The Marcionites were right that Jesus was God; they were wrong that he was not human. The Theodotians were right that Jesus was human; they were wrong that he was not God. The consensus view emerged that he was human and divine, at the same time. Eventually it came to be thought that he was not half of God and half of human. He was fully both things, at one and the same time.

The first official church meeting called to debate theological issues concerning the nature of Jesus was the famous Council of Nicea (325 CE), a gathering of bishops from around the then Christian world. Contrary to what you sometimes read—in such inestimable authorities as *The Da Vinci Code*—everyone at the council already wholeheartedly agreed that Christ was both God and human.[21] But how could he be God if God was God and there was only one God? Was Christ a secondary divinity, subordinate to God the Father and created by him at some point in eternity past? Or, instead, was he fully equal with God the Father in every way, and coexistent with him with no beginning in time? These were the two leading options. In the end it was the latter view that won the day at the Council and eventually became the orthodox, dominant view of the church at large.

It should be obvious that anyone who thinks Jesus was God in the flesh, fully equal for all time with the Father but become a flesh-and-blood human, will remember Jesus's life differently from someone who thinks that he was human and only human (but empowered by God) or that he was divine and only divine (in merely the appearance of humanity). For the bishops who agreed to the Creed of Nicea

287

Jesus was indeed God in the flesh. The life and teachings of Jesus, his death and resurrection, were obviously those of a human—but not of a mere mortal; they were the works of a man who was the God-man. As a result, these bishops and their followers no longer remembered aspects of Jesus's life that would have made him unmistakably fallible and human like the rest of us—aspects of his life that would have been known, say, by his original family and friends and even the later disciples. These earthly associates of Jesus either did not pass along such information, or if they did so, it was eventually lost in the tradition.

The memory of Jesus as an eternal God walking as a man on the earth was thus affected by the theological investments of a later day. It is very different from the memory of Jesus in any of the first- and second-century authors I have mentioned in this chapter and the one preceding.[22] Then again, all these earlier views are also different from one another. We have already seen the reason: in no small measure it is because of the nature of memory. Memory is not simply information and experiences from an earlier time. It is also, at least as much, about what is happening now. How we remember the past is intricately connected with what we are experiencing in the present. In a very real sense, we do not have any direct, unmediated access to the past. We have access to it, in our minds, only through the fallible and malleable processes of memory.

CHAPTER 8

In Conclusion:
A Paean to Memory

LIKE MOST AUTHORS, I get a lot of email from people who have read my books. I find one of the comments I repeatedly receive somewhat disheartening. It involves the importance of memory. To explain the comment, I need to provide a bit of background.

Most of my professional career—as a teacher, researcher, lecturer, and writer—is centered around historical issues and concerns. Whenever I discuss the New Testament from a historical perspective, as I frequently do, I refer to the problems of our sources. The Gospels were written decades after Jesus's death by people who were not eyewitnesses and had probably never laid eyes on an eyewitness. They are filled with discrepancies and contradictions. They represent different perspectives on what Jesus said and did. For that reason, to know what actually happened in Jesus's life we have to apply rigorous historical criteria to these sources to reconstruct historical realities from later distorted memories.

I present these views because at heart I am a historian, interested in seeing what we can know about the past. I have presented some such views here, in this book. But my focus in the book has been on memory, including, of course, distorted memories of Jesus's life, but also memories that are closely related to history—for example, some of the "gist" memories found throughout the Gospels. Memory is not only faulty: most of the time it is pretty good. So too with the memories of Jesus. We can know a good deal about Jesus's historical life based on what our sources say.

Moreover, I have tried to emphasize that the study of memory is not at all limited to what comes to be distorted over time. It is possible to engage in memory-history (what Jan Assmann calls mnemohistory) to see how recollections of Jesus can help us understand the people who were remembering him in one way or the other, why Mark, John, or Thomas recalled Jesus the way he did, how their present circumstances can explain their memories of the past.

The comment I sometimes get from readers that I find disheartening is this: they often tell me that if there is something in the Gospels that is not historical, then it cannot be true (in any respect), and if it is not true, then it is not worth reading.

My sense is that many readers will find it puzzling that I find this view disheartening. But I do.

It is true that to do the work of the historian requires one to be extremely critical about the sources of information available from, and about, the past. Some readers seem to think this approach to sources is taken only by atheistic, hardheaded, liberal historians with anti-supernaturalist biases who are out to destroy religion. But in fact, it is the approach all historians take to all of their materials. The reason some readers find this approach to the Gospels objectionable is that they simply aren't accustomed to dealing with the Bible as history.

But even though I do deal with the Bible as a historian, I do not personally think that is the *only* way to deal with the Bible, and I find it unsettling when readers think that once the Gospels are shown to have discrepancies, implausibilities, and historical mistakes, we should just get rid of them and move on to other things.

I do understand that Christianity is widely seen as a "historical" religion, and that if there are historical problems with Christianity, then Christianity has problems. I understand that very well indeed. But in my judgment there is more to Christianity than history. And there is more to life, and meaning, and truth than the question of whether this, that, or the other thing happened in the way some ancient text says it did.

In my view, the early Christian Gospels are so much more than historical sources. They are memories of early Christians about the one they considered to be the most important person ever to walk the planet. Yes, these memories can be recognized as distorted when seen from the perspective of historical reality. But—at least for me—that doesn't rob them of their value. It simply makes them memories. All memories are distorted.

And yes, the New Testament memories are all different from one another in one way or another. But that doesn't mean that we should then throw them all away because they are not completely trustworthy. Everyone's memories—even of the same event—will be different from everyone else's. That's just how memory works.

And yes again, these memories have all been shaped by the lives, histories, and concerns of the people who recorded them, so that the "present" of these authors affected what they remembered about the past and how they remembered it. But that doesn't mean that we should just go on to read other books instead. All memories of the past are chosen and shaped by the present.

At the end of the day, I find it troubling that so many people think that history is the only thing that matters. For them, if something didn't happen, it isn't true, in any sense. Really? Do we actually live our lives that way? How can we? Do we really spend our lives finding meaning only in the brute facts of what happened before, and in nothing else?

Think about the things that matter to us: our families, friends, work, hobbies, religion, philosophy, country, novels, poetry, music, good food, and good drink. Do we really think that the brute facts about the past are the only things that matter?

To pick only one of these examples, one far removed from the New Testament, to make my point. Is literature unimportant because it does not deal with the brute facts of history? Is Dickens's great novel *David Copperfield* of no value because its main character didn't actually live? Well, that's different, you say, because it's fiction. Yes indeed, it's fiction. And fiction can be life-transforming because it is full of meaning, even though it never happened.

Or consider further: can historical discoveries undermine the power of great literature? Does the earth-shattering force of *King Lear* evaporate if it can be historically proved that someone other than Shakespeare wrote it? Does *Dover Beach* really fail to grip us with its powerful pathos if we learn that these were not actually the author's thoughts the last time he was looking out over the English Channel?

Literature speaks to us quite apart from the facts of history. So does music. So does sculpture. So do all the arts. The Gospels are not simply historical records about the past. They are also works of art.

In addition, they are written forms of memory. The truth is that most of us deeply cherish our memories: memories of our childhood, of our parents, of our friends, of our romantic relationships, of our accomplishments, of our travels, of our pleasures, of our millions of experiences. Other memories, of course, are terribly wrenching:

memories of pain, of suffering, of misunderstandings, of failed relationships, of financial strain, of violence, of lost loved ones, of yet
millions of other experiences.

When we reflect on our past lives, when we remember all that has
happened to us, all the people we have known, all the things we have
seen, all the places we have visited, all the experiences we have had,
we do not decide, before pondering the memory, to fact-check our
recall to make sure we have the brute facts in place. Our lives are not
spent establishing the past as it really happened. They are spent calling
it back to mind.

When we do so our memories may be frail, and faulty, and even
false. But they are how we remember. And that is how we live our
lives, with these memories. If someone tells us that something happened to us differently from how we remember, we may change how
we think about it. But that's not usually what happens. More often
we simply say we don't remember it that way. And we stick to our
memories. If we do shift what we think about our remembered past,
we don't jettison our memories but transform them.

We live not only with our own memories, but also with the
memories of others. We share our lives. Others share their lives with
us. The only way to share a life outside of that nonexistent nanosec-
ond of the present is to share a life of memory. Our presents are affected by these pasts, both our own and those of others. Just as these
pasts are molded by our presents. And our reflections about the future
are molded by both. Living life is never a matter of isolation from
either our pasts or the pasts of others. The living and sharing of memories are what make up our lives.

The Gospels are shared memories of the past. Yes, they can be
scrutinized by historians who want to get a better sense of what actually happened in the life of Jesus. That's what I do for a living. But if
they were only that, they would be dry, banal, and frankly rather

uninteresting to anyone except people with rather peculiar antiquarian interests. The Gospels are more than historical sources. They are deeply rooted and profound memories of a man, memories that ended up transforming the entire world.

It is easy to make the argument that the *historical* Jesus did not transform the world. He does not transform the world today. You may wonder how that could possibly be, if Christianity became the religion of the West. Look at it this way. There are two billion people today who are committed to the memory of Jesus. How many of those two billion have what I, as a historian, would consider to be a historically accurate recollection of the basic facts of Jesus's real life and ministry? Some thousands? It's a tiny fraction. The historical Jesus did not make history. The remembered Jesus did.

For me as a historian it goes without saying that we should pay close attention to what can be learned about the historical Jesus. But we should not neglect the remembered Jesus.

Does it matter if Jesus really delivered the Sermon on the Mount the way it is described in Matthew 5–7? It matters to me historically. But if Jesus didn't deliver the sermon, would it be any less powerful? Not in the least. It is, and in my view deserves to be, one of the greatest accounts of ethical teaching in the history of the planet.

Does it matter if Jesus really healed the sick, cast out demons, and raised the dead? Does it matter if he himself was raised from the dead? To me as a historian it does. But if these stories are not historically accurate, does that rob them of their literary power? Not in my books. They are terrifically moving accounts. Understanding what they are trying to say means understanding some of the most uplifting and influential literature the world has ever seen.

Does it matter if Jesus considered himself to be God on earth? As a historian, it matters to me a great deal. But if he did not—and I think he did not—the fact that he was remembered that way by later followers is terrifically important. Without that memory of Jesus, the faith founded on him would never have taken off, the Roman Empire would not have abandoned paganism, and the history of our world would have transpired in ways that are unimaginably different.[1] History was changed, not because of brute facts, but because of memory.

Memory can certainly be studied to see where it is accurate and where it is frail, faulty, or even false. It should be studied that way. It needs to be studied that way. I spend most of my life studying it that way. But it should also be studied in a way that appreciates its inherent significance and power. Memory is what gives meaning to our lives, and not only to our own personal lives, but to the lives of everyone who has ever lived on this planet. Without it we couldn't exist as social groups or function as individuals. Memory obviously deserves to be studied in its own right, not only to see what it preserves accurately about the past, but also to see what it can say about those who have it and share it.

Christian memory is particularly and uniquely important. Christian memory transformed our world. Christian memory brought about a revolution in the history of Western civilization. Christian memory continues to influence billions of lives in our world today. Ultimately, of course, Christian memory goes back to the earliest memories of Jesus. These too need to be studied for what they can tell us about the historical person who stands behind the memory. But they should also be studied for what they reveal about those who came in his wake, who remembered him and passed along their memories to those of us living today.

ACKNOWLEDGMENTS

BECAUSE THIS BOOK RANGES over so many fields, I am unusually indebted to colleagues with significant expertise who have read all or parts of it to let me know where I botched it, either making mistakes or failing to provide much-needed nuance. One always hopes that all the problems have been taken care of. If not, it's entirely my fault.

I am especially grateful to Daniel L. Schacter, William R. Kenan Jr. Professor and former Chair of the Department of Psychology at Harvard University. He is one of the premier psychologists of memory in our day, arguably the leading expert in the world on the phenomenon of false memory. His books and articles made a large impact on my thinking from the very beginning of my research. Among his many other fine qualities, Professor Schacter is a onetime Tar Heel (he did his undergraduate degree at the University of North Carolina, where I now teach). Professor Schacter graciously agreed to read the manuscript of this book to tell me if and how I went astray. I am deeply in his debt.

I was fortunate to have two New Testament scholars who have worked extensively in the field of collective memory read the manuscript and make very useful comments: Zeba Crook of Carleton University and Chris Keith of St. Mary's University. They both provided significant assistance on matters both major and minor, and I am greatly appreciative. In addition, I asked my good friend and local expert in all things Gospels, Mark Goodacre, of crosstown rival Duke, to work over a draft for embarrassing errors, misstatements, and general infelicities. He was especially generous and helpful in his numerous insights.

Three of my colleagues at UNC read portions of the book that deal with their fields of expertise, and I very much appreciate their willingness to help out a colleague in need: William L. Barney in the Department of History, and Jodi Magness and Evyatar Marienburg, both in my own Department of Religious Studies. May their tribes increase.

I am also grateful to three of my graduate students at UNC who are working on various aspects of New Testament and early Christian studies and who provided me with considerable research assistance for the project: Luke Drake, Shaily Patel, and Travis Proctor. Any professor in the field would be lucky to have student-scholars such as these.

I decided to solicit yet other readers for the book, and in doing so have done something rather unusual. This one will take a bit of explaining.

First the background: I started the Bart Ehrman blog just over three years ago. The blog covers all the areas of my expertise: the New Testament, the historical Jesus, the writings of Paul, the early Christian apocrypha, the Apostolic Fathers, the manuscript tradition of the early Christian writings, and, well, just about everything else related to the history and literature of early Christianity. I post about a thousand words a day on the blog, five to six times a week. The only hitch is that to read my posts, a person has to join the blog, and to join costs money (but not much).

I do the blog, and charge the money, not to line my own pockets but to raise funds for those in need. Every penny goes to charities—two local to me, two international—that deal with hunger and homelessness. The blog keeps growing, as do the moneys we raise through it.

This past year we raised over $110,000. I'm hoping to do significantly better this year. For those interested in joining, it is at www.ehrman blog.org.

As I was finishing this book I decided to try something out of the ordinary: I would offer readers of the blog the right to read the book and make comments on it prior to publication in exchange for a donation of a set amount. Several readers took me up on it. I provided them with the manuscript; they read it; they made remarks; and I took the remarks seriously in making my final revisions.

I am deeply thankful for these contributors and readers. They are Steve and Gabby Walrath, Eric Brown, James and Jeremy Granada, Steve Leonard, Greg Matthews, Ronald Taska, and my two good friends and recent traveling companions Gabriela Laranjeira and Bill Sutherland.

I am especially in the debt of my new editor at HarperOne, Michael Maudlin, who read the manuscript several times with extraordinary care and made extremely insightful and helpful comments on it. The book is much improved as a result.

Finally my friend, onetime editor, and now literary agent, Roger Freet, read the entire manuscript and provided me with savvy comments on style and substance. This is the seventh book we've done together (six while he was an editor for HarperOne). We both dream of many more to come. I am very much in his debt and someday may even think about paying it off.

NOTES

Introduction

1. We will be exploring this issue at length in chapter 3.
2. See http://www.washingtonpost.com/blogs/monkey-cage/wp/2015/02/16/new-ranking-of-u-s-presidents-puts-lincoln-1-obama-18-kennedy-judged-most-over-rated/
3. *Abraham Lincoln and the Forge of National Memory* (Chicago: University of Chicago Press, 2000), p. 31.
4. *The Collected Works of Abraham Lincoln*, ed. Roy Basler (New Brunswick, NJ: Rutgers University Press, 1953–55), vol. 3, pp. 145–46. I owe his quotation to Barry Schwartz; see the preceding note.
5. Schwartz, *Abraham Lincoln*, p. 4.
6. Some scholars make neat differentiations among the phenomena known as "collective memory," "social memory," and "cultural memory." For my purposes in this book, I will simply be using the terms synonymously.
7. Many memory experts would argue that memories are *always* distorted. We do not have video cameras in our head that record exactly what happens; we make a selection of what to remember, and various parts of the event are stored in different parts of the brain, to be (re)constructed later at the point of recollection, as I will discuss in chapter 4. This means that memories are never fully and precisely what we originally experienced. In part for that reason, "distortion" is not necessarily a negative term.
8. *Abraham Lincoln*, p. 6.
9. James W. Loewen, *Lies My Teacher Told Me: Everything Your American History Textbook Got Wrong* (New York: Simon & Schuster, 1995), p. 53.
10. Loewen, *Lies My Teacher Told Me*, p. 64.

Notes

Chapter 1: Oral Traditions and Oral Inventions

1. Engel Tulving, "Episodic and Semantic Memory," in *Organization of Memory*, ed. E. Tulving and W. Donaldson (New York: Academic Press, 1972), pp. 381–403.

2. See pp. 140–43.

3. Memory experts often use "false " and "distorted" interchangeably when referring to incorrect recollections—whether of your personal past (episodic memory) or of factual information about the world (semantic memory). Some people may be inclined simply to call the latter kind of distorted memory "mistakes." That particular terminological distinction will not have any effect on my argument in this book. I will be using the terms "false" and "distorted" as synonyms in my discussions.

4. Reza Aslan, *Zealot: The Life and Times of Jesus of Nazareth* (New York: Random House, 2013).

5. Bill O'Reilly and Martin Dugard, *Killing Jesus: A History* (New York: Henry Holt, 2013).

6. See the review by Candida Moss in the *Daily Beast:* http://www.thedaily beast.com/articles/2013/09/27/the-gospel-according-to-bill-o-reilly-s -new-book-killing-jesus.html

7. For an antimaterialist Jesus, see, for example, John Dominic Crossan, *The Historical Jesus: The Life of a Mediterranean Jewish Peasant* (San Francisco: HarperSanFrancisco, 1991) and Richard Horsley, *Jesus and the Spiral of Violence: Popular Jewish Resistance in Roman Palestine* (Minneapolis: Fortress, 1993).

8. The well-deserved classic in this field is Elisabeth Schüssler-Fiorenza, *In Memory of Her: Feminist Theological Reconstruction of Christian Origins* (New York: Crossroad, 1994).

9. See my book Bart D. Ehrman, *Jesus: Apocalyptic Prophet of the New Millennium* (New York: Oxford University Press, 1993) and Dale Allison, *The Historical Jesus: Millenarian Prophet* (Minneapolis: Fortress, 1998).

10. It is important to point out, however, that scholars who provide these reconstructions are not unconsciously remembering Jesus, but critically trying to establish what he said and did based on surviving evidence. For some reflections on the relationship of history and memory see chapter 7.

11. The Acts of Peter and all the apocryphal episodes of the lives of the Apostles that I refer to here can be found in William Schneemelcher, *New Testament Apocrypha,* vol. 2; Louisville, KY: Westminster/John Knox, 1992. The quotations of these various accounts come from this edition.

12. The translation of all these Pilate Gospels is in Bart D. Ehrman and Zlatko Pleše, *The Other Gospels: Accounts of Jesus from Outside the New Testament* (New York: Oxford Univ. Press, 2014).

13. The translation cited here is in Ehrman and Pleše, *The Other Gospels*. All of the Gospels referred to in this section can be found in that volume.

14. Psalm 148:7, as quoted in *Pseudo-Matthew*, chap. 18.

15. In my view there is a simple answer. Like 97 percent of everyone else in his Palestinian world (see p. 80) Jesus almost certainly never learned how to write.

16. For a discussion of why scholars view this passage as a later addition to John's Gospel, rather than original, see my book Bart D. Ehrman, *Misquoting Jesus: The Story Behind Who Changed the Bible and Why* (San Francisco: HarperOne, 2005), pp. 63–65.

17. One of the documents in the collection is clearly not Christian: it is a fragment of Plato's *Republic*.

18. For one of the most recent and competent discussions of what the Gnostics stood for, see David Brakke, *The Gnostics: Myth, Ritual, and Diversity in Early Christianity* (Cambridge, MA: Harvard Univ. Press, 2010). To read the most important Gnostic texts for yourself, see the translation of Marvin Meyer, ed., *The Nag Hammadi Scriptures* (San Francisco: HarperOne, 2007). For discussion and explanation of these various texts, see Nicola Denzey Lewis, *Introduction to "Gnosticism": Ancient Voices, Christian Worlds* (New York: Oxford Univ. Press, 2013).

Chapter 2: The History of Invention

1. When, that is, they are speaking about distorted episodic memories. Distorted semantic memories would be recollections of information about the world that are incorrect. See note 3 in chapter 1.

2. Daniel J. Simons and Christopher F. Chambris, "Gorillas in Our Midst: Sustained Inattentional Blindness for Dynamic Events," *Perception* 28 (1999): 1059–74; a more accessible, popular version of the article can be found in their book *The Invisible Gorilla: How Our Memory Deceives Us* (New York: Crown, 2009).

3. "Gorillas in Our Midst," p. 1059.

4. For a handy English translation see *Reimarus: Fragments*, ed. Charles H. Talbert (London: SCM Press, 1970). The book was later republished by Wipf and Stock Publishers (Eugene, OR).

5. Quoted in Talbert, ed., *Reimarus: Fragments*, p. 1.

6. See pp. 21–22.

7. I will not detail various discrepancies and contradictions of the New Testament here, as I have covered the subject in my earlier book *Jesus Interrupted: Revealing the Hidden Contradictions of the Bible (and Why We Don't Know About Them)* (New York: Oxford Univ. Press, 2009).

8. There are several excellent introductions to the history of biblical scholarship during the nineteenth century. One that is quite readable for laypeople is Stephen Neil, *The New Testament 1861–1961* (London: Oxford University Press, 1972), which was later updated by N. T. Wright, *The New Testament 1861–1986* (New York: Oxford Univ. Press, 1988). A more thorough treatment is Werner Georg Kümmel, *The New Testament: A History of the Investigation of Its Problems* (Nashville: Abingdon, 1972). The most recent in-depth study is William Baird, *History of New Testament Research*, vol. 2, *From Jonathan Edwards to Rudolf Bultmann* (Minneapolis: Fortress, 2003).

9. See note 7 for this chapter.

10. For a summary of the evidence that most scholars continue to find convincing that Mark was the earliest of the Gospels, see the discussion in my textbook Bart D. Ehrman, *The New Testament: A Historical Introduction to the Early Christian Writings*, 5th ed. (New York: Oxford Univ. Press, 2012), pp. 106–9.

11. For a brilliant analysis of these nineteenth-century lives of Jesus, see the classic by Albert Schweitzer, *The Quest of the Historical Jesus*. Published in German in 1906, the book has appeared numerous times in English (e.g., Minneapolis: Fortress, 2001).

12. Published in German, 1901. For an English translation, see *The Messianic Secret*, tr. J. C. Greig (Minneapolis: Fortress, 1983).

13. See my fuller discussion of Mark's presentation of Jesus in chapter 6.

14. The three classic books are Karl Ludwig Schmidt, *Der Rahmen der Geschichte Jesus* (Darmstadt: Wissenschaftliche Buchgesenschaft, 1919), never translated into English; Martin Dibelius, *From Tradition to Gospel* (New York: Scribner, 1965; German original, 1919); and Rudolf Bultmann, *History of the Synoptic Tradition* (New York: Harper & Row, 1963; German original, 1921).

15. For an informed discussion of the form critics see Edgar McKnight, *What Is Form Criticism?* (Philadelphia: Fortress, 1969).

16. This is not to discount the possibility that our Gospel authors had access to written sources that have since been lost; Luke himself indicates that he did (Luke 1:1–4). But even these sources would have been based ultimately on oral traditions in circulation for months—probably decades—and apart from these verses in Luke there is no hard evidence that the other Gospels

utilized earlier written accounts (though see what I have to say about "Q" on pp. 59–60).

17. See the preceding note.

18. Birger Gerhardsson, *Memory and Manuscript: Oral Tradition and Written Transmission in Rabbinic Judaism and Early Christianity,* 2nd ed. Grand Rapids, MI: Eerdmans, 1998; first edition, 1961.

19. These are sacred texts from centuries later. See my discussion on p. 68.

20. *Memory and Manuscript,* p. 133.

21. See E. P. Sanders and Margaret Davies, *Studying the Synoptic Gospels* (Philadelphia: Trinity Press International, 1989), pp. 129–32.

22. James D. G. Dunn, *Jesus Remembered* (Grand Rapids, MI: Eerdmans, 2003), pp. 203–9.

23. For example, *Poet & Peasant and Through Peasant Eyes: Combined Edition* (Grand Rapids, MI: Eerdmans, 1976, 1980, 1983); and *Jesus Through Middle Eastern Eyes* (Downers Grove, IL: Intervarsity Press, 2008).

24. Kenneth Bailey, "Informal Controlled Oral Tradition and the Synoptic Gospels," *Asia Journal of Theology* 5 (1991): 34–54.

25. "Informal Controlled Oral Tradition," p. 54.

26. For a discussion on what we know about the church in Corinth and Paul's relationship with it, see my textbook *The New Testament,* pp. 340–54.

27. Paul indicates that he later met with other apostles in Jerusalem, including the disciple John (Gal. 2:9).

28. See Rebecca G. Thompson, "Collaborative and Social Remembering," chap. 9 of Gillian Cohen and Martin Conway, *Memory in the Real World,* 3rd ed. (New York: Psychology Press, 2008).

29. William Hirst, Alexandrau Cuc, and Dana Wohl, "Of Sins and Virtues: Memory and Collective Identity," in Dorthe Berntsein and David C. Rubin, chap. 8 of *Understanding Autobiographical Memory: Theories and Approaches* (Cambridge, UK: Cambridge Univ. Press, 2012), p. 148.

30. See Micah Edelson, Tali Sharot, Raymond Dolan, and Yadin Dudai, "Following the Crowd: Brain Substrates of Long-Term Memory Conformity," *Science* 333 (2011): 108–11.

31. See Theodore J. Weeden, "Kenneth Bailey's Theory of Oral Tradition: A Theory Contested by Its Evidence," *Journal for the Study of the Historical Jesus* 7 (2009): 3–43.

32. Weeden, "Kenneth Bailey's Theory of Oral Tradition," pp. 10 and 12.

33. Catherine Hezser, *Jewish Literacy in Roman Palestine* (Tübingen: Mohr Siebeck, 2001); for the 97 percent figure see p. 498.

34. Kent D. Harber and Dov J. Cohen, "The Emotional Broadcaster Theory of Social Sharing," *Journal of Language and Social Psychology* 24 (2005): 382–400.

35. "The Emotional Broadcaster Theory of Social Sharing," p. 393.

36. I should also point out that the idea that eyewitnesses were the ultimate authorities in the early church appears to run counter to the evidence. You might think that such persons would be inestimable authorities to whom everyone would submit in reverence. But if we take Paul's word for it, it wasn't that way at all. Paul himself indicates that when Peter came to the city of Antioch and found Paul there with his gentile converts, he joined them in their table fellowship. That is to say, he ate his meals with them, without being afraid that this would infringe on his need, as a Jew, to keep kosher. But when some representatives of the Jerusalem church came, apparently at the injunction of James, the brother of Jesus, the leader of the Jerusalem church, Peter thought better of his decision to eat with gentiles and withdrew from doing so. How did Paul respond? He publicly rebuked Peter and called him a hypocrite. There was a massive parting of the ways (see Gal. 2:11–14). And so one needs to ask: how much authority did eyewitnesses to the life of Jesus exercise in Paul's churches? In the one instance in which a non-eyewitness confronted an eyewitness over how to understand the significance of Jesus, the non-eyewitness verbally attacked the eyewitness and maligned his character and understanding of the gospel.

37. In the book of Acts he is present when the first people in the city of Caesarea were converted based on his preaching (see Acts 10). Whether there is a historical kernel behind this account is much debated among scholars.

Chapter 3: Eyewitness Testimonies and Our Surviving Gospels

1. This episode is recounted in Elizabeth F. Loftus, *Eyewitness Testimony*, 2nd ed. (Cambridge, MA: Harvard Univ. Press,1996), pp. 20–21.

2. The best-known and very large study is Richard Bauckham, *Jesus and the Eyewitnesses: The Gospels as Eyewitness Testimony* (Grand Rapids, MI: Eerdmans, 2006).

3. See Richard J. McNally, *Remembering Trauma* (Cambridge, MA: Harvard Univ. Press, 2003).

4. Daniel L. Schacter, "Constructive Memory: Past and Future," *Dialogues in Clinical Neuroscience* 14 (2012): 7–18.

5. Hans F. M. Crombag, Willem A. Wagenaar, and Peter J. Van Koppen, "Crashing Memories and the Problem of 'Source Monitoring,'" *Applied Cognitive Psychology* 1 (1996): 95.

6. "Crashing Memories," p. 103.

7. See especially the enlightening discussion of Daniel L. Schacter, *The Seven Sins of Memory: How the Mind Forgets and Remembers* (Boston: Houghton Mifflin, 2001).

8. John E. Mack, *Abduction: Human Encounters with Aliens* (New York: Scribner, 1994). Controversially, Mack indicates that he believes in many instances these were real encounters with aliens.

9. Cambridge, MA: Harvard Univ. Press, 2005.

10. *Abducted*, p. 66.

11. *Abducted*, p. 62.

12. Quin M. Chrobak and Maria S. Zaragoza, "Inventing Stories: Forcing Witnesses to Fabricate Entire Fictitious Events Leads to Freely Reported False Memories," *Psychonomic Bulletin and Review* 15 (2008): 1190–95.

13. "Inventing Stories," p. 1194.

14. John Seamon, Morgan Philbin, and Liza Harrison, "Do You Remember Proposing Marriage to the Pepsi Machine?," *Psychonomic Bulletin and Review* 13 (2006): 752–56.

15. "Do You Remember Proposing Marriage," p. 755.

16. Schacter, "Constructive Memory," p. 10.

17. See, for example, Haya Bar-Izhak, "Modes of Characterization in Religious Narrative: Jewish Folk Legends about Miracle Worker Rabbis," *Journal of Folklore Research* 27 (1990): 205–30; Moshe Rosman, *Founder of Hasidism: A Quest for the Historical Ba'al Shem Tov* (Oxford, UK: Littman Library of Jewish Civilization, 2013); and the introduction to Dan Ben-Amos and Jerome R. Mintz, eds., "In Praise of the Baal Shem Tov [Shivhei ha-Besht]" (Northvale, NJ: Jason Aronson, 1993).

18. *Founder of Hasidism*, p. 141.

19. Ben-Amos and Mintz, eds., writer's preface, *In Praise of the Baal Shem Tov.*

20. See note 2 above.

21. *Jesus and the Eyewitnesses*, p. 6.

22. For a review of the book that focuses in large part on the question of the accuracy of eyewitness testimony see Judith Redman, "How Accurate Are Eyewitnesses? Bauckham and the Eyewitnesses in the Light of Psychological Research," *JBL* 129 (2010): 177–97. For a number of critical responses to Bauckham, and his reply, see *Journal for the Study of the Historical Jesus* 7 (2008).

23. See again Hezser, *Jewish Literacy in Roman Palestine.*

24. Critical scholars are unified in thinking that even if the Gospel writers occasionally came up with a story themselves, they inherited the great

majority of their accounts from the oral tradition. On their possible use of earlier written accounts, see note 16 on p. 304.

25. See above, pp. 74–76. That 1 and 2 Peter were not actually written by Peter is widely acknowledged by critical scholars. See my discussion in *Forged: Writing in the Name of God—Why the Bible's Authors Are Not Who We Think They Are* (San Francisco: HarperOne, 2012), pp. 66–77.

26. See my discussion in *Forged*, pp. 92–114.

27. See my discussion in *The New Testament: A Historical Introduction to the Early Christian Writings*, 5th ed. (New York: Oxford University Press, 2012) pp. 387–91.

28. See my discussion of Papias on pp. 110–17.

29. See the discussion on pp. 257–59.

30. For a translation of their writings, with introductions see Bart D. Ehrman, *The Apostolic Fathers*, 2 vols. (Cambridge, MA: Harvard Univ. Press, 2003). I have used this translation for all my quotations.

31. See the introduction and the collection of all the fragments of Papias that I give in *The Apostolic Fathers*, vol. 2, pp. 85–118.

32. That is obvious if Matthew was based in large part on the Gospel of Mark, as is almost everywhere conceded. Matthew agrees with the Greek text of Mark verbatim throughout his account. The only way that would be possible is if he was copying the Greek text into his Greek text.

33. For a full study see Arthur Bellinzoni, *The Sayings of Jesus in the Writings of Justin Martyr* (Leiden: E. J. Brill, 1967).

34. For a translation of the text and a fuller discussion see Bart D. Ehrman, *Lost Scriptures: Books That Did Not Make It into the New Testament* (New York: Oxford Univ. Press, 2003), pp. 331–33.

35. See the preceding note.

36. Mark 2:13–17 and Luke 5:27–32 both have the call of the tax collector to be Jesus's disciple, but in those versions his name is Levi, not Matthew.

37. For difficulties accepting the claim that one of Paul's traveling companions wrote Luke and Acts, see my study Bart D. Ehrman, *Forgery and Counterforgery: The Use of Literary Deceit in the Early Christian Tradition* (New York: Oxford Univ. Press, 2013), pp. 165–80.

38. As it turns out, the Gospel of Peter is the one Gospel that Justin actually names (*Dialogue with Trypho*, 106, 3). Another reason not to assign the book to Peter may have been the one we've already seen. There was a decades-old tradition that Peter needed an interpreter since either he didn't speak Greek or was not fluent in it, so that it was his interpreter, Mark, who

translated/interpreted his words to a wider audience. Of course, that did not stop *other* Christian authors from writing books in Greek, claiming to be Peter. That is probably true, for example, of 1 and 2 Peter in the New Testament. For discussion of the authorship of these and other Petrine books see my discussion in *Forged*.

39. For a discussion of this passage in Tertullian, see my book *Forgery and Counterforgery*, pp. 117–18.

40. For the written sources behind the Gospel of John see my discussion in *The New Testament*, pp. 185–88.

Chapter 4: Distorted Memories and the Death of Jesus

1. Ebbinghaus's experiments and his forgetting curve are discussed in most surveys of the history of memory studies; see, for example, Daniel L. Schacter, "Memory Distortion: History and Current Status," in Daniel L. Schacter, ed., *Memory Distortion: How Minds, Brains, and Societies Reconstruct the Past* (Cambridge, MA: Harvard Univ. Press, 1995), pp. 1–43.

2. Frederic C. Bartlett, *Remembering: A Study in Experimental and Social Psychology* (Cambridge, UK: Cambridge Univ. Press, 1932).

3. *Remembering*, pp. 204–5, 213.

4. *Remembering*, p. 63.

5. *Remembering*, p. 93.

6. *Remembering*, p. 175.

7. *Remembering*, p. 175.

8. E. Tulving, "Episodic Memory and Common Sense," in Alan Baddeley, Martin Conway, and John Aggleton, *Episodic Memory: New Directions in Research* (Oxford, UK: Oxford Univ. Press, 2001), p. 273.

9. See Daniel L. Schacter, "Suggestibility," chap. 5 in *The Seven Sins of Memory*, and Elizabeth Loftus, "Planting Misinformation in the Mind: A Thirty-Year Investigation of the Malleability of Memory," *Learning and Memory* 12 (2005): 631–66.

10. Elizabeth Loftus, "The Reality of Repressed Memories," *American Psychologist* 48 (1993): 524.

11. R. Brown and J. Kulik, "Flashbulb Memories," *Cognition* 5 (1977): 73–99. For responses some fifteen years later, when the theory had been put through a number of tests, see Eugene Winograd and Ulric Neisser, eds., *Affect and Accuracy in Recall: Studies of "Flashbulb" Memories* (Cambridge, UK: Cambridge Univ. Press, 1992). More recently see Olivier Luminet and Antonietta Curci, *Flashbulb Memories: New Issues and New Perspectives* (New York: Psychology Press, 2009).

12. Ulric Neisser and Nicole Harsch, "Phantom Flashbulbs: False Recollections of Hearing the News About *Challenger,"* in Winograd and Neisser,
eds., *Affect and Accuracy in Recall,* pp. 9–31.

13. Neisser and Harsch, "Phantom Flashbulbs," p. 19.

14. Neisser and Harsch, "Phantom Flashbulbs," p. 21.

15. Neisser and Harsch, "Phantom Flashbulbs," p. 30.

16. "Flashbulb Memories Result from Ordinary Memory Processes and Extraordinary Event Characteristics" in Luminet and Curci, *Flashbulb Memories,* p. 92.

17. Ulric Neisser, "John Dean's Memory: A Case Study," *Cognition* 9 (1981):
1–22.

18. "John Dean's Memory," p. 9. Italics his.

19. "John Dean's Memory," p. 10.

20. "John Dean's Memory," p. 13.

21. Elizabeth Loftus and Katherine Ketcham, *Witness for the Defense: The Accused, the Eyewitness, and the Expert Who Puts Memory on Trial* (New York: St.
Martin's Press, 1991), p. 20.

22. See my discussion of the sermon on pp. 195–202.

23. For a discussion of how scholars establish what probably happened in the
life of Jesus, based on sources (the Gospels) that are often problematic, see
my book *Jesus: Apocalyptic Prophet of the New Millennium* (New York: Oxford
Univ. Press, 1999), especially chap. 2 and 6.

24. For an argument that all these memories are basically historical, see Ehrman, *Jesus: Apocalyptic Prophet,* chap. 7–12.

25. I should stress here a point I made earlier: it is possible that an author who
records an episode from the life of Jesus is actually inventing it himself,
or consciously changing one that he inherited. Even if that is the case,
however, a distorted memory is still involved, since those who take his
account to be accurate from then on "remember" the event in this distorted way.

26. For the basic historicity of Jesus's trial and crucifixion, see my fuller discussion in *Jesus: Apocalyptic Prophet.*

27. See Ehrman, *Jesus: Apocalyptic Prophet,* pp. 221–23.

28. Exodus 1:37 indicates that there were six hundred thousand men, which
does not include the women and children.

29. See the discussion in E. P. Sanders, *Jesus and Judaism* (Philadelphia: Fortress, 1985).

30. See Sanders, *Jesus and Judaism.*

31. See my discussion in Bart D. Ehrman, *How Jesus Became God: The Exaltation of a Jewish Preacher from Galilee* (San Francisco: HarperOne, 2014), pp. 161–64.

Chapter 5: Distorted Memories and the Life of Jesus

1. A. R. Luria, *The Mind of a Mnemonist: A Little Book About a Vast Memory* (New York: Basic, 1968).
2. Jan Vansina, *Oral Tradition: A Study of Historical Methodology* (New Brunswick, NJ: Transaction, 2006; reprint, with additional introductory materials of 1965 original; trans. from French by H. M. Wright. French original 1961), p. 40.
3. David Henige, *Oral Historiography* (New York: Longman, 1982), p. 5.
4. *Oral Historiography*, p. 5.
5. Albert B. Lord, *The Singer of Tales* (Cambridge, MA: Harvard Univ. Press, 1960). The summary of Parry and Lord's work that follows comes from this classic work.
6. *Singer of Tales*, p. 4.
7. *Singer of Tales*, p. 99.
8. Jack Goody, *The Interface Between the Written and the Oral* (Cambridge, UK: Cambridge Univ. Press, 1987), p. 84.
9. Goody, *Interface Between the Written and the Oral*, pp. 84, 86.
10. *Singer of Tales*, p. 5.
11. Jack Goody, *The Domestication of the Savage Mind* (Cambridge, UK: Cambridge Univ. Press, 1977), p. 29.
12. Walter J. Ong, *Orality and Literacy: The Technologizing of the Word*, 30th anniversary edition (London: Routledge, 2002; original edition London: Methuen, 1982), p. 61 (summarizing Goody's findings).
13. *Domestication of the Savage Mind*, pp. 98–99.
14. *Orality and Literacy*, p. 57.
15. See note 22.
16. This sense of tradition obviously maps very nicely on the experiments that F. C. Bartlett performed on "serial reproduction." See p. 137.
17. *Oral Tradition*, p. 76.
18. David C. Rubin, *Memory in Oral Traditions: The Cognitive Psychology of Epic, Ballads, and Counting-out Rhymes* (New York: Oxford Univ. Press, 1995), p. 130.
19. *Oral Tradition*, p. 43.
20. *Oral Tradition*, p. 109.
21. *Oral Tradition*, p. 109.

22. Jan Vansina, *Oral Tradition as History* (Rochester, NY: Broydell & Brewster, 1985), p. 65.

23. Luke does have a similar sermon that Jesus delivers on a plain (rather than a mountain; see Luke 6:17–49), but it is much shorter than the Sermon on the Mount and different in numerous other ways.

24. See the preceding note.

25. For a general discussion about the sermon, see Warren Carter, *What Are They Saying About Matthew's Sermon on the Mount?* (New York: Paulist, 1994).

26. Werner H. Kelber, *The Oral and the Written Gospel: The Hermeneutics of Speaking and Writing in the Synoptic Tradition, Mark, Paul, and Q,* 2nd ed. (Philadelphia: Fortress, 1997), p. 30. Emphasis his.

27. Most commentaries will give possible explanations for this peculiar ending to the parable. See the options as cited, for example, in W. D. Davies and Dale Allison, *A Critical and Exegetical Commentary on the Gospel According to Saint Matthew,* vol. 3 (Edinburgh: T&T Clark, 1988).

28. See my fuller discussion in Bart D. Ehrman, *Jesus: Apocalyptic Prophet of the New Millennium* (New York: Oxford Univ. Press, 1999), chap. 8–9.

29. See my discussion of the passage in Bart D. Ehrman, *Misquoting Jesus: The Story Behind Who Changed the Bible and Why* (San Francisco: HarperOne, 2005), pp. 158–61.

30. For the text see Bart D. Ehrman and Zlatko Pleše, *The Other Gospels: Accounts of Jesus from Outside the New Testament* (New York: Oxford Univ. Press, 2014), pp. 110–11.

31. For example, E. P. Sanders, *The Historical Figure of Jesus* (London: Penguin, 1995).

32. See Bart D. Ehrman, *How Jesus Became God: The Exaltation of a Jewish Preacher from Galilee* (San Francisco: HarperOne, 2014), pp. 143–51, and, specifically with respect to Jesus's activities, Bart D. Ehrman, *The New Testament,* chap. 16.

33. See the preceding note.

Chapter 6: Collective Memory: Our Earliest Gospel of Mark

1. Maurice Halbwachs, *On Collective Memory,* ed. and tr. Lewis A. Coser (Chicago: Univ. of Chicago Press, 1992; French original, 1925).

2. *On Collective Memory,* p. 169.

3. *On Collective Memory,* p. 49.

4. *On Collective Memory,* p. 38.

5. See the discussion of F. C. Bartlett in chapter 4.

6. *On Collective Memory,* p. 61.

7. Lewis A. Coser, in the introduction to *On Collective Memory,* p. 25.

8. *On Collective Memory,* p. 119.

9. From his work "On the Topography of the Gospels," as quoted in Barry Schwartz, Yael Zerubavel, and Bernice M. Barnett, "The Recovery of Masada: A Study of Collective Memory," *Sociological Quarterly* 27 (1986): 149.

10. Jan Assmann, *Moses the Egyptian: The Memory of Egypt in Western Monotheism* (Cambridge, MA: Harvard Univ. Press, 1997), pp. 8–9.

11. *Moses the Egyptian,* p. 10.

12. *Moses the Egyptian,* p. 10.

13. For a historian's analysis of the reliability of Josephus's report see Shaye J. D. Cohen, "Masada: Literary Tradition, Archaeological Remains, and the Credibility of Josephus," *Journal of Jewish Studies* 33 (1982): 385–405.

14. I will not be discussing the views of Masada among other social groups, such as Israeli non-Jews or Jews in America or elsewhere.

15. "The Recovery of Masada." See note 26.

16. "The Recovery of Masada," p. 154.

17. "The Recovery of Masada," p. 151.

18. "The Recovery of Masada," p. 150.

19. Yael Zerubavel, *Recovered Roots: Collective Memory and the Making of Israeli National Tradition* (Chicago: Univ. of Chicago Press, 1995).

20. *Recovered Roots,* p. 63.

21. *Recovered Roots,* p. 67.

22. *Recovered Roots,* p. 68.

23. *Recovered Roots,* p. 69.

24. Nachman Ben-Yehuda, *The Masada Myth: Collective Memory and Mythmaking in Israel* (Madison: Univ. of Wisconsin Press, 1995), pp. 13–14.

25. *Recovered Roots,* p. 69.

26. It is interesting to note that the way Masada is presented today, especially since the end of the twentieth century, is different yet again—different from how it was told by Josephus and from how it was related in the "national founding myth" of Israel in the mid-twentieth century. For a variety of reasons explored intriguingly by Paul A. Cohen in his study *History and Popular Memory: The Power of Story in Moments of Crisis* (New York: Columbia Univ. Press, 2014), pp. 33–36, today Israelis are far less inclined to feel outmanned and in danger of imminent destruction, in part because of their amazing military successes and current power. As a result, the Masada myth

has faded in importance, and is seen less as "a positive symbol to be emulated than as a negative metaphor for a situation to be avoided at all costs" (p. 62).

27. It is sometimes said that Mark does not have a resurrection narrative, since the final twelve verses (16:9–20) are lacking in our best and earliest manuscripts. It is true that Mark appears to have ended his Gospel with what is now 16:8, but that does not mean that he lacks an account of Jesus's resurrection. Jesus is indeed raised from the dead in Mark's Gospel, as the women visiting the tomb learn. What Mark lacks is any account of Jesus appearing to his disciples afterward; in this it is quite different from the other three canonical Gospels.

28. For a discussion of the term in antiquity see Helmut Koester, *Ancient Christian Gospels: Their History and Development* (Philadelphia: Trinity Press International, 1990), pp. 1–4.

29. For an authoritative overview see John Collins, *The Scepter and the Star: Messianism in Light of the Dead Sea Scrolls* (Grand Rapids, MI: Eerdmans, 2010).

30. This is a difficult passage to translate, but the Greek is clarified by the context; those who come to rescue Jesus from the public eye are his family (see v. 31), and their stated reason is that he "stands outside himself"—that is, he is beside himself, out of his mind.

Chapter 7: The Kaleidoscopic Memories of Jesus: John, Thomas, and a Range of Others

1. See my discussion in *How Jesus Became God,* pp. 69–75.
2. See the discussion on pp. 220–26 in chapter 5.
3. As to why John calls Jesus's enemies "the Jews," see pp. 265–67.
4. Above all see Raymond E. Brown, *The Community of the Beloved Disciple* (New York: Paulist, 1979) and J. Louis Martyn, *History and Theology in the Fourth Gospel,* 3rd ed. (Nashville: Abingdon, 2003).
5. See the works cited in the preceding note.
6. See especially *The Community of the Beloved Disciple.*
7. See above, pp. 40–42.
8. I am using the translation found in Ehrman and Pleše, *The Other Gospels.*
9. See my discussion in Bart D. Ehrman, *Lost Christianities: The Battles for Scripture and the Faiths We Never Knew* (New York: Oxford Univ. Press, 2003), pp. 39–41.
10. See p. 59.
11. For this interpretation see my discussion in Bart D. Ehrman, *Forgery and Counterforgery: The Use of Literary Deceit in Early Christian Polemics* (New York: Oxford Univ. Press, 2013), pp. 415–16.

12. As suggested to me by my colleague Zlatko Pleše; see my discussion in *Forgery and Counterforgery,* pp. 340–41.

13. Other antiapocalyptic views are found scattered throughout the Gospel in sayings 18, 37, and 51.

14. See the discussion of Q on pp. 59–60.

15. That was for an important reason. The only way to know for certain what was in Q is when Matthew and Luke share material that is not found in Mark. But they do not have any such material in their Passion narratives.

16. For an accessible discussion see the collection of essays in Rodolphe Kasser, Marvin Meyer, and Gregor Wurst, *The Gospel of Judas,* 2nd ed. (Washington, DC: National Geographic, 2008).

17. See p. 40.

18. See p. 40. For a very insightful, readable, and up-to-date discussion of Gnosticism see David Brakke, *The Gnostics: Myth, Ritual, and Diversity in Early Christianity* (Cambridge, MA: Harvard Univ. Press, 2010).

19. For a fuller discussion, see Ehrman, "Lost Christianities," pp. 103–9.

20. For a fuller discussion see Bart D. Ehrman, *The Orthodox Corruption of Scripture: The Effect of Early Christological Controversies on the Text of the New Testament* (New York: Oxford Univ. Press, 1993), pp. 51–52.

21. For a fuller discussion of the council, in response to that wonderful source of misinformation, Dan Brown's bestselling novel, see Bart D. Ehrman, *Truth and Fiction in the Da Vinci Code* (New York: Oxford Univ. Press, 2005), especially chapter 5.

22. It is closest, of course, to the view of the Gospel of John; but that Gospel certainly does not present Jesus in the even more highly exalted terms that were adopted by the theologians at the Council of Nicea more than two centuries later.

Chapter 8: In Conclusion: A Paean to Memory

1. This is my argument in Bart D. Ehrman, *How Jesus Became God* (San Francisco: HarperOne, 2014).

INDEX

Index

Joseph (husband to Mary), 33–36
Josephus, 171, 236, 240, 241
Judaism: "divine hypostases" of God in, 258–59; Justin's "dialogue" with Trypho on Christianity and, 118; law of Moses, 67, 164, 194, 279, 281; rabbinic, 67; Sabbath law of, 36, 63, 64, 170, 264–65, 275
Judas Iscariot, 28–30, 114–15, 149, 218
Judas Thomas, 39
Jude, brother of Jesus, 270
Justin, 118–19

Kelber, Werner, 198–99
Ketcham, Katherine, 147
Killing Jesus (O'Reilly), 22
Kingdom of God: gist memories of Jesus on the coming, 194, 207, 208–11, 253–54; John's community on salvation and the, 266–68; miracles of Jesus validating his identify and teachings about coming, 222–23, 224–26; Reimarus on meaning of Jesus's referral to the, 54. *See also* Jesus's teachings; salvation
Kulik, James, 140, 141

Lamb of God, 158, 214, 215–16, 259
Lamdan, Yitzhak, 238–39
law of Moses, 67, 164, 194, 279, 281
Lazarus, 218
Lessing, G. E., 53, 56–57
Letter of Pilate to Herod, 30
Lincoln, Abraham, 5–8, 10, 20, 233
Loftus, Elizabeth, 139–49, 147
Lord, Albert, 183, 184–87, 191
Lord's Prayer, 188, 196, 197
Luke the "beloved physician," 125, 126–27
Luria, Alexandre R., 179–80

Mack, John E., 92
Marcion, 284–85, 286, 287

Mark (companion to Peter), 125, 127–28
marriage and divorce, 200–202
Mary and Martha, 218
Mary Magdalene, 23
Mary, mother of Jesus, 23, 32, 33–35, 214
Masada fortress, 236–42
"Masada" (Lamdan), 238–39
The Masada Myth: Collective Memory and Mythmaking in Israel (Ben–Yehuda), 241
Masada the event: changing meaning of the memory of, 238–42; as "founding myth" of modern State of Israel, 236, 238, 239–42
Matthew the text collector, 125–26
memories: distorted memories as indistinguishable from factual, 139–43; "flashbulb," 140–42; "group memory" phenomenon, 75–76, 229; how and why they are changed over time, 13–14; psychology of episodic versus semantic, 17–20, 228; the relevance of the past that make us remember our, 64, 291; remembering as process of filling in the gaps in, 134–38, 145–46; the value of even imperfect, 292–93, 295. *See also* Christian memories; distorted/false memories; gist memories; remembering
memory: defining and limitations of, 3–4; oral cultures and, 12, 181–93; techniques for developing better, 131–32; understanding the different types of, 17–21. *See also* collective memory
Memory and Manuscript (Gerhardsson), 66–67
memory–history memories: approaching the Gospel of Mark as a, 243–54; description and task of, 229, 230, 233–35, 290; of Masada event, 236–42. *See also* history
Memory in Oral Traditions (Rubin), 191

Index

Polycarp of Smyrna, 111
Pontius Pilate: appointing Roman
guards to watch tomb of Jesus, 44;
historical sources on, 160, 171–72;
trial and sentence passed on Jesus by,
29–32, 47, 55, 83, 149, 150, 151–59,
171–73, 195–96, 263
Protevangelium Jacobi (Proto–Gospel of
James), 32–34, 35

Q source: apocalyptic proclamations of
the coming kingdom in, 208; comparison between Coptic Gospel of
Thomas and, 280; providing sayings
of Jesus in the New Testament, 60,
80, 129, 197, 198; Sermon on the
Mount inclusion of Q sayings from
the, 197, 198, 199, 279–80

*Recovered Roots: Collective Memory and
the Making of Israeli National Tradition*
(Zerubavel), 239
Reimarus, Hermann Samuel, 52–54, 56,
57, 168
Remembering (Bartlett), 134
remembering: factual versus procedural
memory, 133–34; the "gist" of things
issue of, 143–59; "mnemo–history"
or "memory–history" of, 229; as
process of filling in memory gaps,
134–38, 145–46; "repeated" and
"social" production of, 136, 137–38.
See also memories
remembering Jesus: Apostle Peter on,
25–28; Coptic Gospel of Thomas
on, 268–76; Council of Nicea on
Jesus as God in the flesh, 287–88;
Gospel of John on, 256–68; Gospel
of Judas on, 283–84; Gospel of Mark
on, 245–52; Gospel of Matthew,
280–81; Marcion on nature of Jesus,
284–85, 286, 287; Paul's memories
of Jesus, 278–79; Q source, 279–80;

similarities and differences in the
New Testament, 281–83; Theodotus
on nature of Jesus, 285–88. *See also*
Christian memories; Jesus
Report of Pilate, 30
resurrection, 174, 262, 278–79
Riesenfeld, Harald, 69, 70
ripping the Temple curtain, 173–76
Roman Empire: destruction of Masada
by, 236–42; Kingdom of God misunderstood as freedom from, 22, 54; Jesus
promoting submissive nonviolence vs.
armed rebellion against, 168–71
Rubin, David, 142, 191

"S" (Luria's memory study subject),
179–80
Sabbath law, 36, 63, 64, 170, 264–65, 275
Salome (midwife), 33–34
salvation: disciples's invention, 56; Gnos-
tic knowledge of the, 40, 283–84;
Gospel of Thomas on the path to,
211, 273; Jesus's teachings on his
role in the, 47, 210, 251, 252; John's
community and their understanding of the, 266–68; proclaiming the
"good news" on, 44, 45. *See also*
Jesus's teachings
Schacter, Daniel, 89, 94–95, 139
Schmidt, Karl Ludwig, 61, 62, 65
Schwartz, Barry, 5–8, 233
Seamon, John, 94
semantic memories, 18, 19–20
Semler, Johann S., 57
September 11, 2001 memories, 18, 140,
143, 229
Sermon on the Mount sermon: different
versions of marriage, divorce, and
adultery found in, 200–202; Gospel
of Luke's account of some of the
aspects of, 197–98; Gospel of
Matthew's account of, 147, 195–202;
as one of the greatest accounts of

325

Index

Sermon on the Mount sermon: (*cont.*)
ethical teaching, 294; Q sayings
founds in, 197, 198, 199, 280
the Sicarii (Jewish assassins), 241
sight-blindness experiment, 50–51
Simon, 27, 219
Simon (a Pharisee), 218–19
Simon Peter (Apostle Peter), 215–16,
246, 260
Simons, Daniel, 50–51
Simon the leper, 217, 218
The Singer of Tales (Lord), 184
sins: baptism for forgiveness of, 212;
Jesus as the Lamb of God taking
away everyone's, 158, 214, 215–16,
259; problem of baptism of Jesus for
his, 212–13
social memory: Abraham Lincoln and
construction of his, 5–8; Christopher
Columbus and construction of his,
8–10; shaped by our present interests
and concerns, 10, 15, 20–21. *See also*
collective memory
"Son of the Father," 173
Synoptic Gospels: debate over the
"Synoptic problem," 59–60; Jesus as
remembered in the Gospel of John
compared to the, 256–68. *See also*
Gospel of Luke; Gospel of Mark;
Gospel of Matthew

Talarico, Jennifer, 142
Talmud, 67
Tatian, 119
Tertullian, 30, 128
Thaddaeus (or Addai), 39
Theodotus, 285–88

Tiberius (Roman emperor), 30, 31
tomb of Jesus, 44–45, 251–52
Torah, 194
trial of Jesus: Barabbas released in honor
of Passover during, 150, 153, 157,
171–73; Pontius Pilate and the,
29–32, 47, 55, 83, 149, 150, 151–59,
195–96, 263
truth representation, 45–48
Trypho, Rabbi, 118
Tulving, Endel, 18, 139

Vansina, Jan, 182, 189–92, 193
von Liszt, Professor, 87–88

Watergate hearings, 144–46
Weeden, Theodore, 76, 77
Wise and Foolish Virgins parable,
204–5, 208
Wolfenbüttel Fragments ("Fragments")
[Lessing], 53
women: Jesus's "without sin among
you" statement on adulterous, 38;
Protevangelium Jacobi (Proto–Gospel
of James) principally about, 32–34;
significant role in life of Jesus by, 23,
215, 217–19, 251–52
Word of God, 257–59, 266–67
World Trade Center attacks (2001)
memories, 18, 140, 143, 229
Wrede, William, 60–61

Yadin, Yigael, 240

Zealot (Aslan), 21–22
Zenon, 37
Zerubavel, Yael, 239, 240, 241